the Woman's Day
book of Knitted Sweaters

by

The Editors of Woman's Day

Simon and Schuster • New York

Copyright © 1970, 1971, 1972, 1973, 1974, 1975, 1976
by Fawcett Publications, Inc.
All rights reserved
including the right of reproduction
in whole or in part in any form
Published by Simon and Schuster
A Gulf+Western Company
Rockefeller Center, 630 Fifth Avenue
New York, New York 10020

Designed by Beri Greenwald
Manufactured in the United States of America

1 2 3 4 5 6 7 8 9 10

Library of Congress Cataloging in Publication Data

Main entry under title:

The Woman's day book of knitted sweaters.

   1. Sweaters.   I. Woman's day.   II. Title: Book of
knitted sweaters.
TT825.W64   746.4'32   75-40460
ISBN 0-671-22204-X

contents

Colorful Favorites 105

Special Sweaters 135

6

foreword

Here are seventy-five fabulous sweaters for you to knit, in a marvelous collection of designs for men, women, and children. With clear and complete directions, worked in extravagant or subtle colors and a wide variety of yarns, each project is sure to please the most discerning knitter.

The editors of Woman's Day have gone to great lengths to bring together in this book the most outstanding examples from the magazine's extensive sweater collection for you to make and enjoy for their enduring beauty. The patterns chosen have proven to be so popular that to this day they are still in great demand.

You will find designs that appeal to expert and beginner alike, from textured country tweeds to glittery evening tops. There are rugged sweaters for outdoor wear, worked in the timeless, traditional designs of European fishermen, and delicate little smocks made of the finest yarns to keep tiny tots warm.

For the beginner, there are directions and illustrative diagrams for learning the basic steps and stitches from which all knitting is derived. In addition, there are tips on how to read directions, how to check your gauge, what size needle works best with what weight yarn, helpful hints on how to work different hems and selvages, how to pick up that dropped stitch, how to block your finished pieces, and the many ways to sew a fine seam. Careful explanations of such techniques as Fair Isle and Argyle knitting have also been included.

introduction

Knitting has been done through the ages. It is one of the oldest, most practical crafts, and today, as always, it is one of the most satisfying.

The word knit *is derived from the Anglo-Saxon* cnittan, *which means "threads woven by hand." This is accomplished by means of needles, or "pins," as they used to be called. With one thread, one loop is pulled through another loop and passed from one needle to another, and that is all there is to it. All the other steps evolve from this simple procedure.*

Interestingly, up until the nineteenth century knitting was mainly done by men. It is generally believed to have originated among the ancient nomadic tribes of the Near East. Arab traders, "knitting" their way across the desert, brought the craft to ancient Egypt, where fragments of knitted fabric have been found in the tombs. From there it spread to Italy, Spain, and the rest of Europe. The skilled craft of knitting was brought to its height of refinement during the Middle Ages when the Knitters' Guilds flourished. A young man aspiring to become a member would have to apprentice to the Guild for at least six years to acquire the basic skills, and travel to study techniques and patterns in faraway lands. Only after passing an extensive examination of his knowledge and skills by the Guild would he be accepted as a Master Knitter.

Even today the notion that knitting is a manly art still persists in parts of northern Europe, the British Isles, and areas of the Mediterranean where shepherds carry on this time-honored tradition. Moreover, it was the sailors and fishermen of Ireland's rugged Aran Islands who originated what we today classify as fisherman knits—those sweaters worked in hand-spun, natural-colored yarns, that stand out for their beautiful, deeply carved and textured patterns. They felt it was a womanly task to spin the wool, but a man's privilege to knit it!

Around the turn of the century, knitting socks and bedspreads was our grandmothers' favorite pastime. We have come a long way since. Fashion and sports have inspired an infinite variety of new knitted garments. And today the endless selection in yarns, in their rainbow of colors and fascinating textures, inspire the creative knitter to do her—or his—own thing.

the Woman's Day

book of
Knitted Sweaters

KNITTING EQUIPMENT, YARNS AND TECHNIQUES

Equipment

KNITTING NEEDLES

The most essential equipment for knitting is the needles. They come in a wide variety of sizes, types, and lengths and are made of various materials.

STRAIGHT NEEDLES with single points are used when you work back and forth in rows. They come in pairs in 10- and 14-inch lengths.

DOUBLE-POINTED NEEDLES come in sets of four and are usually 7 or 9 inches long. They are used for socks, mittens, and other items to be worked in rounds.

CIRCULAR NEEDLES are used for knitting skirts or other seamless garments. However, they may also be used to work back and forth when a straight needle is not long enough to hold a large number of stitches. Circular needles come in 11- to 36-inch lengths. Knitting needles are made of steel, aluminum, plastic, or wood. They used to be made of bone, but haven't been manufactured in that material for over a century in this country. So if you happen to find a pair in some tucked-away knitting basket, treasure them.

The instructions in this book specify the type and size needle to be used to execute the designs. Always remember to choose needles to suit the type of work you are doing and the yarn you are using. In most cases, large needles are used for heavy yarn and smaller needles for thinner yarn. The length of needle is mainly determined by the total number of stitches it will have to carry. However, if you feel more comfortable knitting, say, only 5 stitches on 14-inch needles, that is perfectly fine, too.

Needle sizes are indicated by numbers found on the head of the needle. Unfortunately, the standardization of sizes leaves something to be desired, and therefore it is wise to choose from well-distributed brand names. Also, because the sizing of needles is not the same in the United States as in England and Canada, a listing of comparative sizes is given below. Sizes 15 and 000 are largest.

Comparative sizes in knitting needles

U.S.	0	1	2	3	4	5	6	7	8	9	10	11	13	15
Eng./Can.	13	12	11	10	9	8	7	6	5	4	3	2	0	000

17

ACCESSORIES

STITCH HOLDERS look like simplified safety pins. They come in various sizes and materials and are meant to hold stitches that are set aside to be worked later. However, if you don't have any at hand, do not despair. Use a crochet hook or tapestry needle to pull an extra length of yarn through these stitches and tie the two ends of yarn together. This way the stitches are set aside as securely as with holders.

RING MARKERS are used to separate sections of work, or to indicate where increases and/or decreases are to be made. You can buy markers (small plastic or metal rings) or make your own by tying a contrasting color yarn around the needle. You can also use small safety pins or paper clips as markers. The markers should be slipped from one needle to the other as you go along.

CABLE-STITCH HOLDERS: When working cables, in which whole sections of knitting exchange places, some stitches must be temporarily held while others are worked. Cable holders are available at the needlework counters in various types and sizes, but you may equally effectively use the plastic pins that come with hair rollers, which become handy mini-needles. Or, if the cable is small, use a toothpick or a bobby pin.

RULER OR TAPE MEASURE: One of these is necessary to check your gauge and measure the progress of your work.

BOBBINS: These are used when knitting with more than two colors. They are often made of plastic. However, instead of using plastic bobbins, it is very easy and practical to wind separate bobbins that pull from the center. Directions and diagrams on how to wind these balls are given on page 36.

TAPESTRY NEEDLE: This is a large-eyed needle with a blunt point used for sewing seams, weaving two pieces together (see kitchener stitch, page 32), and working embroidery in duplicate stitch (see page 33).

18

Yarns and Threads

Today an almost endless variety of yarns is available from which to choose. They come in a rainbow of colors and in many new and exciting textures, from fluffy mohairs to smooth and nubby finishes and on to sparkly metallic-look threads. We used to think that only wool yarns were for knitting and tended to associate cotton with crochet. But not any longer. The yarn or thread used can be of any fiber, natural or synthetic. The latter are often machine-washable, a quality especially important in garments that need a lot of washing, such as children's and babies' clothes. But almost anyone can appreciate the unsurpassed beauty of a hand-spun, natural-colored wool yarn that requires tender, loving care.

The weight of yarn to be used is determined by the style of the garment you wish to make.

The materials mentioned in the directions have been specifically chosen to suit the garment which is being made. If at all possible, do *not* substitute other yarns for those recommended, unless you are an absolutely expert knitter. Directions have been written especially for the yarn mentioned, which has been knitted to a certain gauge on a certain size needle to obtain a particular size garment.

When you buy yarn, always make sure to buy enough to complete the entire garment and check that the dye-lot numbers are all the same. Despite sophisticated dyeing processes, there is always the slightest color variation between two dye lots.

If, however, one day you have the problem of two different dye lots, you can eliminate an obvious line in your work and merge the two dye lots as follows: Before finishing the last skein of the original dye lot, start with the new dye lot, and for about 10 rows work alternate rows of each dye lot. This way the two blend almost invisibly.

Basic Knitting Techniques

HOW TO READ INSTRUCTIONS

Before embarking on a project, go over the directions from beginning to end. Read each paragraph completely, watching especially for such sentences as "and at the same time . . ." and "for a specific size only. . . ."

Before you begin, draw a circle throughout the directions around each number that applies to your size.

If you select a design in a new and unfamiliar pattern and you are not sure whether or not you will be able to follow its instructions, make a sample swatch to try it out. Use any available yarn and make the swatch big enough so that you can repeat the pattern a couple of times; e.g., if the pattern is a multiple of 4 stitches plus 1, cast on 17 stitches for the swatch.

It is a good idea when following complicated directions to mark where you are in the instructions when you put your work down. It is also a good idea as you work to put a piece of paper or a ruler below the row you are working on, especially on patterns which have more than 6 rows to a repeat. That way you can prevent skipping from one row to the wrong one, especially when you are looking back and forth from directions to your knitting.

GAUGE

At the beginning of all knitting directions a gauge is given. Gauge simply means the number of stitches to 1 inch and the number of rows to 1 inch obtained with a specific yarn on a specific size needle. Based on these two factors, the fit of a knitted garment is calculated. So it is *most important* that you knit to the gauge specified, so that your finished product will be the correct size.

To check *your* gauge, make a sample swatch of at least 4 inches square, using the needles and yarn recommended in the directions. With a ruler measure the number of stitches and rows per inch. If you have the same number of stitches as given in the directions, you are knitting to the same gauge and you can work the design on the size needle recommended.

If the number of stitches does not correspond to that given in the gauge, you may have to try needles of a different size.

If you have *more* stitches to the inch than specified, you are working more tightly and you should try *larger* needles.

If you have *fewer* stitches, you are working more loosely and should try using *smaller* needles.

Although it is possible to get the correct gauge by changing your tension (this is knitting looser or tighter), it is not a good idea. The way you knit is so personal that any effort to change it for an entire garment would mean to really strain yourself and it would probably result in uneven work. It is almost like trying to change your voice or your handwriting. Keep changing the size needles until your gauge is exactly the same as that specified. The size needle used is not important as long as you obtain the correct gauge. *Always* check it first, before you begin a new project.

Gauge: 6 stitches = 1 inch

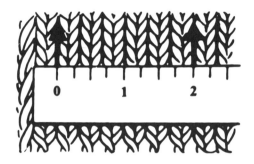

HOW TO MAKE THE RIGHT SIZE

To determine size, you should take careful measurements of yourself, or of whomever the garment is intended for.

Measure children around the chest, just under the arms. Measure pre-teens around the chest, the waist, and the hips. (Note that pre-teens' sizes are larger than similar children's sizes, smaller than misses' or men's.)

Measure misses and women around the fullest part of the bust, the waistline, and the hips about 7 inches down. Be sure the person measured is wearing the same girdle and bra she will wear with the garment.

Measure men around the chest, just under the arms. Sleeve length may be noted for future reference, but does not determine the size.

Now compare the measurements you have taken with those in the chart, find the column most like yours. Immediately above it, in bold numerals, is the size you should make.

BODY MEASUREMENTS

MISSES AND WOMEN

SIZE:	8	10	12	14	16	18
Bust:	31½″	32½″	34″	36″	38″	40″
Waist:	23″	24″	25½″	27″	29″	31″
Hips:	33½″	34½″	36″	38″	40″	42″

PRE-TEENS

SIZE:	8	10	12	14
Chest:	28″	29″	31″	33″
Waist:	23″	24″	25″	26″
Hips:	31″	32″	34″	36″

MEN

SIZE:	34	36	38	40	42	44	46
Chest:	34″	36″	38″	40″	42″	44″	46″

CHILDREN

SIZE:	4	6	8	10	12	14
Chest:	23″	24″	26″	28″	30″	32″

INFANTS AND TODDLERS

SIZE:	6-mo.	1	2	3	4
Chest:	19″	20″	21″	22″	23″

HOW TO ALTER A KNITTED GARMENT

If you have carefully followed directions, knitted according to gauge, and used yarn and needles as specified, you should have a sweater knitted in the selected size.

However, sometimes, despite all best intentions, you may knit a little tighter or looser than planned, and there you are with a sweater that doesn't quite fit. Sometimes you may have no other choice but to pull out the sections that are too small or too big. But first, if your sweater is too small, try to stretch and block it to the correct measurements and size. Sew the seams with an overhand stitch instead of a backstitch; this will add about a quarter of an inch to each seam.

If your sweater is too big, you can sometimes alter it in the same manner you would a sewn garment. Put the sweater on wrong side out. Have someone take in the seams where necessary with pins, baste, then with a fine hand or machine stitch sew along the basted line. Stitch again close along first stitching line. Trim the excess. This method of alteration is advisable only on fine and medium weight yarn.

KNITTING TERMS AND THEIR ABBREVIATIONS

Many people are intimidated by knitting directions. Directions have to be abbreviated for space's sake and yet should remain decipherable.

Here are the most common abbreviations and an explanation of the terms and symbols most frequently used in knitting.

beg—beginning (of a row or round)

dec—decrease

dp—double pointed (needles)

inc—increase

k—knit

k-wise—knit-wise, as if to knit

p—purl

pat (t)—pattern

psso—pull or pass the slipped stitch over the next stitch

p-wise—purl-wise, as if to purl

rep—repeat

rnd—round

sl—slip a stitch from left-hand needle to right-hand needle without working it.

sl st—slip stitch

sl 1, k 1, psso—slip 1 stitch, knit 1 stitch, and pass the slipped stitch over the knit stitch

sl 1 y f (b)—slip 1 stitch, holding yarn in front (back)

sl 1, k 2 tog, psso—slip 1 stitch, knit 2 stitches together, and pass the slipped stitch over the 1 stitch resulting from the knit 2 stitches together

st (s)—stitch(es)

tog—together

yo—yarn over. Wrap the yarn over the needle to make a new stitch (see page 30).

*—An asterisk means repeat the instructions following the asterisk as many times as specified, *in addition* to the first time.

[ ]—Brackets are used to indicate a change in size when directions are given, as they often are, for more than one size. The figure in front of the brackets refers to the smallest size.

Even—When the directions say "work even," this means continue working without increasing or decreasing, always keeping pattern as established.

Multiple of stitches—A pattern often needs an exact number of stitches to be worked correctly. When directions say "multiple of," it means the number of stitches must be divisible by this number. For example: Multiple of 6 would be: 12, 18, 24, etc.; multiple of 6 plus 3 would be: 15, 21, 27, etc.

( )—Parentheses mean repeat instructions in parentheses as many times as specified. For example: (k 3, p 2) 5 times, means to work all that is in parentheses 5 times *in all*.

Place a marker in work—This term means to mark with a safety pin or a thread a certain point in the work itself to use as a guide in taking future measurements.

Place a marker on needle—This term means to place a stitch marker *on the needle* between the stitches. It is slipped from one needle to the other as you work across the row.

Slip a stitch—When directions say "slip a stitch" or "sl 1," insert right needle in stitch to be slipped as if to purl and simply slip it from left to right needle without working it.

HOW TO KNIT

To make a little practice swatch use knitting worsted and a pair of No. 6 knitting needles.

TO CAST ON: To cast on means to put the stitches on the needle; this will serve as the foundation for the work. This should always be done loosely to keep the elasticity of the work. If you find you are casting on too tightly, use a larger size needle for casting on only. There are various ways of casting on:

Casting-on in slip stitch. This is the easiest way, using only one needle.

Make a slip knot at the free end of the yarn (Diagram 1). Place loop on needle, which is held in the right hand, and tighten (Diagrams 2 and 3).

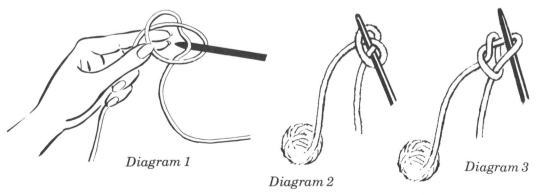

Diagram 1

Diagram 2

Diagram 3

Work a loop of yarn from front to back around the left forefinger, insert the needle into the back of the loop just made, crossing the thread, slip loop from finger onto the needle, and pull thread tight with left hand (Diagram 4). Repeat this procedure as many times as necessary for the required number of stitches.

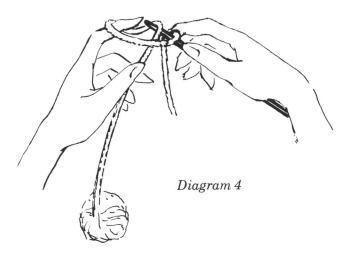

Diagram 4

This method is often used by beginners, or when casting on a small number of stitches in the course of the work; e.g., when making button-holes, or when adding a larger number of stitches at the end of a row, when making a sleeve.

Casting on using 2 lengths of yarn and 1 needle. Make a slip knot as in Diagram 1 at about 2 yards from the "free" end of the yarn. (**Note:** The length of this "free end" varies and is determined by the number of stitches you want to cast on and the weight of the yarn you are using. As a rule, figure 1 inch of yarn per stitch for heavy yarn and large needles, ½ inch per stitch for lighter-weight yarn and smaller needles.) Hold free yarn end in palm of left hand (Diagram 5).

Diagram 5

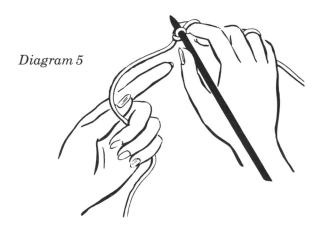

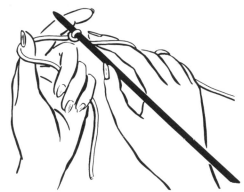

Diagram 6

Loop end of yarn around your left thumb from front to back; wind yarn leading to ball loosely around fingers of right hand.

Diagram 7

Holding needle in right hand as you would hold a pencil, insert the needle into loop on thumb from front to back.

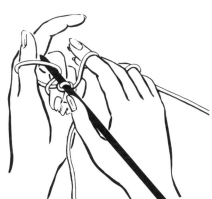

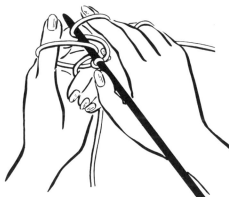

Diagram 8

Pass the yarn in your right hand around the needle from back to front.

Diagram 9

Draw yarn through, slip loop off thumb, pull to tighten. One stitch is cast on.

Repeat this procedure as many times as necessary for the required number of stitches.

If you ever run out of yarn before you have cast on the needed stitches, here is another way of doing it: Use 2 skeins of yarn, one to make the loop with and a second one to pull through to form another loop. After you have cast on the required number of stitches, just break off one (it doesn't matter which one).

Casting on using 2 needles. Make a slip knot as in Diagram 1, but hold needle in left hand. Hold second needle in right hand, with yarn in working position as shown in Diagram 10. Insert point of right needle into loop on left needle as shown. With index finger bring the yarn over the point of right needle (Diagram 11).

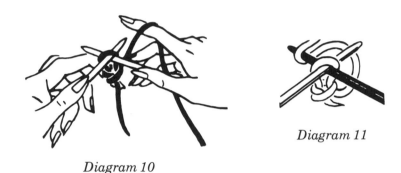

Diagram 11

Diagram 10

Draw the yarn through the loop (Diagram 12). Insert left needle through new loop (Diagram 13) and remove right needle. You now have 2 stitches cast on. You can make the next and all succeeding stitches in the same way, or for a stronger edge, you can insert right needle between stitches, just below left needle, instead of through loops (Diagram 14).

Diagram 12   Diagram 13   Diagram 14

Using any of these three techniques of casting on, cast on 15 stitches for a sample swatch, and we'll show you how to do the knit stitch.

KNIT STITCH: Hold needle with cast-on stitches in left hand. Keep yarn at back of work. Insert right needle into first stitch on left needle, as shown, front to back. With right hand bring yarn under and over the point of right needle and draw the yarn through the stitch; slip the old stitch off the left needle. This completes the first stitch of the row. Repeat in each stitch (Diagram 15) until all the stitches have

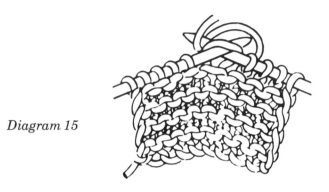

Diagram 15

been knitted off left needle. Always push work along left needle so that stitch to be worked is near tip. When row is completed, you should have 15 stitches on right needle as you had on left originally. Count stitches occasionally to make sure that you keep the same number. At the end of row, turn work so needle with stitches is in your left hand. Continue working rows in this manner until work is uniform and you feel familiar with the stitch. When you knit each stitch in each row, it's called **garter stitch.**

TO BIND OFF

You are now ready to finish off your practice piece. This process is called binding off.

Loosely knit 2 stitches. With point of left needle pick up first stitch and slide it over second; slip it off needle. * Knit next stitch and slip preceding one over it. Repeat from * across (Diagram 16).

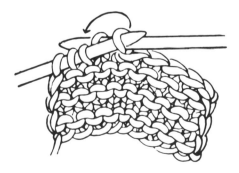

Diagram 16

Basic Knitting Techniques

When you come to your last stitch, cut yarn about 3 inches from the needle. Bring loose end through last stitch and pull tightly. Darn in end with tapestry needle so that it will not show. If you find yourself binding off too tightly, use a knitting needle one size bigger. You should usually bind off in pattern. For example, the knit row in stockinette stitch (see below) is bound off in knit stitch, the purl row in purl stitch. The same goes for ribbing, to preserve its stretch.

Note: How to count bound-off stitches. When directions say "Bind off 5 stitches at beginning of a row," knit the first 2 stitches, pick up first stitch and pull it over the second. This counts as 1 stitch bound off. So, to bind off 5 stitches, you actually knit 6 stitches, but the 6th stitch, already knitted, is on the right needle.

PURL STITCH: To make this stitch, hold needle with stitches in left hand and second needle in right, with yarn in front of work. Insert the right-hand needle into first stitch from right to left, back to front. With right hand bring yarn over and under right-hand needle and draw yarn through the stitch, slip the stitch just made off left-hand needle. This completes first purl stitch. Keeping yarn in front of work, proceed in this manner in each stitch across (Diagram 17).

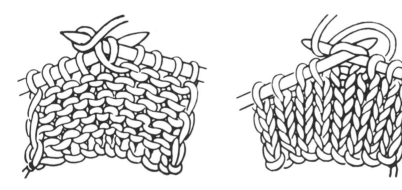

Diagram 17   Diagram 18

STOCKINETTE STITCH: This stitch is produced by alternating knit and purl rows. It has two different surfaces. The bumpy surface (Diagram 17) is the purl side or back of the stockinette stitch. The smooth surface, and this is the knit side (Diagram 18), is usually considered as the right side of the work.

Reverse stockinette means that the bumpy purl side is used as the front or right side of the work.

RIBBING: This is a combination of knitting and purling in which you alternate a specific number of stitches of each across the row. The most common combination is k 1, p 1 and k 2, p 2. If the row ends with p st(s), begin the next row with k st(s), and vice versa. Because of its elasticity, it is often used for waistbands, cuffs, and neckbands.

TO INCREASE: Increases are usually made to shape a garment. There are two ways of doing this.

Knit or purl twice in the same stitch. Knit (or purl) the stitch as usual, but do not slip the stitch just worked in off left-hand needle. Then knit (or purl) into the back of this same stitch. This second stitch will have a small horizontal thread crossing it on the knit side.

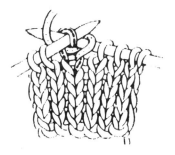

Increase in purling

Increase in knitting

Make a yarn over. A yarn over automatically increases a stitch and is used mostly in lace patterns since it produces a hole in the work.

On a knit row, bring yarn forward under tip of right needle, up and over needle to the back, then work next stitch (Diagram 19).
On a purl row, loop yarn over right needle, around and to the front again, then work next stitch (Diagram 20).

Yarn overs should be worked as other stitches on the next row.

Note: If for any reason no hole in the work is wanted, work into the back of the yarn over on the next row.

Diagram 19   *Diagram 20*

TO DECREASE: There are two ways of decreasing and directions always tell you which method to use. The first and most often used direction will say "dec 1" and indicate where to do this.

Knit or purl 2 stitches together. If you do this as shown in Diagram 21, the decrease will slant to the right; however, if you knit 2 stitches together through the back side of the first and second stitch, the decrease slants to the left.

30

Slip 1 stitch, knit 1 stitch, pull slipped stitch over. This method is used only on knit rows. Directions say sl 1, k 1, psso. To do this, slip 1 stitch by simply passing the stitch as if to knit from left needle to right without working it. Knit the next stitch, insert left needle into slipped stitch and pull it over the knit stitch. Decrease will slant to the left (Diagram 22).

Note: Increases and decreases should always be made in second or third stitch in or before end of row to keep edge even.

Diagram 21

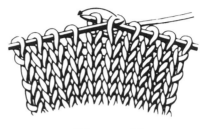
Diagram 22

TO ATTACH A NEW STRAND OF YARN: Plan to attach a new skein of yarn at the beginning of a row. With a new strand make a slip knot around working strand. Move slip knot close to edge of work and continue with new skein.

If you run out of yarn in the middle of the row, you can either pull out the row to the beginning, or leave a 4-inch end of yarn from old skein, work next stitch with new skein, leaving a 4-inch end also. Work a couple of rows and tie the ends together without pulling the work in and weave them invisibly into work.

TO PICK UP DROPPED STITCHES: Everybody drops a stitch or stitches sometime. They must be picked up or they will "run" just like a stocking.

Use a crochet hook. Catch the loose stitch and draw the horizontal thread of the row above through it (Diagram 23). Repeat until you reach the row on which you are working. Then place the stitch on the needle. Diagram 23 shows picking up a knit stitch. Diagram 24 shows a purl stitch.

Diagram 23

Diagram 24

TO PICK UP AND KNIT STITCHES ALONG AN EDGE: This is usually done around a neck or sleeve edge, where additional knitting, such as ribbing, is to be done.

With right side of work facing you, tie yarn to spot where picking up is to begin. Working with one needle only, held in the right hand, insert point of needle through work a short distance from the edge, wrap yarn around needle as if to knit, and draw loop through work. Continue in this manner until the required number of stitches has been picked up. When working along a bound-off or cast-on edge, pick up and knit 1 stitch in each stitch, inserting needle under 2 top loops of each stitch (Diagram 25).

Diagram 25

TO HEM—Knit-In Hem: Cast on the required number of stitches. Work a number of rows in stockinette stitch for the desired depth of the hem facing, ending on the wrong side of work. Then purl 1 row on the right side to mark the folding line for the hem. Starting with a purl row, continue in stockinette stitch and work the same number of rows as for the hem facing, ending on the wrong side of work.

With right side of work facing you, fold work along hem line. Insert right-hand needle into first stitch on left-hand needle and into corresponding stitch of cast-on edge you are holding right behind it; knit these 2 stitches together. Continue in this manner across the row.

Picot Hem: This is a pretty and very elastic way of finishing a hem. Work in same manner as for knit-in hem above. But instead of working the purl row on the right side, work an eyelet row as follows: k 1, * yo, k 2 tog. Repeat from * across row. This row is the folding line for hem. Count your stitches to make sure you have the same number you started with. Complete as for knit-in hem. Or you may sew the cast-on edge to the wrong side of work later.

GRAFTING: This is a method of weaving two pieces of knitting with an invisible seam, such as on the toe of a sock, a shoulder seam, or any place where it is desirable to give a continuous effect. It is done with the **kitchener,** or **weaving,** stitch: Use 2 needles and a tapestry needle. Break off the yarn coming from the knitting itself, leaving a 15-inch end. Thread yarn into tapestry needle and work as follows: Hold the 2 knitting needles, each with an equal number of stitches on it, even and parallel with yarn coming from the right end of back needle. * Draw tapestry needle through first stitch of front needle as if to knit and slip stitch off needle; draw tapestry needle through second stitch as if to purl, but leave stitch on needle; draw tapestry needle through first stitch on back needle as if to purl and slip stitch off needle; draw tapestry needle through second stitch of back needle as if to knit, leaving stitch on needle. Repeat from * until all stitches are joined in this manner. Draw end through last remaining loop and fasten.

DUPLICATE STITCH: This is used to embroider a design on top of stockinette stitch, simulating the knit stitch. With a contrasting color yarn and tapestry needle work as follows: Draw yarn from wrong to right side through center of lower point of stitch. Insert needle at top right-hand side of same stitch. Then holding needle in horizontal position, draw through to top left side of stitch (Diagram 26). Insert again into base of same stitch. Keep your tension even so that the knit stitch is covered completely. Almost any design that appears on a chart or graph can be worked in this stitch.

Diagram 26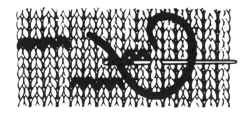

JACQUARD KNITTING OR WORKING WITH TWO OR MORE COLORS: The best-known techniques in this category are Fair Isle and Argyle, or bobbin, knitting.

Fair Isle Knitting: This term is used for an item worked in stockinette stitch, in a design where two or more colors are used across the row and the colors change every few stitches. The yarn not being used is carried and "held" in place on the wrong (purl) side throughout the whole pattern. The color yarn used for most of the stitches on a row is held in the right hand in the usual way; the other colors are held together in the left hand and worked with the left hand where required.

If the yarn is carried more than 3 stitches, catch the carried yarn in order to avoid having a long loop at the back of your work. Accomplish this as follows: * Insert right needle in regular manner, but before picking up yarn to work this stitch, slip point of right-hand needle under the carried yarn(s). (Diagram 27 shows how yarn is caught behind stitches on a knit row.) Work stitch in usual manner, slipping off carried yarn(s) as stitch is completed. Work next 2 stitches in regular manner (Diagram 28). Repeat from * across. Be careful neither to draw yarn too tightly as work will pucker, nor to work too loosely as loops will hang at back of work. Diagrams 29 and 30 show how yarn is caught in front of stitches on a purl row.

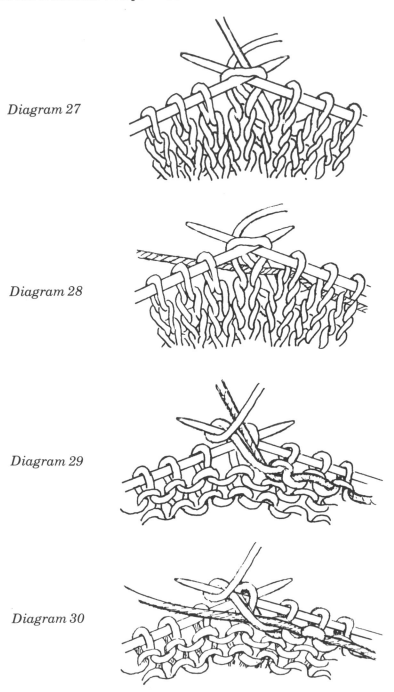

Diagram 27

Diagram 28

Diagram 29

Diagram 30

Argyle or Bobbin Knitting: When a design or motif appears in a knitted garment and the design is not repeated continuously across the row (as in Fair Isle knitting), a bobbin of yarn is attached, where specified in the directions, to knit each color of the motif, or wherever you need one to work separate motifs or vertical stripes.

In order to avoid holes in the work when changing colors, work as follows: Mark right side of work with a safety pin. Make sure that both colors are hanging on wrong side of work. Drop the old color, pick up and tie on a new color and bring it up from under the old color. Knit next stitch (Diagram 31). Old color will be caught through loop of new color on wrong side (Diagram 32). If wrong side is facing you, twist yarns by bringing old color to the left side and new color to the right side between points of needles. Break off bobbin when color unit has been completed, leaving a 5-inch end to weave into work. Never carry any color yarn across back of work.

Diagram 31

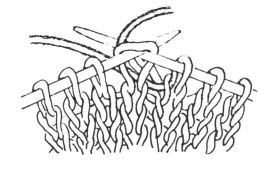

Diagram 32
Back of knitted
red/white swatch.

Make Your Own Bobbins: Instead of wrapping yarn around plastic bobbins, which have a tendency to get tangled, we have found that it is much more convenient to work with bobbins made by winding a few yards of yarn into small balls that pull from the center. Following are directions and diagrams on how to wind these little balls:

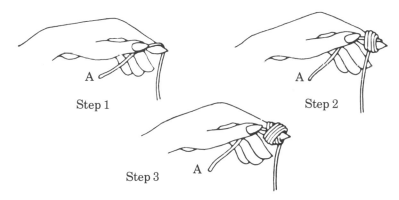

Step 1   Step 2

Step 3

Step 1. Hold yarn in left hand with thumb and index finger in position as shown in drawing.

Step 2. While holding end A firmly in left hand, with right hand wind yarn around index finger about 4 times.

Step 3. With right hand, wind yarn 4 times at an angle over strands on finger, being careful not to catch A.

Continue to wind yarn around finger 6 times more at a different angle.

Remove ball of yarn from index finger and, holding it between thumb and index finger, continue to wind ball, turning it every 4 or 5 winds, being always careful not to catch end A into winding. Break off and tuck outside end into last winding. End A will now pull from center.

To rewind: After most of the yarn is used from these balls, they become loose and will drop down and need rewinding. Without breaking off ball from work, start with end of yarn that is attached to work and rewind ball following Steps 1 through 3.

HOW TO READ CHARTS: When working duplicate stitch, Fair Isle, or Argyle knitting, a chart is given with the directions. Follow the chart for design and key for colors. Simply think of each little square on the chart as one stitch in your work. On knit rows follow the chart from right to left, on purl rows from left to right.

SELVAGES: The edge stitches form the selvages on knitted fabric and they may be worked in various ways:

Chain Stitch Selvage (for stockinette stitch): Slip the first stitch of each row, knit-wise on the knit rows and purl-wise on the purl rows. A chain, the equivalent of 2 rows, is formed along each edge.

Moss Stitch Selvage (for stockinette stitch): Knit the first and last stitch on every row. This makes a nice edge for a seam allowance.

Garter Stitch Selvage (for stockinette stitch): This selvage is slightly narrower than moss stitch. On knit rows: With yarn in front, slip first stitch purl-wise, bring yarn to back between points of needles, knit across row. On purl rows: With yarn in front, slip first stitch knit-wise, bring yarn around to back and then to front between points of needles, purl across row.

Chain Stitch Selvage (for garter stitch): On each row, with yarn in front of work, slip first stitch purl-wise, bring yarn to back between points of needles, knit across.

Note: When working any of the garments in this book, you may want to apply any one of these selvage treatments to your work; unless specific directions are given, use whichever one you find most suitable.

FINISHING

This is the process of steaming, or pressing and shaping a garment before sewing it together.

LAUNDERING KNITTED GARMENTS: To prevent work from getting dirty, especially an item made of light-colored yarn, it is a good idea to wash your hands every time before picking it up. Keep your work in a plastic bag or pillowcase to keep the dust and dirt out.

If your work has gotten dirty, you must wash pieces before block-ing. Many manufacturers print laundering instructions on the yarn wrapper. DO READ THEM. There are so many types of yarn—natural, synthetic or a combination of both—that it is advisable to check for these instructions. Nowadays, many synthetic yarns and specially treated wool yarns are machine washable and dryable.

Wash 100 percent wool yarns by hand, using lukewarm water and a good-quality soap which dissolves well in cool water. Gently swish the garment through the suds; do not rub or twist.

Wash and rinse several times until all soap suds have been rinsed out.

Gently squeeze out water, never wring. To speed up drying, put the item on a heavy bath towel, roll it up tightly and press down on it firmly. Spread the garment on a flat surface. If you hang up a wet knitted garment, the weight of the water will pull it out of shape. An exception is linen knitwear, and special washing directions are given for those within the book. Shape garment according to desired meas-urements. Block when still moist.

Never dry in direct sunlight or near artificial heat, or discoloration and shrinkage may occur.

Many synthetic yarns can be machine washed with warm water and the machine set on the gentle cycle. Synthetic yarns don't have the "crimp" or natural elasticity of wool yarns and need more careful shap-ing after washing to prevent stretching.

BLOCKING: If a garment is made in separate pieces, such as back, front, and sleeves, two similar pieces should be blocked together before sewing seams.

First, lay single piece to be blocked face down or two similar pieces together with right sides facing each other, on a padded board. Place *rust-proof* pins all around outer edges of pieces, about ¼ inch apart, adjusting them to desired proportions by giving a tuck here and there. Do not pin out ribbing.

Place a damp cloth over them. On smooth surfaces such as stockinette stitch, press hot iron very gently on damp cloth; do it quickly enough not to dry out the pressing cloth. Remove cloth and let pieces dry thoroughly before unpinning them.

Pieces worked in any raised pattern or fluffy yarns should, of course, never be pressed but steamed. Pin pieces out as before. Hold steam iron as close as possible above work without touching it. Move it around above entire piece. Unpin when dry.

Sometimes it is convenient not to have to use an iron at all. Sometimes it just isn't necessary. Pin out pieces, and with a spray bottle or plant mister, dampen them well. Again, let them dry well before you unpin them. And that's all you'll have to do.

TO SEW EDGES TOGETHER: Seams should be as invisible as possible.

Backstitching is the most common method of seaming knitwear. Use the yarn in which the garment was made, unless it is very bulky or the instructions specify otherwise, and a blunt, large-eyed tapestry needle. (**Note:** Sometimes it is possible to split yarn. Knitting worsted, for example, consists of 4 strands of yarn that are twisted together; untwist them and use 2 strands to sew with.) Pin pieces to be sewn together, with right sides facing, matching patterns or stripes where necessary. Backstitch (Diagram 33) close to the edge, being careful not to pull the yarn too tight or seam will pucker and lose its elasticity.

Diagram 33

Weaving is also a method to invisibly join two top edges that have the same number of stitches and have not been bound off. (See weaving, or kitchener, stitch directions, page 32.)

Overhand Stitch: Place two pieces to be joined side by side, flat on surface, and with right sides up. Draw sewing yarn through first stitch at bottom edge of one piece, then draw through corresponding stitch of other piece. Continue in this manner, just picking up edge stitch of each piece until seam is completed.

Picking Up the Eye: The "eye" is the little horizontal thread between two stitches. With right side of work facing you, place side edges in position for sewing. Following Diagram 34, pick up the eye between first and second stitches from edge. Remember, you can only do this on an edge without decreases, and it only works well on stockinette stitch when you have the same number of rows on each side.

Diagram 34

TO SEW IN SLEEVES: With right sides together, pin sleeve in armhole, with center of sleeve cap at shoulder seam and matching underarm seams, easing in any fullness. Backstitch in place.

Note: The length of a sleeve is always measured from wrist to armhole along underarm seam.

FINISHING TOUCHES IN CROCHET

Some of the directions in this book indicate crochet finishes on a knitted garment. In each case a specific size is given, but here is some general information on crochet hooks and step-by-step directions to show you the basic steps of crochet.

Crochet hooks are available in many materials and sizes. Aluminum and plastic hooks are generally used for wool yarn.

Their sizes are indicated either by a number—1 through 10½—or a letter—B through K—or both, K and 10½ being the largest size.

Steel hooks are mostly used with cotton yarns for such fine work as laces, doilies, and delicate edgings. Their size is indicated by a number only. They range from 00 to 15, a hair-fine hook.

Just as for knitting needles, there is a difference in sizing between the U.S. and England and Canada. Here are their comparative sizes.

Aluminum or Plastic Hooks

U.S.	1(B)	2(C)	3(D)	4(E)	5(F)	6(G)	7(H)	8(I)	9(J)	10½(K)
Eng./Can.	14	13	12	11	10	9	8	7	6	4

Steel Hooks

U.S.	1	2	3	4	5	6	7	8	9	10	11	12	13	14	15
Eng./Can.	0	1	1½	2	2½	3	3½	4	4½	5	5½	6	6½	7	7½

HOW TO CROCHET

FOUNDATION CHAIN
or chain st (ch)

1

Make a slip knot on hook, held in the right hand. Thread yarn over left ring finger, under middle, and over index fingers, holding short end between the thumb and middle finger.

2

Pass hook under and over yarn and draw it through loop on hook. Repeat for as many stitches as the directions specify.

SINGLE CROCHET (sc)

3

Insert hook into second stitch from hook, under the two upper strands.

4

Pass hook under and over yarn and draw it through the stitch.

5

Pass hook under and over yarn again and draw it through the two loops on hook.

HALF DOUBLE CROCHET (hdc)

6

Pass hook under and over yarn, insert hook into third stitch from hook, under the two upper strands.

7

Pass hook under and over yarn and draw it through the stitch. Pass hook under and over yarn again and draw it through the three loops on hook.

DOUBLE CROCHET (dc)

8

Pass hook under and over yarn, insert hook into the fourth stitch from hook, under the two upper strands.

9

Pass hook under and over yarn and draw it through the stitch, then pass hook under and over yarn again. Draw yarn through the first two loops on hook. Pass hook under and over yarn again and draw it through remaining two loops on hook.

WOMEN'S SWEATERS

The Classics

Soft V-Neck Pullover

This pullover is made with pink punch and periwinkle stripes and garter-stitch details.

SIZES: 8 [10–12–14]. Garment measures 14″ [15″–15″–16″] across bust.

MATERIALS: Bucilla Melody mohair, 4 [5–5–6] (1 oz.) balls champagne No. 4 (color A). 1 ball each pink punch No. 10 (B) and periwinkle No. 5 (C); 1 pair knitting needles No. 7 (or English needles No. 6) **or the size that will give you the correct gauge.**

GAUGE: 5 sts = 1″; 13 rows = 2″.

Note: Check your row gauge carefully.

BACK: Starting at lower edge with A, cast on 72 [78–78–82] sts. Work garter-st border for ¾″.

Now work in stockinette st. With A, work for 2″. Break off A; attach B and work 4 rows. Work 2 rows C and 4 rows B. Attach A and continue to work even until piece measures 11″ from beg or desired length to underarm.

To Shape Armholes: Bind off 6 [7–7–8] sts at beg of next 2 rows. Work even on 60 [64–64–66] sts until armholes measure 6½″ [6¾″–7″–7¼″] from beg.

To Shape Shoulders: Bind off 12 [14–14–15] sts at beg of next 2 rows. Place remaining 36 sts on holder for back neck.

FRONT: Work as for back until piece measures 2½″ less than back to underarm. **Next row:** Work 36 [39–39–41] sts, place remaining 36 [39–39–41] sts on holder.

46

To Shape Neck and Armholes: Working on one side only, dec 1 st at neck edge every 3rd row until piece measures same as back to underarm. Then bind off 6 [7–7–8] sts at armhole edge and continue to dec 1 st at neck edge every 3rd row until 12 [14–14–15] sts remain. Work even on remaining sts, if necessary, until armhole measures same as back. Bind off remaining 12 [14–14–15] sts.

Place 36 [39–39–41] sts from front holder on needle. Work to correspond to other side.

SLEEVES: Starting at lower edge with A, cast on 66 [68–70–72] sts. Work in garter st for 5 rows. Then work in stockinette st for 1". Break off A; attach B and work 4 rows. Work 2 rows C and 4 rows B. Attach A and continue to work until piece measures 7" from beg. Then work garter-st border for ¾". Break off. Work other sleeve in same manner.

FINISHING: Sew shoulder, underarm and sleeve seams. Sew sleeves in place.

Neckband: With dp needles and right side facing you, using A, pick up and k 62 [64–66–68] sts across left front edge; place marker on needle at center point of V neck, pick up and k 62 [64–66–68] sts across right front edge, then pick up and k remaining 36 sts from back neck holder. Work in ribbing of k 1, p 1 for 1", decreasing 1 st at each side of marker on each rnd. Bind off in ribbing.

Polo Pullover

*The pullover is worked
vertically in rust stripes on a
sand-colored background.
The waistband is added on
later and worked
horizontally.*

SIZES: (8–10) [(12–14)—(16–18)]. Sweater measures about 16″
[18″–20″] across back at underarms, 21″ [21½″–22″] from back neck to
lower edge.

MATERIALS: Bucilla Perlette Orlon acrylic yarn, 3 [4–4] (1¾-
oz.) balls sand No. 7 (color A) and 3 balls rust No. 19 (B); knitting
needles, 1 pair No. 4 (or English needles No. 9) **or the size that will
give you the correct gauge.**

GAUGE: 13 sts = 2″; 9 rows = 1″.

Note: Body of sweater is worked vertically in stripes. Waistband
is picked up later around lower edge of sweater and worked horizontally.

PATTERN: Starting with directions for Back (below) and working in stockinette stitch, work stripes as follows: For sizes (8–10) work
¾″ with A. For sizes (12–14) work ½″ with B and 1¼″ with A. For sizes
(16–18) work 1″ with A. Then for all sizes repeat pattern of ½″ B, 1¼″ A,
ending in stripes to match beg of piece.

BACK: Starting at left side edge above waistband with color A
[B–A], cast on 65 sts.

To Shape Left Armhole: Working stripes as specified under Pattern above, work even on 65 sts for ½″, ending with a k row. Inc 1 st at
beg (armhole edge) of next row, then at same edge every other row 2
[3–4] times more (68 [69–70] sts), ending with a p row. **Next row:** K
across, then cast 43 [45–47] sts onto right-hand needle for armhole,
ending at shoulder edge (111 [114–117] sts).

To Shape Shoulders: Work even for 1″ [1¼″–1½″]; inc 1 st at
shoulder edge on next row, then at same edge every 1½″ once more (113
[116–119] sts). Work even until piece measures 8″ [9″–10″] from beg
(side edge) to center back; place marker at neck edge. Continue to work
even until piece measures same as first half from center marker to last

48

inc at left shoulder. Dec 1 st at right shoulder edge on next row, then at same edge every 1½" once more (111 [114–117] sts). Work even for 1" [1¼"–1½"], ending at right shoulder edge.

To Shape Right Armhole: Bind off 43 [45–47] sts for armhole, then work to end of row (68 [69–70] sts). Dec 1 st at armhole edge every other row 3 [4–5] times (65 sts), then work even for ½", finishing in stripe pattern to match left armhole and side edge. Bind off.

Mark center 54 rows (about 6") for back neck edge.

FRONT: Starting at right side edge, work as for back until piece measures same as back to first neck marker, ending at shoulder edge (113 [116–119]).

To Shape Neck: Bind off 8 sts at beg of next row. Dec 1 st at neck edge on each of next 3 rows. Work 1 row even. Working all decs at neck edge, dec 1 st on next row. Work 2 rows even. Dec 1 st on next row. Work 3 rows even. Dec 1 st on next row. Work 4 rows even. Dec 1 st on next row (98 [101–104] sts). Work even for 2 rows, ending at neck edge. **Next row:** P 40 sts and place on holder for right side edge of front opening, then work to end of row. Work even on remaining sts for 11 rows for center front, ending at neck edge. Place sts on a holder. Break off.

Neckband: Place sts for right side edge of front opening from holder onto needle and attach B. Work in ribbing of k 1, p 1 for 1¼". Bind off in ribbing. With B, cast on 40 sts for left edge of opening and work in ribbing for 1¼". Place sts from front holder onto free needle and work across them in stockinette st in pattern stripe color (98 [101–104] sts). Complete front to correspond to other side. Lap end of one neckband over end of other band and sew along center front neck edge.

SLEEVES: Starting at lower edge with B, cast on 85 sts. Work in ribbing of k 1, p 1 for 4". Break off B; attach A. Work in stockinette st for 1¼"; attach B and work ½". Working with A, inc 1 st at beg and end of every other row 1 [2–3] times (87 [89–91] sts). Work even until stripe measures 1".

To Shape Cap: Continuing in stripe pattern, bind off 3 sts at beg of next 2 rows. Dec 1 st at beg and end of every other row 9 [10–11] times, then every row 4 times. Bind off 2 sts at beg of next 6 rows. Bind off remaining 43 sts.

WAISTBAND: With color B, pick up and k 128 [146–164] sts as evenly spaced as possible across lower edge of back. Work in ribbing of k 1, p 1 for 4¼". Bind off loosely in ribbing. Work front waistband in same manner.

FINISHING: Sew shoulder, side and sleeve seams. Sew sleeves in place.

Collar: With B, pick up and k 130 sts around neck edge, including ends of neck ribbing. Work in ribbing of k 1, p 1 for 4". Bind off in ribbing.

The Classics **49**

Springy Openwork Yoke Sweater

A side zipper keeps the high midriff band snug-fitting around the waist. The yoke is worked around without seams.

SIZES: 8 [10–12–14]. Garment width across back at underarms: 16″ [17″–18″–19″].

MATERIALS: Lily Sugar-'n-Cream (100%-cotton yarn), 4 [4–5–5] (125-yard) balls; knitting needles: for body and sleeves, 1 pair single-pointed needles No. 8 (or English needles No. 5), **or the size that will give you the correct gauge;** for yoke and ribbing, 16″ circular needle No. 5 and 1 pair single-pointed needles No. 5 (or English needles No. 8); 10″ neckline zipper; 8 markers (plastic rings or paper clips); aluminum crochet hook size G.

GAUGE: On No. 8 needles: 4 sts = 1″; 6 rows = 1″.

Note: The yoke is worked around without seams. The body of the sweater has side seams to accommodate the zipper. The yoke is made in one size; increases for the various sizes are made at the underarms after the yoke has been completed.

YOKE: Starting at neck edge with circular needle, cast on 112 sts. **1st rnd:** Place marker on right-hand point of needle and, being careful not to twist sts, join them into circle by knitting the first st; k 36 for back, place marker on needle, k 1 (seam st), place marker, k 17 for sleeve, place marker, k 1 (seam st), place marker, k 37 for front, place marker, k 1 (seam st), place marker, k 17 for sleeve, place marker, k 1 (seam st). Work yoke pattern as follows: **2nd rnd:** * Sl marker, y o, k to next marker, y o, sl marker, k 1. Repeat from * 3 times more (8 sts increased). **3rd rnd:** Slipping markers as you work, k 2, (* y o, k 2 tog. Repeat from * to within 1 st of next marker, k 4) 3 times; work in pattern to within 1 st of last marker, k 2. **4th rnd:** Repeat 2nd rnd (8 sts increased). **5th rnd:** Slipping markers as you work, k 2, * p to within 2 sts of next marker, k 5. Repeat from * twice more; p to within 2 sts of last marker, k 3. Repeat 2nd rnd through 5th rnd 6 times more (224 sts).

To Divide Bodice and Sleeves: Changing to single-pointed needles No. 8 and removing markers, k next 65 sts (back), place following 47 sts on a holder for sleeve, place next 65 sts on another holder for front, place remaining 47 sts on 3rd holder for 2nd sleeve. Work back and forth on single-pointed No. 8 needles across back sts only, as follows:

To Shape Back—Underarm Shaping: Working in stockinette st (p 1 row, k 1 row), inc 0 [2–2–2] sts at beg of next 2 rows, then inc 0 [0–2–4] sts at beg of following 2 rows (65 [69–73–77] sts).

Work even in stockinette st until piece measures 3" [3"–3½"–3½"] from yoke. Dec 1 st at beg and end of next row, then every 1½" twice more (59 [63–67–71] sts). Work even until piece measures 7" [7"–7½"–7½"] from yoke.

Change to single-pointed needles No. 5 and work in ribbing as follows: **1st row:** K 1, * p 1, k 1. Repeat from * across. **2nd row:** P 1, * k 1, p 1. Repeat from * across. Repeat last 2 rows until ribbing measures 6". Bind off in ribbing.

To Shape Front: With right side facing you, place the 65 sts from front holder onto left-hand needle No. 8. Attach yarn and k across. Complete front in same manner as back.

Sleeves: With right side facing you, place the 47 sts from right sleeve holder onto left-hand needle No. 8. Attach yarn and k across. Work underarm shaping as for back (47 [51–55–59] sts). Work even in stockinette st for 1" more, ending with a p row. Change to single-pointed No. 5 needles. **Next row:** K across, decreasing 4 [6–8–10] sts evenly spaced across row (43 [45–47–49] sts). Work in ribbing as for back for 1". Bind off in ribbing. Work other sleeve in same manner.

FINISHING: Leaving lower left side open for zipper, sew side and sleeve seams. Sew zipper in place. With hook, crochet 2 rows sc around neck, keeping neckline flat.

Classic Rib-Knit Threesome

Soft Purple Pullover

This soft sweater is done in simple k 2, p 2 stretch ribbing all the way.

Ribbed V-Neck Cardigan

A hip-hugging V-neck cardigan is accented with brass buttons.

Ribbed and Laced Pullover

This red polo shirt laces at the neck, in an unusual raised slip rib pattern.

RIBBED AND LACED PULLOVER

SIZES: Small (8–10) [medium (12–14)—large (16–18)]. Shirt measures approximately 16″ [18″–20″] across at underarms.

MATERIALS: Columbia Minerva Nantuk Sweater and Afghan yarn (100% Orlon acrylic), 6 [7–8] (2-oz.) skeins; knitting needles, 1 pair each No. 6 and No. 8 (or English needles No. 7 and No. 5) **or the size that will give you the correct gauge.**

GAUGE: Using No. 8 needles, 11 sts = 2″; 7 rows = 1″.

BACK: Starting at lower edge with No. 8 needles, cast on 89 [97–109] sts. **1st row (wrong side):** K 2, p 1, * k 3, p 1. Repeat from * across, ending with k 2. **2nd row:** P 2, bring yarn to back, sl next st as if to p, * bring yarn to front, p 3, bring yarn to back, sl next st as if to p. Repeat from * across, ending with p 2. Repeat last 2 rows for pattern until piece measures 15½″ from beg, or desired length to underarms.

To Shape Armholes: Bind off 5 sts at beg of next 2 rows. Dec 1 st at beg and end of every other row 5 [6–7] times (69 [75–85] sts). Work even in pattern until armholes measure 7″ [7¼″–7½″].

To Shape Shoulders: Bind off 6 [6–7] sts at beg of next 4 rows, then 6 [8–10] sts at beg of next 2 rows. Slip remaining 33 [35–36] sts on a st holder for back neck. Break off.

FRONT: Work as for back until piece measures 15″ from beg.

To Shape Front Opening and Armholes—1st row: Work in pattern across 39 [43–49] sts, drop yarn; attach another skein and bind off next 11 sts (center sts), work in pattern to end. **2nd row:** Work in pattern to front opening, drop yarn and skip opening, with first skein work to end. Work even on both sides at once in this manner, keeping in pattern and, **at same time,** when piece measures same as back to armholes, shape armholes as for back. Work even on 29 [32–37] sts on each side until armholes measure 4½″ [5″–5½″].

To Shape Neck: Continuing in pattern, dec 1 st at each neck edge every row 8 [9–10] times, then every other row 3 times (18 [20–24] sts on each side). Work even until armholes measure same as back.

To Shape Shoulders: Bind off 6 [6–7] sts at beg of next 4 rows, then 6 [8–10] sts at beg of next 2 rows. Break off.

SLEEVES: Starting at lower edge with No. 6 needles, cast on 45 sts. Work in pattern for 3″. Change to No. 8 needles. Continuing in pattern, inc 1 st at beg and end of next row, then every 1½″ [1½″–1″] 7 [9–10] times (61 [65–67] sts). Work even until sleeve measures 17″, or desired length to underarm.

To Shape Cap: Bind off 5 sts at beg of next 2 rows. Dec 1 st at beg and end of next 2 rows, then at beg and end of every other row 12 [13–14] times. Bind off 4 sts at beg of next 4 rows. Bind off remaining 7 [9–9] sts.

FINISHING: Block pieces with back neck sts still on holder. Sew shoulder, underarm and sleeve seams. Sew sleeves in place.

Right Front Neckband: With right side facing you, attach yarn at lower right corner of front opening, using No. 6 needles pick up and k 34 [37–40] sts along straight edge of opening, place marker on needle at corner, pick up and k 23 sts along right front neck edge, then k 17 [18–18] sts from back neck holder (74 [78–81] sts). Leave remaining sts on holder. **1st row (wrong side):** Work in ribbing of k 1, p 1 for 1 row, slipping marker. **2nd row (inc row):** Work in rib pattern to within 1 st of marker, inc 1 st in next st, sl marker, inc 1 st in next st, rib to end. **3rd row (eyelet row):** Working added sts in ribbing, rib to marker, sl marker, rib 2 sts, y o, k 2 tog (eyelet made), * rib 8 [9–10] sts, y o, k 2 tog. Repeat from * twice more (4 eyelets), work last st. **4th row:** Rib across, working each y o in pattern. Work 3 more rows in ribbing. Bind off in ribbing.

Left Front Neckband: With right side facing you, attach yarn at center back neck, k remaining 16 [17–18] sts from holder, pick up and k 23 sts along neck edge, place marker on needle, pick up and k 34 [37–40] sts along straight edge of front opening (73 [77–81] sts). Work as for right band for 2 rows. **3rd row (eyelet row):** Working added sts in ribbing, rib 1 st, p 2 tog, y o, * rib 8 [9–10] sts, p 2 tog, y o. Repeat from * twice more (4 eyelets made); rib to end. Complete as for right band.

Sew neck bands tog at center back and to lower edge of front opening.

Lacing: With No. 6 needles, cast on 4 sts. Work in ribbing of k 1, p 1 for 40″. Bind off in ribbing. Lace through eyelets as for lacing a shoe, tie at neck.

RIBBED V-NECK CARDIGAN

SIZES: Small (8–10) [medium (12–14)—large (16–18)]. Cardigan measures approximately 14″ [15″–16″] across at underarms without stretching ribbed pattern.

MATERIALS: Reynold's Mohair No. 1 (85% mohair, 15% Vinyon), 6 [7–9] (40-gram—1½ oz.) balls; knitting needles, 1 pair each No. 6 and No. 8 (or English needles No. 7 and No. 5) **or the size that will give you the correct gauge;** 7 buttons.

GAUGE: Using No. 8 needles and without stretching ribbed pattern, 5 sts = 1″; 6 rows = 1″.

BACK: Starting at lower edge with No. 8 needles, cast on 70 [74–78] sts. **1st row:** P 2, * k 2, p 2. Repeat from * across. **2nd row:** K 2,

* p 2, k 2. Repeat from * across. Repeat last 2 rows until piece measures 19″ from beg, or desired length to underarms.

To Shape Armholes: Bind off 3 sts at beg of next 2 rows. Dec 1 st at beg and end of every other row 6 times. Work even on 52 [56–60] sts until armholes measure 7″ [7¼″–7½″].

To Shape Shoulders: Bind off 5 [6–7] sts at beg of next 2 rows, then 5 sts at beg of next 4 rows. Bind off remaining 22 [24–26] sts in ribbing for back neck.

LEFT FRONT: Starting at lower edge with No. 8 needles, cast on 34 [36–38] sts. Work in ribbing until piece measures same as back to underarm.

To Shape Armhole and Neck: Bind off 2 sts at beg (armhole edge) of next row. Dec 1 st at same edge every other row 6 times, and **at same time,** dec 1 st at neck edge every other row once, then every 4th row 10 times.

Continuing in pattern as established, work even on 14 [16–18] sts until armhole measures same as back armholes, ending at armhole edge.

To Shape Shoulder: Bind off 6 sts at beg of next row, then 4 [5–6] sts at beg of every other row twice. Break off.

LEFT FRONT BAND: Pin shoulder seam. With No. 6 needles cast on 7 sts. **1st row:** K 1, (p 1, k 1) 3 times. **2nd row:** P 1, (k 1, p 1) 3 times. Repeat last 2 rows until band fits along front edge, front neck and to center of back neck. Bind off in ribbing. Sew in place on left front, leaving section for back neck free temporarily. Remove shoulder pins. Mark band for 7 buttons about 3″ apart, with the first button 1½″ from lower edge.

RIGHT FRONT: Work as for left front, reversing shapings.

RIGHT FRONT BAND: Work as for left band, working buttonholes opposite markers on left band as follows: Starting from front edge, work 3 sts, bind off 2 sts, work to end. On following row, cast on 2 sts over bound-off sts.

SLEEVES: Starting at lower edge with No. 6 needles, cast on 32 [34–36] sts. Work in ribbing of k 1, p 1 for 2″. **Next row:** K across, increasing 4 sts as evenly spaced as possible (36 [38–40] sts). Change to No. 8 needles. Work in ribbing of k 2, p 2, increasing 1 st at beg and end of row every 1½″ 6 [7–8] times, working added sts in ribbing.

Work even on 48 [52–56] sts until sleeve measures 18″ from beg, or desired length to underarm.

To Shape Cap: Bind off 3 sts at beg of next 2 rows. Dec 1 st at beg and end of every other row 9 [10–11] times (24 [26–28] sts). Bind off 2 sts at beg of next 4 rows. Bind off remaining 16 [18–20] sts.

FINISHING: Block pieces without stretching (see page 37 for blocking). Sew shoulder, back neckband, side and sleeve seams. Sew sleeves in place. Overcast buttonholes. Sew buttons in place.

SOFT PURPLE PULLOVER

SIZES: Small (8–10) [medium (12–14)—large (16–18)]. Pullover measures approximately 15″ [15½″–16″] across at underarms, without stretching ribbed pattern.

MATERIALS: Bucilla Melody (50% mohair, 50% acrylic), 10 [11–13] (1-oz.) balls; knitting needles, 1 pair each No. 5 and No. 6 (or English needles No. 8 and No. 7) **or the size that will give you the correct gauge.**

GAUGE: Using No. 6 needles and without stretching ribbed pattern, 6 sts = 1″; 7 rows = 1″.

BACK: Starting at lower edge with No. 6 needles, cast on 90 [94–98] sts. **1st row:** P 2, * k 2, p 2. Repeat from * across. **2nd row:** K 2, * p 2, k 2. Repeat from * across. Repeat these 2 rows until piece measures 15½″ from beg, or desired length to underarms.

To Shape Armholes: Bind off 5 sts at beg of next 2 rows. Dec 1 st at beg and end of every other row 3 [4–5] times. Work even on 74 [76–78] sts until armholes measure 7″ [7¼″–7½″].

To Shape Shoulders: Bind off 6 sts at beg of next 6 rows (38 [40–42] sts).

Collar: Change to No. 5 needles and work even in rib pattern over remaining 38 [40–42] sts for 1½″. Bind off loosely in ribbing.

FRONT: Work as for back.

SLEEVES: Starting at lower edge with No. 5 needles, cast on 58 [62–66] sts. Work even in rib pattern for 4″. Change to No. 6 needles and continue in pattern until sleeve measures 18″ from beg, or desired length to underarm.

To Shape Cap: Bind off 5 sts at beg of next 2 rows. Dec 1 st at beg and end of every other row 5 [6–7] times. Bind off remaining 38 [40–42] sts.

FINISHING: Block pieces without stretching (see page 37 for blocking). Sew shoulder, collar, underarm and sleeve seams. Sew sleeves in place.

The Peasant Pullover

The fisherman's sweater softens up with fuller sleeves and a tie at the neck, but the patterns are the traditional diamonds and teardrops against a reverse stockinette and moss stitch background, edged by narrow cables.

SIZES: (8–10) [(12–14)—(16–18)]. Sweater measures about 17" [19"–21"] across back at underarms, 21½" [22"–22½"] from shoulder to lower edge.

MATERIALS: Unger's Scheepjes Natuurwol (100% wool), 9 [10–11] (1⅝-oz.) balls light gray No. 5001; knitting needles, 1 pair each No. 6 and No. 7 (or English needles No. 7 and No. 6) **or the size that will give you the correct gauge;** 1 dp needle.

GAUGE: 5 sts = 1"; 7 rows = 1" in moss st.

Note: Directions for pullover start after pattern directions below.

VERTICAL BAND: Pattern A—Diamond worked over 14 sts with a 24 row repeat.

1st row (wrong side): P across. **2nd row:** P 5; sl next 2 sts to dp needle and hold in front of work, k 2, k 2 sts from dp needle (double cross made), p 5. **3rd row:** K 5, p 4, k 5. **4th row:** P 4; sl next st to dp needle and hold in back of work, k 2, k st from dp needle (right slope made); slip next 2 sts to dp needle and hold in front of work, p 1, k 2 sts from dp needle (left slope), p 4. **5th row:** K 4, p 2, k 1, p 3, k 4. **6th row:** P 3, work right slope over next 3 sts, p 1, k 1, work left slope over next 3 sts, p 3. **7th row and all odd numbered rows through 19th row:** K the k sts and p the p sts. **8th row:** P 2, work right slope over next 3 sts, (p 1, k 1) twice; work left slope over next 3 sts, p 2. **10th row:** P 1, work right slope over next 3 sts, (p 1, k 1) 3 times; work left slope over next 3 sts, p 1. **12th row:** P 1, work left slope over next 3 sts, (k 1, p 1) 3 times; work right slope over next 3 sts, purling st from dp needle, p 1. **14th row:** P 2, work left slope over next 3 sts, (k 1, p 1) twice; work right slope over next 3 sts, purling st from dp needle, p 2. **16th row:** P 3, work left slope over next 3 sts, k 1, p 1, work right slope over next 3 sts, purling st from dp needle, p 3. **18th row:** P 4, work left slope over next 3 sts, work right slope over next 3 sts, purling st from dp needle, p 4. **20th row:** Repeat 2nd row. **21st through 25th rows:** Starting with a k row, work 5 rows in reverse stockinette st (k on wrong side rows, p on right side rows).

Teardrop worked over 14 sts with a 22 row repeat.

26th row (right side): P 3, k 1, y o, p 6, y o, k 1, p 3. **27th row:** K 3, p 2, k 6, p 2, k 3. **28th row:** P 3, k 2, p 6, k 2, p 3. **29th row:** Repeat 27th row. **30th row:** Repeat 28th row. **31st row:** K 3, p 2 tog, k 6, p 2 tog, k 3. **32nd through 35th rows:** Starting with a p row, work 4 rows in reverse stockinette st.

Repeat 26th through 31st rows once more, then starting with a p row, work 6 rows in reverse stockinette st.

Repeat 2nd through 47th rows for vertical band pattern.

Pattern B—Single Cable Rib worked over 2 sts with a 2 row repeat.

1st row (wrong side): P 2. **2nd row:** Sl next st to dp needle and hold in front of work, k 1, k st from dp needle (left slope made).

Repeat these 2 rows for pattern.

Pattern C—Moss st worked on an even number of sts with a 4 row repeat.

1st row (wrong side): * K 1, p 1. Repeat from * across. **2nd row:** K across. **3rd row:** * P 1, k 1. Repeat from * across. **4th row:** K across.

Repeat first through 4th rows for pattern.

BACK: Starting at lower edge with No. 6 needles, cast on 84 [94–104] sts. Work in k 1, p 1 ribbing for 2½", increasing 4 sts evenly spaced on last row (88 [98–108] sts). Change to No. 7 needles and work even in pattern C until piece measures 14½" or desired length to underarms.

To Shape Armholes: Bind off 6 [7–8] sts at beg of next 2 rows. Dec 1 st at beg and end of every other row 6 [7–9] times. Work even on 64 [70–74] sts until armholes measure 7" [7½"–8"].

To Shape Shoulders: Bind off 6 [7–8] sts at beg of next 4 rows. Bind off remaining 40 [42–42] sts.

FRONT: Cast on and work ribbing as for back. Change to No. 7 needles and establish patterns as follows:

1st row (wrong side): Work first row of pattern C over first 14 [18–22] sts, place a marker on needle, p 1, k 2, work first row of pattern B over next 2 sts, work first row of pattern A over next 14 sts, work first row of pattern B over next 2 sts, k 2, p 1, place marker, work first row of pattern C over next 12 [14–16] sts, place marker, p 1, k 2, work first row of pattern B over next 2 sts, work first row of pattern A over next 14 sts, work first row of pattern B over next 2 sts, k 2, p 1, place marker, work first row of pattern C over last 14 [18–22] sts.

Using diagram as a guide, following each pattern separately and slipping markers on each row, work even in pattern until piece measures same as back to underarms, ending with a wrong side row. Keep the 3 sts next to each pattern B in ribbing as indicated. (**Note:** Rows 26 through 30 of pattern A have added sts; do not count these sts when checking the number of sts on a row.)

To Shape Armhole and Front Opening: Bind off 6 [7–8] sts, work in pattern across 34 [38–42] sts, (k 1, p 1) twice for front border, place remaining 44 [49–54] sts on a holder. **Next row:** (K 1, p 1) twice; work in pattern across. Working on one side only, continuing in pattern and keeping 4 sts at front opening in ribbing, dec 1 st at arm edge every other row 6 [7–9] times. Work even on remaining 32 [35–37] sts until armhole measures 4½" [5"–5½"], ending at front opening.

To Shape Neck: Bind off 10 [11–11] sts at beg of next row, work across. Bind off 2 sts at neck edge every other row 5 times. Work even on 12 [14–16] sts until armhole measures same as back, ending at armhole edge.

To Shape Shoulder: Bind off 6 [7–8] sts at beg of next row. Work 1 row even. Bind off remaining 6 [7–8] sts.

Attach yarn at center front and work other side to correspond, reversing shaping.

SLEEVES: Starting at lower edge with No. 6 needles, cast on 48 [50–52] sts. Work in ribbing of k 1, p 1 for 3", increasing 16 sts evenly spaced on last row (64 [66–68] sts). Change to No. 7 needles. Working in pattern C, work 2" even, then dec 1 st at beg and end of next row. Repeat this dec every 2" twice more (58 [60–62] sts); then inc 1 st at beg and end of row every 2" 4 times. Work even on 66 [68–70] sts until sleeve measures 18" or desired length to underarm.

To Shape Cap: Bind off 6 [7–8] sts at beg of next 2 rows. Dec 1 st at beg and end of every other row 12 times. Bind off 2 sts at beg of next 4 rows. Bind off remaining sts.

FINISHING: Sew shoulder, side and sleeve seams. Sew in sleeves.

Neckband: With right side of work facing you, using No. 6 needles, pick up and k 100 [104–104] sts around neck edge. Work in ribbing of k 1, p 1 for 1". Bind off in ribbing.

Ties (make 2): Using No. 6 needles, cast on 4 sts. Work even in stockinette st until piece measures 7". Bind off. Sew ties to neckband.

14 [18–22]	3	2	14	2	3	12 [14–16]	3	2	14	2	3	14 [18–22]	stitches
C	rib	B	A	B	rib	C	rib	B	A	B	rib	C	patterns

Pullover Diagram

Raglan in the Round

This sweater is worked from the neck down in one piece, alternating knit and purl rounds in white and green.

SIZES: (6–12) [14–18]. At underarms pullover will stretch to fit 30″ to 34″ [35″ to 39″].

MATERIALS: Unger's Roly-Poly acrylic yarn, 2 [3] (3½ oz.) balls white No. 8001 (color W) and 2 balls green No. 8352 (G); knitting needles, 1 set (4) dp needles No. 8 and one 29″ circular needle No. 8 (or English needles No. 5) **or the sizes that will give you the correct gauge.**

GAUGE: In garter st: 4 sts = 1″.

Note: Sweater is knitted from the neck down in one piece. Change to circular needle when dp needles become crowded.

Starting at turtleneck with dp needles and W, cast on 72 sts. Divide sts evenly on 3 needles. Join in circle, being careful not to twist sts. Work around in ribbing of k 1, p 1 for 7½″.

Next rnd: With W k 8 sts for sleeve, place marker on needle, k 28 sts for back, place marker, k 8 sts for other sleeve, place marker, k last 28 sts for front, place marker. Drop W; attach G.

Working in rounds as before, slipping markers on each rnd, work in garter-stitch stripe pattern as follows: **1st rnd:** With G p around. Drop G; pick up W. **2nd rnd:** With W k around, increasing 1 st before and after each of the 4 markers (8 sts inc on rnd). Drop W; pick up G.

60

Repeat first and 2nd rnds for pattern until there are 50 [60] sts on each sleeve section and 70 [80] sts each on back and front sections (240 [280] sts in all), ending with a G rnd.

To Divide Work: Using two small stitch holders or a length of yarn as holder for each sleeve, slip next 50 [60] sleeve sts to holder, remove marker; with W k across next 70 [80] sts, remove marker, slip next 50 [60] sleeve sts to another set of holders, remove marker, k across last 70 [80] sts.

BODY: Continue in garter-st stripe pattern, working around as before; work even on 140 [160] sts for 10″ [11″]. Break off G. With W k next rnd, decreasing 14 [20] sts evenly spaced around, then work around in ribbing of k 1, p 1, for 4″. Bind off loosely in ribbing.

SLEEVES: Starting at underarm, divide 50 [60] sts from holders for one sleeve evenly on 3 dp needles. Mark underarm and attach W at marker; working around in pattern as established, work even for 3″ [4″]. **Next rnd (dec rnd):** Dec 1 st at beg and end of rnd at underarm. Repeat dec rnd every 1″ [¾″] until 30 [34] sts remain. Work even until sleeve measures 14″ from underarm or 2½″ less than desired length. Break off G. With W work in ribbing of k 1, p 1 for 2½″. Bind off loosely in ribbing.

Bright Blue Sweaters

The sweater with the deeply ribbed turtleneck and sleeve decoration is worked in knitting worsted, with ribbing details adding an unusual textured pattern. The V-neck cardigan is worked in stockinette stitch with fine rib details on shoulder, sleeves, and pockets.

DEEPLY RIBBED TURTLENECK SWEATER

SIZES: Misses' 10 [12–14–16]. Garment width around underarms, about 35″ [37″–39″–41″].

MATERIALS: Knitting worsted, 26 [26–28–30] ozs. Knitting needles No. 8 and No. 9, **or the size that will give you the correct gauge.**

GAUGE: 4 sts and 6 = 1".

PATTERN—Row 1 (right side): * P 2, k 3; repeat from *, end p 2. **Row 2:** * K 2, p 3; repeat from *, end k 2. Repeat these 2 rows for rib pat.

BACK: With No. 9 needles, cast on 80 [84–88–92] sts. Work in k 1, p 1 ribbing for 3 rows. **Next row:** K 16 [18–19–21], 12 sts in rib pat, k 24 [24–26–26], 12 sts in rib pat, k 16 [18–19–21] sts. **Next row:** P 16 [18–19–21], 12 sts in rib pat, p 24 [24–26–26], 12 sts in rib pat, p 16 [18–19–21] sts. Repeat these 2 rows for pat. Dec 1 st each edge every 2" 5 times—70 [74–78–82] sts. Work until 16" [16½"–16¾"–17"] from beg, inc 1 st each edge every row 10 times working added sts in stockinette st (k on right side, p on wrong side)—90 [94–98–102] sts.

To Shape Sleeves: At each edge, cast on 52 [52–57–57] sts for sleeves, also working these sts in stockinette st—194 [198–212–216] sts. Work until sleeve measures 4" [4¼"–4½"–5"]. With center 24 [24–26–26] sts in stockinette st, continue the 12 sts at each side of center sts in established rib pat, and with care to continue rib correctly, work rib pat on the 73 [75–81–83] sleeve sts at each side. Work until sleeve measures 8" [8½"–9"–9½"].

To Shape Shoulders and Neck: At each edge bind off 21 [22–23–24] sts twice. Mark center 18 [18–20–20] sts. **Next row:** Bind off first 21 [22–23–24] sts. Work to first marker, join another ball of yarn and bind off center 18 [18–20–20] sts, finish row. Working both sides at once, bind off 21 [22–23–24] sts at beg of next sleeve edge, then 22 [21–24–23] sts at beg of next sleeve edge on each piece; **at the same time,** dec 1 st at each neck edge every row 3 times.

FRONT: Work same as back until sleeve measures 6¼" [6½"–7"–7½"], starting rib pat on sleeve sts at same point as on back— 194 [198–212–216] sts.

To Shape Shoulders and Neck—Next row: Work 90 [92–98–100] sts, join another ball of yarn and bind off center 14 [14–16–16] sts, finish row—90 [92–98–100] sts each side. Working both sides at once, dec 1 st at each neck edge every row 5 times—85 [87–93–95] sts each side. Work until sleeve measures 8" [8½"–9"–9½"]. At each sleeve edge, bind off 21 [22–23–24] sts 3 times, 22 [21–24–23] sts once.

FINISHING: Sew right shoulder and sleeve seam. **Turtleneck:** Right side facing, with No. 8 needles, pick up 87 [87–92–92] sts around neck edge. Work in rib pat so that when collar is folded outwards right side of pat will be on right side of garment. Work for 10". Bind off. Seam collar and shoulder.

Cuff: Right side facing, with No. 8 needles, pick up 47 [52–52–57] sts along bottom edge of each sleeve. Work in rib pat so that when cuff is folded outwards right side of pat will be on right side of sleeve. Work for 6½". Bind off in pat. Sew side and sleeve seams.

V-NECK CARDIGAN

SIZES: 8 [10–12–14]. Garment width around underarms, about 31½″ [33½″–35″–37″].

MATERIALS: Sport yarn, 18 [18–20–20] ozs. Knitting needles No. 4, **or the size that will give you the correct gauge.** 7 buttons.

GAUGE: 6 sts and 8 rows = 1″.

PATTERN—Row 1 (right side): * P 2, k 1; repeat from *, end p 2. **Row 2:** * K 2, p 1; repeat from *, end k 2. Repeat these 2 rows for rib pat.

BACK: With double strand of yarn, cast on 104 [110–116–120] sts. Change to single strand of yarn. Work in k 1, p 1 ribbing for 3 rows. **For sizes 8 and 10 only:** Inc 1 st at end of last row—105 [111–116–120] sts. Work in pat as follows: **Row 1 (right side):** P 47 [50–51–53] sts for reverse stockinette st; p 2, * k 1, p 2, repeat from * 2 [2–3–3] more times, p last 47 [50–51–53] sts. **Row 2:** K 47 [50–51–53] sts; k 2, * p 1, k 2, repeat from * 2 [2–3–3] more times, k to end. Repeat these 2 rows for pat, dec'ing 1 st each edge every 2″ 5 times—95 [101–106–110] sts. Work even until 15½″ [16″–16½″–16¾″] from beg, end wrong side. Start working 3 sts more on each side of center 11 [11–14–14] sts in rib pat until the entire row is in rib pat. **At the same time,** when 18″ [18½″–18¾″–19″] from beg, at each armhole edge bind off 4 [5–5–4] sts once, 2 sts twice, 1 st once—77 [81–86–92] sts. Work until 6½″ [7″–7½″–7¾″] above beg of armhole shaping.

To Shape Neck and Shoulders: Mark center 25 [25–26–28] sts. **Next row:** Keeping to pat, bind off 7 [9–8–9] sts, finish row. **Next row:** Bind off 7 [9–8–9] sts, work to first marker, join another ball of yarn and bind off center 25 [25–26–28] sts, finish row. Working both sides at once, at each armhole edge bind off 8 [8–9–10] sts twice; **at the same time,** dec 1 st at each neck edge every row 3 [3–4–3] times.

LEFT FRONT: With double strand of yarn, cast on 65 [67–71–73] sts. Change to single strand of yarn. **Row 1 (right side):** Work in k 1, p 1 ribbing for 48 [50–54–56] sts, k 8 sts, sl 1 with yarn in back for folding edge, k 8 sts (facing). **Row 2:** P 17, work next 48 [50–54–56] sts in established ribbing. **Row 3:** Repeat Row 1. Continue 17 sts at front edge in stockinette st (k on right side, p on wrong side), slipping center st on every right side row and 48 [50–54–56] sts in reverse stockinette st (p on right side, k on wrong side), dec 1 st at side edge every 2″ 5 [4–5–5] times—60 [63–66–68] sts. Work even until 15½″ [16″–16½″–16¾″] from beg. On next row, begin working 3 sts in rib pat next to front edge sts, then 3 sts more in rib pat every right side row until all but 17 sts at front edge are in rib pat; **at the same time,** dec 1 st inside 17 front edge sts for neck every 4th row 11 [11–13–13] times and when 18″ [18½″–18¾″–19″] from beg, at each armhole edge, bind off 4 [5–5–4] sts once, 2 sts twice, 1 st once—40 [42–43–46] sts. Work until 6½″ [7″–7½″–7¾″] above beg of armhole shaping.

To Shape Shoulder: At armhole edge bind off 7 [9–8–9] sts once, then 8 [8–9–10] sts twice—17 sts. Work even on remaining sts to fit to center back of neck when band is slightly stretched. Bind off. Mark position of 6 buttons evenly spaced on left front with the first one ¾″ from lower edge and the last one at beg of neck shaping.

RIGHT FRONT: Work to correspond to left front, reversing shaping and marking buttonholes opposite markers, as follows: Work 3 sts from front edge, bind off 2 sts, work until 7 sts beyond bound-off sts, bind off 2 sts, finish row. On next row, cast on 2 sts over bound-off sts.

SLEEVES: With double strand of yarn, cast on 60 [64–68–72] sts. Change to single strand of yarn. Work in k 1, p 1 ribbing for 3 rows. **Row 1 (right side):** P 8 [10–12–14]; k 1, p 2, k 1; p 36 center sts; k 1, p 2, k 1; p 8 [10–12–14] sts. **Row 2:** K 8 [10–12–14]; p 1, k 2, p 1; k 36 center sts; p 1, k 2, p 1; k 8 [10–12–14] sts. Repeat these 2 rows for pat, inc 1 st each edge every 2½″ 5 times, working added sts in reverse stockinette st—70 [74–78–82] sts. Work until 15½″ [16″–16½″–16¾″] from beg or desired length to underarm.

To Shape Cap: At each edge bind off 5 [5–5–6] sts once, 3 sts once, 2 sts once. Dec 1 st at beg of every row 22 [26–30–32] times—28 sts. Bind off 2 sts at each edge 3 times—16 sts. Bind off.

POCKETS: Make 2. With single strand of yarn, cast on 32 sts. Work in rib pat, inc 1 st each edge every row 3 times—38 sts. Work in rib pat until 4″ from beg. Change to stockinette st and dec 10 sts evenly spaced across first row—28 sts. Continue in stockinette st for 1½″, end right side. K next wrong side row for folding edge. Continue in stockinette st for 1½″ more. Bind off.

FINISHING: Sew shoulder, side and sleeve seams. Sew in sleeves. Join front band and facing at back of neck and sew to neck. Fold front edge along slip st and tack facing to wrong side of cardigan. Overcast buttonholes. Fold pocket hem along folding edge and tack to inside of pocket. Sew on pockets as pictured. Sew a button on each pocket as pictured. Sew buttons on left front edge.

Belted Wrap Jacket

A classic to wear forever. Tweedy, gray wool yarn is knitted in simple stockinette stitch with wishbone cable detail on front. It has a ribbed shawl collar, pockets, and belt.

SIZES: (6–8) [(10–12)—(14–16)—(18–20)]. Sweater measures 17″ [18″–20″–22″] across back at underarms and 27½″ [28″–28½″–29″] from shoulder to lower edge.

MATERIALS: Bernat Blarney-spun, 11 [12–12–13] (2-oz.) balls country gray No. 7997; knitting needles, 1 pair No. 9 (or English needles No. 4) **or the size that will give you the correct gauge;** 1 dp needle for cable pattern.

GAUGE: 4 sts = 1″; 6 rows = 1″ in stockinette st.

WISHBONE CABLE PATTERN: Worked on 13 sts. **1st row (right side):** K 2 tog, y o, k 9, y o, k 2 tog. **2nd row:** P 13. **3rd row:** Repeat first row. **4th row:** Repeat 2nd row. **5th row:** K 2 tog, y o, sl next 3 sts to dp needle and hold in front of work, k 3, bring the sts on dp needle to back of work, k 3, k sts from dp needle, y o, k 2 tog. **6th row:** P 13. **7th row:** Repeat first row. **8th row:** Repeat 2nd row. Repeat first through 8th rows for pattern.

BACK: Starting at lower edge, cast on 80 [84–92–100] sts. Work in k 1, p 1 ribbing for 3 rows. Establish pattern as follows: **1st row (right side):** K 13 [15–17–19], work first pattern row over next 13 sts, k 28 [28–32–36], work first pattern row over next 13 sts, k 13 [15–17–19]. **2nd row:** P 13 [15–17–19], work 2nd pattern row over next 13 sts, p 28 [28–32–36], work 2nd pattern row over next 13 sts, p last 13 [15–17–19] sts. Keeping cable pattern as established and working other sts in stockinette st, work even until piece measures 5″ from beg, ending with a wrong side row. Dec 1 st at beg and end of next row, then every 4″ twice more (74 [78–86–94] sts). Work even until piece measures 20″ from beg, or desired length to underarms.

To Shape Armholes: Bind off 4 [5–6–6] sts at beg of next 2 rows, bind off 2 [2–2–3] sts at beg of next 2 rows, then dec 1 st at beg and end of every other row 2 [1–3–4] times. Work even on 58 [62–64–68] sts until armholes measure 7″ [7½″–8″–8½″].

To Shape Shoulders: Bind off 7 [8–8–9] sts at beg of next 4 rows. Bind off remaining 30 [30–32–32] sts.

LEFT FRONT: Starting at lower edge, cast on 49 [51–55–59] sts. **1st row:** K 1, * p 1, k 1. Repeat from * across. **2nd row:** K 1, * k 1, p 1. Repeat from * to within last 2 sts, k 2. Repeat first row once. Establish pattern as follows: **1st row (right side):** K 13 [15–17–19], work first pattern row over next 13 sts, k 16 [16–18–20], (p 1, k 1) 3 times; k 1 for front border. **2nd row:** K 1, (p 1, k 1) 3 times for front border; p 16 [16–18–20], work 2nd pattern row over next 13 sts, p 13 [15–17–19]. Mark end of row for side edge. Continuing to work in stockinette st and pattern, and keeping rib st border at front edge, work even until piece measures 5″ from beg, ending at side edge. From side edge, dec 1 st at beg of next row, then every 4″ twice more. Work even on 46 [48–52–56] sts until piece measures 18″ from beg, ending at side edge.

To Shape Neck and Armhole: Work in pattern across to within last 2 sts, k 2 tog. Dec 1 st at neck edge every other row 18 times more, then every 4th row 5 [5–6–6] times and, **at same time,** when piece measures same as back to underarm, shape armhole as follows: At side edge, bind off 4 [5–6–6] sts once, bind off 2 [2–2–3] sts once, then dec 1 st every other row 2 [1–3–4] times. Work even on 14 [16–16–18] sts until armhole measures same as back to shoulder.

To Shape Shoulder: At arm edge, bind off 7 [8–8–9] sts every other row twice.

RIGHT FRONT: Starting at lower edge, cast on 49 [51–55–59] sts. Work first 3 rows as for left front. Establish pattern as follows: **1st row (right side):** K 1, (k 1, p 1) 3 times for front border; k 16 [16–18–20], work first pattern row over next 13 sts, k 13 [15–17–19]. Mark end of row for side edge. **2nd row:** P 13 [15–17–19], work 2nd pattern row over next 13 sts, p 16 [16–18–20], k 1, (p 1, k 1) 3 times for front border. Continuing to work in stockinette st and pattern, and keeping rib st border at front edge, complete right front to correspond to left front, reversing all shaping.

SLEEVES: Starting at lower edge, cast on 50 [50–52–54] sts. Work in k 1, p 1 ribbing for 3 rows. Starting with a k row and working in stockinette st, inc 1 st at beg and end of row every 6″ twice. Work even on 54 [54–56–58] sts until sleeve measures 17″ from beg, or desired length to underarm.

To Shape Cap: Bind off 4 [5–6–6] sts at beg of next 2 rows, 2 sts at beg of next 2 rows, then dec 1 st at beg and end of every other row 9 [9–10–10] times. Bind off 2 sts at beg of next 4 rows. Bind off remaining 16 [14–12–14] sts.

Sew shoulder seams.

COLLAR: With right side of work facing you, pick up and k 58 [60–62–64] sts along right front neck edge, pick up and k 30 [30–32–32] sts along back neck edge, pick up and k 58 [60–62–64] sts along left front neck edge 146 [150–156–160] sts. Work 1 row even in k 1, p 1 ribbing. **Short Rows—1st row:** Work in ribbing to within last 4 sts; do not work last 4 sts; turn. **2nd row:** Sl 1, work in ribbing to within last 4 sts; turn. **3rd row:** Sl 1, work in ribbing to within last 8 sts; turn. **4th row:** Sl 1, work in ribbing to within last 8 sts; turn. Continue to work 4 less sts each row for 17 rows in all and, *at same time,* when 6 rows have been completed, place 2 markers evenly spaced across 6th row and inc 1 st each side of each marker on next row (4 sts inc), being careful to keep added sts in ribbing. When 16 rows have been completed, place 4 markers evenly spaced across 16th row and inc 1 st each side of each marker on next row (8 sts inc), being careful to keep added sts in ribbing. **18th row:** Work in ribbing across. Work 6 more rows even in ribbing. Bind off in ribbing.

POCKETS: Cast on 32 sts. Work in k 1, p 1 ribbing for 6″. Bind off in ribbing (top edge).

BELT: Cast on 10 sts. Work in k 1, p 1 ribbing for 44″, or desired length. Bind off in ribbing.

FINISHING: Sew side and sleeve seams. Sew sleeves in place. Following photograph for placement, sew pockets in place.

Camel Cables

This stunning cardigan coat
has a deeply carved
cabled front, back, and
sleeves on a reverse stockinette
stitch background. It
buttons in front.

SIZES: (8–10) [(12–14)—(16–18)]. Cardigan measures 17″ [19″–21″] across back at underarms when stretched for a snug fit. Length is 26″ [27″–28″] from shoulder.

MATERIALS: Bear Brand Winsom Orlon acrylic yarn, 16 [18–20] (2-oz.) skeins camel No. 368; knitting needles, 1 pair No. 10 (or English needles No. 3) **or the size that will give you the correct gauge;** 1 dp needle for cable pattern; 6 wooden buttons ¾″ in diameter.

Note: Work with 2 strands of yarn held together throughout.

GAUGE: When stretched, 9 sts = 2″.

BACK: Starting at lower edge with 2 strands of yarn, cast on 84 [94–104] sts. Work in ribbing of k 1, p 1 for 1¾″; on last row inc 1 st (85 [95–105]) sts. Change to cable pattern as follows: **1st row (right side):** P 8 [11–14], k 3, p 3, k 3, * k 6 [7–8], k 3, p 3, k 3. Repeat from * across, ending p 8 [11–14]. **2nd row:** K 8 [11–14], p 3, k 3, p 3, * k 6 [7–8], p 3, k 3, p 3. Repeat from * across, ending k 8 [11–14]. Repeat 1st and 2nd rows 4 times more.

11th row (right side): P 8 [11–14], sl next 3 sts to dp needle and hold in front of work, k next 3 sts, p next 3 sts, then k 3 sts from dp needle (cable twist made), * p 6 [7–8], work cable twist over next 9 sts. Repeat from * across, ending p 8 [11–14]. **12th row:** Repeat 2nd row. **13th through 30th rows:** Repeat 1st and 2nd rows 9 times.

Repeat last 20 rows (11th row through 30th row) for cable pattern until piece measures 8″ [8½″–9″] from beg, ending with a wrong-side row.

Next row (dec row): P 6 [9–12], p 2 tog for dec and, keeping cable pattern as established, work across row to within last 8 [11–14] sts, p 2 tog for another dec, p 6 [9–12].

Always decreasing on inner edge of both side panels as before, repeat dec row every 2″ twice more, then every 3″ once. Work even on 77 [87–97] sts until piece measures 18″ [18½″–19″] from beg.

Put marker in work at beg and end of last row to mark beg of armholes. Continue to work even until piece measures 8″ [8½″–9″] from markers. Entire piece should measure 26 ″ [27″–28″] from beg.

To Shape Shoulders: Bind off 8 [9–10] sts at beg of next 4 rows, then 9 [11–12] sts at beg of next 2 rows. Place remaining 27 [29–33] sts on holder for collar.

LEFT FRONT: Starting at lower edge, cast on 46 [50–56] sts. **1st row (right side):** * K 1, p 1. Repeat from * across, ending k 2. **2nd row:** * K 1, p 1. Repeat from * across. Repeat 1st and 2nd rows for 1¾″, ending with a wrong-side row; on last row inc 0 [1–0] st (46 [51–56]) sts.

Change to cable pattern as follows: **1st row (right side):** P 8 [11–14], * k 3, p 3, k 3, p 6 [7–8]. Repeat from * once more, then (k 1, p 1) 3 times; k 2 for front border. **2nd row:** (K 1, p 1) 4 times for border, * k 6 [7–8], p 3, k 3, p 3. Repeat from * once more, end k 8 [11–14].

Repeat 1st and 2nd rows 4 times more. Mark end of last row for side edge. **11th row (right side):** P 8 [11–14], * work cable twist over 9 sts, p 6 [7–8]. Repeat from * once more, work ribbed border as established. **12th row:** Repeat 2nd row.

Continuing to work in pattern as established (working cable twist every 20th row as for back and keeping ribbed border at front edge), work even until piece measures 8″ [9″–10″] from beg, ending at side edge.

Next row (dec row): P 6 [9–12], p 2 tog for dec; complete row, keeping pattern as established.

Always decreasing on inner edge of side panel as before, repeat this dec every 2″ twice more, then every 3″ once. Work even on 42 [47–52] sts until piece measures 18″ [18½″–19″] from beg. Put marker in work at side edge for armhole and continue in pattern as before for 1″ more, ending at front edge. **Next row (wrong side):** Work ribbed border, then k 1, p 1 (2 extra sts are worked in front border pattern and 2 sts less in cable pattern as established); complete row.

For Lapel: Working even on 42 [47–52] sts, at front edge work 2 extra sts in ribbing after border sts (and 2 sts less in cable pattern) every 4th row until 18 [18–20] sts are worked in ribbing (this includes border sts).

Continue in pattern as established until piece measures same length as back to shoulder, ending at side edge.

70

To Shape Shoulder: At arm edge only, bind off 8 [9–10] sts twice; then 9 [11–12] sts once. Place remaining 17 [18–20] sts on holder for collar.

Mark left front border for 6 buttonholes, placing the first one 1½" above lower edge, the last one 2" above armhole marker and spacing the others evenly between.

RIGHT FRONT: Work to correspond to left front, reversing shaping and working buttonholes opposite markers on left front border as follows: Starting at front edge and working in ribbing, work 2 sts, bind off 4 sts, work to end of row. On next row, cast on 4 sts over bound-off sts.

SLEEVE: Starting at lower edge, cast on 43 [47–51] sts for cuff. Starting with a k row, work in stockinette st for 4", ending with a p row. Change to cable pattern as follows: **1st row (right side):** P 2 [3–4], k 3, p 3, k 3, * p 6 [7–8], k 3, p 3, k 3. Repeat from * once more, ending p 2 [3–4]. **2nd row:** K 2 [3–4], p 3, k 3, p 3, * k 6 [7–8], p 3, k 3, p 3. Repeat from * once more, ending k 2 [3–4].

Work in pattern as established until 10 rows are completed. **11th row (right side):** Work cable twist over each group of 9 sts.

Continuing to work in pattern as established, work cable twist every 20th row and, **at same time,** inc 1 st at beg and end of row every 1¼" 11 times, keeping inc sts in pattern as established. Work even on 65 [69–73] sts until sleeve measures 21½" from beg (this includes 3½" for turned-back cuff), or desired length to underarm plus cuff. Bind off all sts.

FINISHING: Sew shoulder seams. Sew top edge of sleeve between armhole markers. Sew side and sleeve seams. **Collar:** Place all sts from holders onto needle. Attach yarn and, working in ribbing as established on front lapels, k 1, p 1 in ribbing for 3". Bind off all sts in ribbing.

Sew on buttons. Block lightly.

Car Coat for the First Chilly Fall Days

A comfy car coat in warm brown and rust tones, this cardigan is worked from the top down; the hood is sewn on afterward.

SIZES: Small (6–8) [medium (10–12)—large (14–16)]. Garment width across back at underarms: 17" [19"–21"].

MATERIALS: Bucilla de Luxe knitting worsted 3 [3–4] (4-oz.) skeins copper No. 330 (color A), 2 skeins medium oxford No. 71 (B), 1 [1–2] skeins rustone No. 29 (C), 1 skein winter white No. 375 (D); knitting needles: For yoke, body, sleeves and hood, 24" circular needle No. 7 and 1 pair single-pointed needles No. 7 (or English needles No. 6), **or the size that will give you the correct gauge;** for ribbing and hems, 1 pair single-pointed needles No. 6 (or English needles No. 7); 7 buttons; 1¾ yards 1½"-wide grosgrain ribbon; 4 markers (plastic rings or paper clips).

GAUGE: On No. 7 needles: 11 sts = 2"; 7 rows = 1".

Note: The yoke is worked back and forth, in one piece, on circular needle. The body of the coat has side seams.

YOKE: Starting at neck edge with circular needle and color A, cast on 66 [68–70] sts. Do not join sts in a ring, but work back and forth in stockinette st as follows: **1st row (wrong side):** P 10 for left front, place marker on needle, p 6 [7–8] for sleeve, place marker, p 34 for back, place marker, p 6 [7–8] for sleeve, place marker, p 10 for right front. **2nd row:** K to within 1 st of first marker, * k in front and in back of next st (1 st inc), sl marker, inc in next st, k to within 1 st of next marker. Repeat from * twice more; inc in next st, sl marker, inc in next st, k to end, cast on 3 sts at right front edge (11 sts inc in row). **3rd**

row: P across, slipping markers, cast on 3 sts at end of row (left front edge). Repeat last 2 rows 3 times more (26 sts on each front—122 [124–126] sts in all).

Next row: (K 1, p 1) 4 times for border; k to last 8 sts, increasing before and after each marker as before, (p 1, k 1) 4 times for front border (8 sts inc). **Following row:** (P 1, k 1) 4 times; p to last 8 sts, slipping markers, (k 1, p 1) 4 times. Repeat last 2 rows 24 [26–28] times more (322 [340–358] sts).

To Divide Bodice and Sleeves: Keeping border pattern, work first 51 [53–55] sts and place them on a holder for left front, remove marker, k next 64 [69–74] sts and place them on another holder for left sleeve, remove marker, k across 92 [96–100] sts for back, remove marker, place next 64 [69–74] sts on a 3rd holder for sleeve, remove marker, place remaining 51 [53–55] sts on 4th holder for right front. Work only on back sts as follows:

To Shape Back: Underarm Shaping—1st row: Cast on 2 [4–6] sts for left underarm, p across, cast on 2 [4–6] sts for right underarm (96 [104–112] sts).

Work even until piece measures 4½" from underarm. Break off. Attach B and work 8 rows. Break off. Work 8 rows C and 8 rows D. Attach A, * work 1 row. Inc 1 st at beg and end of next row; then work even for 4". Break off *. Attach B and repeat from * to * once more. Attach C and repeat from * to * once more, ending with a k row (102 [110–118] sts). Now, work hem as follows, or make coat longer, if you wish, before working hem.

HEM: K 1 row across wrong side for hemline. Change to No. 6 needles and, starting with a k row, work even for 1". Bind off.

LEFT FRONT: With wrong side facing you, place sts from left front holder onto left-hand single-pointed needle No. 7 and attach A at underarm edge. Cast on 2 [4–6] sts for underarm, p across, working border (53 [57–61] sts). Keeping 8 border sts, work even as for back to first B stripe. Do not break off A; attach B. Work border sts with A and remainder of row with B, being careful to twist colors so as to avoid a hole. Continue in stripe pattern as for back, increasing at side edge at beg of the 4" stripes as before and keeping border sts in color A. End with a wrong-side row just before hemline.

HEM—NEXT ROW: Bind off border sts; p across right side for hemline. Change to No. 6 needles and complete hem. Bind off.

RIGHT FRONT: With right side facing you, place sts from right front holder onto left-hand No. 7 needle and attach A at underarm edge. Cast on 2 [4–6] sts for underarm, k across, working border sts (53 [57–61] sts). Complete to correspond to left front.

SLEEVES—Left Sleeve: With wrong side facing you, place sts from left sleeve holder onto left-hand No. 7 needle and attach A. Cast on 2 [4–6] sts for underarm, p across, cast on 2 [4–6] sts for underarm (68 [77–86] sts). Work in stripe pattern of 5" A, 8 rows each B, C and D,

3½" A, and **at same time** dec 1 st at beg and end of row every 1" twelve times (44 [53–62] sts). With B, work 3½" or until sleeve is desired length. Work hem. Bind off.

Right Sleeve: With right side facing you, place sts from right sleeve holder onto needle and attach A. Cast on 2 [4–6] sts, k across, cast on 2 [4–6] sts. Work as for other sleeve.

FINISHING—Neck Ribbing: Attach A at front neck edge; with No. 6 needles, pick up 94 sts along neck edge. Work in ribbing of k 1, p 1 for 1". Bind off in ribbing.

Sew side and sleeve seams. Turn up sleeves and lower edge at hemlines and sew in place. Face front borders with grosgrain ribbon. Sew buttons, evenly spaced, to left front border. Make buttonholes by machine on right border.

HOOD: The hood is composed of 3 pieces: 1 rectangular piece that covers the top and back of the head, and 2 side panels.

Rectangular Piece: Starting at back neck edge with single-pointed needles No. 7 and A, cast on 44 sts. Work even in stockinette st for 15". Bind off.

Left Panel: Starting at neck edge with A, cast on 30 sts. Work even in stockinette st for 8½", ending with a p row. Bind off 3 sts at beg of next row, then at same edge every other row twice more for shaped corner at top back edge (21 sts). Bind off.

Right Panel: Work as for left panel for 8½", ending with a k row. Shape corner as before. Bind off.

Finishing: Sew bound-off edge, shaped corner and 1 long edge of left panel to a long edge of rectangle. Sew right panel to opposite edge of rectangle in same manner. Hood now forms cap shape.

Facing: With No. 6 needle, pick up 46 sts along face edge of a side panel, 42 sts along end (face edge) of rectangle and 46 sts along face edge of other side panel. Attach A. Work even in stockinette st for 2". Bind off. Turn facing to inside and sew in place. Sew hood to inside neck edge of jacket so that ribbing extends above edge of hood.

Long, Sleeveless Cabled Vest

This vest is worked in a combination of cables and a lacy fishtail pattern, with low, knit-in hip pockets.

SIZES: (6–8) [(10–12)—(14–16)—(18–20)]. Vest measures 15″ [17″–19″–21″] across at underarms without stretching and 26″ from shoulder to lower edge.

MATERIALS: Bear Brand Soufflé (90% acrylic fiber, 10% Vinyon), 4 [5–5–5] (1¾-oz.) balls violite No. 479; knitting needles, 1 pair each 14″ No. 6 and No. 7 (or English needles No. 7 and No. 6) **or the size that will give you the correct gauge;** 6 buttons ¾″ in diameter; 1 dp needle for cable.

GAUGE: 17 sts = 3″; 8 rows = 1″.

BACK: Starting at lower edge with No. 6 needles, cast on 83 [95–107–119] sts. Work in ribbing of k 1, p 1 for 1″. Change to No. 7 needles and work in pattern as follows: **1st row (right side):** P 1 [2–3–4], k 6, p 1 [2–3–4], * k 7, p 1 [2–3–4], k 6, p 1 [2–3–4]. Repeat from * across. **2nd row and all even-numbered rows:** K 1 [2–3–4], p 6, k 1 [2–3–4], * p 7, k 1 [2–3–4], p 6, k 1 [2–3–4]. Repeat from * across. **3rd row:** P 1 [2–3–4], k 6, p 1 [2–3–4], * y o, sl 1, k 1, psso, k 3, k 2 tog, y o, p 1 [2–3–4], k 6, p 1 [2–3–4]. Repeat from * across. **5th row:** P 1 [2–3–4], k 6, p 1 [2–3–4], * k 1, y o, sl 1, k 1, psso, k 1, k 2 tog, y o, k 1, p 1 [2–3–4], k 6, p 1 [2–3–4]. Repeat from * across. **7th row:** P 1 [2–3–4], sl next 3 sts on cable needle and hold in back of work, k next 3 sts, k 3 sts from cable needle (cable crossed), p 1 [2–3–4], * k 2, y o, sl 1, k 2 tog, psso, y o, k 2, p 1 [2–3–4], sl next 3 sts on cable needle and hold in back of work, k 3, k 3 sts from cable needle, p 1 [2–3–4]. Repeat from * across. **8th row:** Repeat 2nd row.

Repeating 1st through 8th rows for pattern, work even until piece measures 18″ from beg, ending with an 8th pattern row.

To Shape Armholes: Bind off 5 [6–7–8] sts at beg of next 2 rows. Dec 1 st at beg and end of every other row 5 [6–8–9] times. Work even in pattern on 63 [71–77–85] sts until armholes measure 7¾″ [8″–8¼″–8½″].

To Shape Shoulders: Bind off 5 [6–7–8] sts at beg of next 6 rows. Bind off remaining 33 [35–35–37] sts.

POCKET LINING: With No. 7 needles, cast on 22 [24–26–28] sts. Work in ribbing of k 1, p 1 for 4″. Place sts on st holder. Make another pocket lining and place on separate holder.

LEFT FRONT: Starting at lower edge with No. 6 needles, cast on 38 [44–50–56] sts. Work in ribbing of k 1, p 1 for 1″. Change to No. 7 needles and work even in pattern as for back until piece measures 5″ from beg, ending with an 8th pattern row. Mark end of this row for side edge.

POCKET OPENING: Work in pattern across first 8 [10–12–14] sts, sl next 22 [24–26–28] sts to a holder, sl pocket lining sts from holder onto left-hand needle, work in pattern across pocket lining sts and remaining 8 [10–12–14] sts of front. Continue to work even in pattern until piece measures same as back to underarm, ending at side edge.

To Shape Armhole and Neck: Bind off 5 [6–7–8] sts, work in pattern across to within last 2 sts, k 2 tog. Work 1 row even. Dec 1 st at armhole edge on next row, then every other row 4 [5–7–8] times more and, **at same time,** dec 1 st at neck edge every other row 12 [13–13–14] times more (15 [18–21–24] sts). Work even in pattern until armhole measures same as back, ending at armhole edge.

To Shape Shoulder: Bind off 5 [6–7–8] sts at beg of next row, then every other row twice more.

RIGHT FRONT: Work to correspond to left front, reversing all shaping.

FINISHING: Sew shoulder seams.

Left Front Band: With right side of work facing you, attach yarn to center of back neck edge. Using No. 6 needles, pick up and k 158 [161–163–166] sts along back neck edge and front. Work in ribbing of k 1, p 1 for 1¼″. Bind off in ribbing.

With pins, mark front border for placement of 6 buttons, the first one about 1¼″ from lower edge, the rest spaced about 3½″ apart.

76

Right Front Band: With right side of work facing you, attach yarn at corner of lower edge. Using No. 6 needles, pick up and k 158 [161–163–166] sts to center of back neck edge, work 4 rows in ribbing. Mark placement of buttonholes, following pins on right front. On next row make buttonholes as follows: Work in ribbing to pin, * bind off 2 sts, work in ribbing to next pin. Repeat from * to end. On following row cast on 2 sts over bound-off sts, keeping in ribbing as established. Work even in ribbing until band measures 1¼″. Bind off in ribbing.

Armhole Ribbing: With right side of work facing you, using No. 6 needles, pick up and k 94 [98–102–106] sts around armhole edge. Work in k 1, p 1 ribbing for 1¼″. Bind off in ribbing.

Pocket Borders: With right side of work facing you, sl pocket sts onto left-hand No. 6 needle. Attach yarn and work in ribbing of k 1, p 1 for 1″, increasing 1 st at beg and end of first row. Bind off in ribbing. Sew border and lining in place.

Sew on buttons. Sew ends of bands together at neck. Sew side and armhole ribbing seams. Sew pocket linings in place.

Pretty Pink Mohair Jacket

This is a jacket in tiny, all-over cable pattern.

SIZES: Small (8–10) [medium (10–12)—large (14–16)]. Sweater measures 16″ [18″–20″] across back at underarms, 21″ [21½″–22″] from back of neck to lower edge.

MATERIALS: Bucilla Melody (50% mohair, 50% acrylic), 12 [13–15] (1 oz.) balls; 1 pair No. 7 knitting needles (or English needles No. 6) **or the size that will give you the correct gauge;** 1½ yards 1¼″-wide grosgrain ribbon.

GAUGE: 5 sts = 1″; 6 rows = 1″.

CABLE PATTERN: Multiple of 4 sts plus 2. **1st row (right side):** P 2, * skip first st on left-hand needle, k 2nd st on left-hand needle, then k the skipped st and slip both sts off needle (twist made), p 2. Repeat from * across. **2nd row:** K 2, * p 2, k 2. Repeat from * across. **3rd row:** P 2, * k 2, p 2. Repeat from * across. **4th row:** Repeat 2nd row. Repeat these 4 rows for pattern.

BACK: Starting at lower edge, cast on 82 [90–98] sts. Work even in pattern until piece measures 13½″, or desired length to underarms.

To Shape Armholes: Bind off 2 [3–4] sts at beg of next 2 rows. Dec 1 st at beg and end of every other row 6 [7–8] times. Work even on 66 [70–74] sts until armholes measure 7″ [7½″–8″].

To Shape Shoulders: Bind off 8 sts at beg of next 4 rows, 6 [7–8] sts at beg of next 2 rows. Bind off remaining 22 [24–26] sts.

LEFT FRONT: Starting at lower edge, cast on 50 [54–58] sts. **1st**

row: Starting with twist st, work in cable pattern to within last 6 sts, k 6 (front border). **2nd row:** K 6, work pattern to end. Working 6 front border sts in garter st (k every row) and remaining sts in cable pattern as established, work even until piece measures same as back to underarm, ending at side edge.

To Shape Armhole: Bind off 2 [3–4] sts at beg of next row, then from armhole edge dec 1 st every other row 6 [7–8] times. Work even on 42 [44–46] sts until armhole measures 4″ [4½″–5″], ending at front edge.

To Shape Neck: Bind off 14 [14–15] sts at beg of next row, then dec 1 st at neck edge every other row 6 [7–7] times. Work even on 22 [23–24] sts until armhole measures same as back to shoulder, ending at arm edge.

To Shape Shoulder: (Bind off 8 sts at beg of next row; work 1 row even) twice. Bind off remaining 6 [7–8] sts.

RIGHT FRONT: Work as for left front, reversing all shaping.

SLEEVES: Starting at lower edge, cast on 46 sts. Work as for back in cable pattern, increasing 1 st at beg and end of row every 1″ 12 [14–16] times, working added sts in pattern. Work even on 70 [74–78] sts until sleeve measures 18″, or desired length to underarm, including turned-up cuff if desired.

To Shape Cap: Bind off 6 sts at beg of next 2 rows, then dec 1 st at beg and end of every other row 16 [18–20] times. Bind off 5 sts at beg of next 4 rows. Bind off remaining 6 sts.

FINISHING: Sew shoulder, side and sleeve seams. Sew in sleeves. **Neckband:** Pick up and k 77 [81–85] sts along neck edge. **1st row:** K 1, * p 1, k 1. Repeat from * across. **2nd row:** P 1, * k 1, p 1. Repeat from * across. Repeat last 2 rows for 1″. Bind off in ribbing. Sew ribbon to wrong side of front bands from top of neckband to lower edge.

A Golden Classic

This hip-length cardigan is in wide, over-all ribbing with low-slung patch pockets.

SIZES: 10 [12–14–16–18]. Garment width around underarms, about 36″ [37½″–39″–40½″–42¼″].

MATERIALS: Sport yarn, 18 [20–20–22–22] ozs. Knitting needles No. 2 and 4, **or the size that will give you the correct gauge;** 11 buttons.

GAUGE: 13 sts and 17 rows = 2″.

BACK: With No. 2 needles, cast on 117 [122–127–132–137] sts. **Row 1 (wrong side):** K 2, * p 3, k 2, repeat from *. **Row 2:** K the k sts and p the p sts as they face you. Repeat these 2 rows for rib pat. Work until 7 rows from beg. Change to No. 4 needles. Work even until 17¾″ [18¼″–18½″–18¾″–19″] from beg, end wrong side.

To Shape Armholes: Keeping to pat, at each edge bind off 6 [7–5–5–6] sts once, 2 [2–3–3–3] sts 2 [2–1–1–1] times, 1 [1–2–2–2] sts 1 [1–2–3–3] times, 1 st 1 [1–2–2–2] times—93 [96–99–100–103] sts. Work even in rib pat until 6¾″ [7¼″–7½″–7¾″–8″] above beg of armhole shaping, end wrong side.

To Shape Shoulders: Keeping to pat, at each edge bind off 6 sts 4 times, 7 [8–9–9–10] sts once—31 [32–33–34–35] sts. Place sts on holder.

LEFT FRONT: With No. 2 needles, cast on 66 [68–71–73–76] sts. **Row 1 (wrong side):** K 2, p 4 for front bands, * k 2, p 3, repeat from * across, end **size 12 and 16 only** with k 2. **Row 2:** Beg sizes **12 and 16 only** with p 2, work on all sizes: * k 3, p 2, repeat from * to within last 6 sts at front edge, k 6. The 2 sts at front edge are kept in garter st (k every row). Continue in above established pat, working to same length as back to underarm.

To Shape Armhole: Keeping to pat, at armhole edge bind off 6 [7–5–5–6] sts once, 2 [2–3–3–3] sts 2 [2–1–1–1] times, 1 [1–2–2–2] sts 2 [1–2–3–3] times, 1 st 3 [1–5–3–5] times—51 [55–54–56–56] sts. Work even until 4¼″ [4½″–4½″–4¾″–5″] above beg of armhole shaping, end at front edge.

To Shape Neck: Keeping to pat, bind off 2 sts at front edge, place 10 [11–11–12–12] sts beyond bound-off sts on a strand of yarn, finish row. Continue in pat, dec 1 st at neck edge on next 3 rows, then 1 st at same edge every other row until 31 [32–33–33–34] sts remain. Work even until same length as back to shoulder.

To Shape Shoulder: Keeping to pat, at armhole edge bind off 6 sts 4 times, then 7 [8–9–9–10] sts once. Mark position of 9 buttons evenly spaced with the first one ¾″ from lower edge and the last one ½″ before neck shaping.

RIGHT FRONT: Work to correspond to left front, reversing shaping and pat, making buttonholes opposite markers, as follows: Work 4 sts from front edge, bind off next 2 sts, finish row. On next row, cast on 2 sts over bound-off sts.

SLEEVES: With No. 2 needles, cast on 52 [57–57–62–62] sts. Work in rib pat as on back for 7 rows. Change to No. 4 needles. Continue in pat, inc 1 st each edge of next row, then every 6th row 16 [15–16–15–16] times more, working added sts in rib pat—86 [89–91–94–96] sts. Work even in pat until 15¾″ [16¼″–16½″–16¾″–17¼″] from beg, or desired length to underarm, end wrong side.

To Shape Cap: Keeping to pat, at each edge bind off 5 sts once. Dec 1 st each edge on next 5 rows, then every other row 13 [14–15–16–17] times, then each edge on next 10 rows—20 [21–21–22–22] sts. Bind off.

POCKETS: Make 2. With No. 4 needles, cast on 35 sts. **Row 1 (wrong side):** K 1 (edge st), p 3, * k 2, p 3, repeat from * across, end k 1 (edge st). **Row 2:** K 1 (edge st), k 3, * p 2, k 3, repeat from * across, end k 1 (edge st). Repeat these 2 rows for rib pat. Work until 5¼″ from beg. Change to No. 2 needles. Continue in rib pat for 8 rows, making a buttonhole across center 3 sts on row 2. Bind off.

FINISHING: Sew shoulder seams. Fold garter st edgings on each front to wrong side and sew in place.

Neckband: With right side facing, using No. 2 needles, pick up and k 99 [100–101–106–107] sts around neck, including sts on holders. Work in stockinette st (p on wrong side, k on right side) for 4 rows, dec 6 sts evenly spaced across last row. K next row on wrong side for hemline. Beg with a k row, continue in stockinette st for 4 rows more. Bind off.

Sew side and sleeve seams. Sew in sleeves. Work buttonhole st around buttonholes. Sew on buttons. Turning edge sts on pockets to wrong side, sew pockets in place as pictured. Sew button on each pocket as pictured. Turn neckband to wrong side and sew in place.

Raglan Sweater Jacket and V-Neck Pullover Set

A stylish garter stitch jacket with ribbed yoke pairs up with a cap-sleeved V-neck pullover for a smart new look.

SIZES: (8–10) [(12–14)—(16–18)]. Jacket measures about 16″ [18″–20″] across back below armholes, 24½″ [25″–25½″] from back of neck to lower edge. Snug-fitting pullover measures 15″ [17″–19″] across back at underarms, 20½″ [21″–21½″] from back of neck to lower edge.

MATERIALS: Spinnerin Germantown Deluxe (Orlon acrylic knitting-worsted-weight yarn). Jacket: 6 [7–7] (4-oz.) skeins bright gold No. 3245 (color G); knitting needles, 1 pair each No. 8 and No. 4 (or English needles No. 5 and No. 9) or the sizes that will give you the correct gauge. Pullover: 1 skein each bright gold No. 3245 (G), turquoise No. 3215 (T) and brick No. 3257 (B); knitting needles, 1 pair each No. 3 and No. 5 (or English needles No. 10 and No. 8) or the sizes that will give you the correct gauge.

GAUGE: Jacket: In garter st, 9 sts = 2″. Pullover: 5 sts = 1″.

Diagram 1

Diagram 2

JACKET

BACK: Starting at lower edge with No. 8 needles, cast on 87 [95–103] sts. Work in garter st (k each row) for 1″. Continuing in garter st, dec 1 st at beg and end of next row, then every inch 6 times more. Work even on 73 [81–89] sts until piece measures 18″ or 1″ less than desired length to underarms.

To Establish Rib Pattern—(Note: Ribbing will not be apparent until at least 4 rows have been worked.) Change to No. 4 needles and work as follows: **1st row (mark this row for right side):** P 1, * k next st in the row below (see photo diagram 1—k rb made), p 1. Repeat from * across. **2nd row:** K 1, p 1, * k rb (see photo diagram 2, which shows rib st after several rows have been completed), p 1. Repeat from * across to within last st, k 1. Repeat last 2 rows twice more, ending with a wrong-side row.

To Shape Raglan Armhole—1st row (dec row): P 1, k rb, p 2 tog, work across in rib pattern to within last 4 sts, p 2 tog, k rb, p 1. **2nd row:** K 1, p 1, k 1, work across in pattern to within last 3 sts, k 1, p 1, k 1. **3rd row:** P 1, k rb, p 1, work across in pattern to within last 3 sts, p 1, k rb, p 1. **4th row:** Repeat 2nd row.

Repeat last 4 rows 18 [17–16] times more. **For sizes (12–14) [(16–18)] only:** Repeat 1st and 2nd rows 5 [10] times. **For all sizes:** Place remaining 35 sts on a holder for back neck. Break off.

LEFT FRONT: Starting at lower edge with No. 8 needles, cast on 49 [53–57] sts. Work in garter st for 1″. Mark end of last row for side edge. Dec 1 st at beg of next row, then dec 1 st at side edge every 1″ 6 times more. Work even on 42 [46–50] sts until piece measures same as back to beg of rib pattern, ending at side edge.

To Establish Rib Pattern: Change to No. 4 needles. **1st row (mark this row for right side):** * P 1, k rb. Repeat from * to within last 12 sts, k these 12 sts for front border. **2nd row:** K 12 for border, * p 1, k rb. Repeat from * across to within last 2 sts, p 1, k 1. Repeat last 2 rows twice more, ending at side edge.

To Shape Raglan Armhole—1st row (dec row): P 1, k rb, p 2 tog, work in pattern across ribbing, ending with garter-stitch border. **2nd row:** Work border, then rib to within last 3 sts, k 1, p 1, k 1. **3rd row:** P 1, k rb, p 1, work across in pattern. **4th row:** Repeat 2nd row.

Repeat last 4 rows 17 [16–15] times more, ending at arm edge, then dec as before at arm edge every other row 2 [7–12] times and, **at the same time,** when there are 29 [32–35] sts on needle, ending at front edge, shape neck as follows: K across border, slip these sts onto a holder, bind off next 4 sts, complete row. Dec 1 st at neck edge every row 3 times. When raglan shaping is completed, bind off remaining 3 sts.

RIGHT FRONT: Work as for left front to beg of rib pattern, ending at front edge.

To Establish Rib Pattern—1st row (right side): K 12 for border, * k rb, p 1. Repeat from * across. **2nd row:** K 1, p 1, * k rb, p 1. Repeat from * across to within last 12 sts, k 12. Complete to correspond to left front, reversing shaping.

SLEEVES: Starting at cuff with No. 4 needles, cast on 33 [35–35] sts. Repeat 1st and 2nd rows of back rib pattern 12 times. Change to No. 8 needles and k across, increasing 1 st in each st. Work even in garter st on 66 [70–70] sts until sleeve measures 12″ above ribbing, decreasing 1 st on last row (65 [69–69] sts).

To Establish Rib Pattern: Work 6 rows in rib pattern as for back.

To Shape Raglan Cap: Work 1st through 4th rows of back armhole shaping, then repeat 3rd and 4th rows once more. Repeat last 6 rows 9 [10–12] times more, then dec as before at each side every other row 8 [8–5] times. Place remaining 29 [31–33] sleeve sts on a holder.

FINISHING: On wrong side, lightly steam ribbing open. Sew side, sleeve and raglan seams. **Neckband:** With right side of work facing you, with No. 4 needles, pick up and k 149 [153–155] sts around neck edge, including sts from holders. Working in garter st, dec 7 sts as evenly spaced as possible, every other row 7 times. Bind off remaining 100 [104–106] sts.

V-NECK PULLOVER

BACK: Starting at lower edge with No. 3 needles and G, cast on 76 [86–96] sts. Work in ribbing of k 1, p 1 for 4½″. Break off G; attach T. Change to No. 5 needles and work even in stockinette st until T stripe measures 4½″. Break off T; attach B. Continue in stockinette st until B stripe measures 4½″. Break off B.

To Shape Cap Sleeve—Next row: With free No. 5 needle and G, cast on 6 sts; work across 76 [86–96] sts on other needle, cast on 6 sts (88 [98–108] sts). Work even in stockinette st until G stripe measures 4½″. Break off G; attach T. Work even until sleeve measures 7″ [7½″–8″] from beg.

To Shape Shoulder: Bind off 10 [12–14] sts at beg of next 4 rows, then 8 [9–10] sts at beg of next 2 rows. Place remaining 32 sts on a holder for back neck.

FRONT: Work same as for back until piece measures same as back to underarm.

To Shape Cap Sleeve and Divide for V-Neck—Next row: With free needle and G, cast on 6 sts, work across first 38 [43–48] sts. Place remaining 38 [43–48] sts on a holder for other side. Work on one side only from now on. Dec 1 st at neck edge on next row, then every 3rd row 15 times more and, **at same time,** when G stripe measures 4½″, break off G; attach T. When neck shaping is completed, work even until sleeve measures same as back sleeve to shoulder, ending at arm edge.

84

To Shape Shoulder: Starting at arm edge, bind off 10 [12–14] sts at beg of every other row twice. Work 1 row even. Bind off remaining 8 [9–10] sts.

Place 38 [43–48] sts from holder onto needle. Attach yarn at center and work across, then cast on 6 sts. Complete to correspond to other side.

FINISHING: Sew right shoulder seam. **Neckband—1st row:** With right side facing you, with No. 3 needles and G, pick up and k 54 [56–58] sts along left front neck edge, 54 [56–58] sts along right front neck edge, k 32 sts from back neck holder (140 [144–148] sts). Mark center st at point of V-neck. **2nd row:** Work in ribbing of k 1, p 1 to within one st of marked st, work next 3 sts tog in pattern (mark this st), continue across in ribbing. Bind off in ribbing to within one st of marked st, work next 3 sts tog, then continue binding off.

Sew left shoulder seam. With right side facing you, with No. 3 needles and G, pick up and k 82 [84–86] sts along left armhole edge. Work in ribbing of k 1, p 1 for 1 row. Bind off in ribbing. Work right armhole in same manner. Sew side seams.

Classic Sweater Set

Here is a sweater set in a lacy fishtail pattern.

SIZES: (10–12) [(14–16)—(18–20)]. Pullover measures about 16½″ [18″–20″] across back below underarms. Length is 22½″ [23″–23½″] from back neck to lower edge and is adjustable. Jacket measures about 18¼″ [19¼″–21″] across back below underarms. Length is 28½″ from back neck to lower edge and is adjustable.

MATERIALS—Pullover: Bear Brand Winsom (Orlon acrylic yarn), 4 [5–6] (2 oz.) skeins blue No. 312; knitting needles, 1 pair each No. 7 [8–8] and 8 [9–9] (or English needles No. 6 [5–5] and 5 [4–4]) **or the sizes that will give you the correct gauge. Jacket:** Bucilla Melody (50% mohair, 50% acrylic yarn), 10 [11–12] (1 oz.) balls blue No. 7; knitting needles, 1 pair No. 8 [9–8] (or English needles No. 5 [4–5]) **or the size that will give you the correct gauge;** elastic thread and bias tape (optional).

GAUGE—Pullover: 1 pattern repeat (12 sts) on No. 8 needles = 2⅜″. 1 pattern repeat on No. 9 needles = 2½″. **Jacket:** 1 pattern repeat on No. 8 needles = 2⅝″. 1 pattern repeat on No. 9 needles = 2¾″.

Note: Be very careful to get the correct gauge as the garment size is determined, in some cases, on the needle size alone and not on a change in the number of stitches.

Note: Directions for Pullover start after directions for pattern.

LACE PATTERN—1st row: K 1, * y o, k 4, sl 1, k 2 tog, psso, k 4, y o, k 1. Repeat from * across. **2nd row:** P across. **3rd row:** P 1, * k 1, y o, k 3, sl 1, k 2 tog, psso, k 3, y o, k 1, p 1. Repeat from * across. **4th row and all even numbered rows:** K 1, * p 11, k 1. Repeat from * across. **5th row:** P 1, * k 2, y o, k 2, sl 1, k 2 tog, psso, k 2, y o, k 2, p 1. Repeat from * across. **7th row:** P 1, * k 3, y o, k 1, sl 1, k 2 tog, psso, k 1, y o, k 3, p 1. Repeat from * across. **9th row:** P 1, * k 4, y o, sl 1, k 2 tog, psso, y o, k 4, p 1. Repeat from * across. **10th row:** Repeat 4th row. Repeat these last 10 rows for pattern.

PULLOVER

BACK: Starting at lower edge with No. 7 [8–8] needles, cast on 84 [90–96] sts. Work in ribbing of k 3, p 3 for 6″. Inc 1 st at end of last row (85 [91–97] sts). Change to No. 8 [9–9] needles. **For sizes (10–12) and (18–20),** work even in lace pattern until piece measures 16″, or desired length to underarms. **For size (14–16),** k 3 sts, place marker on needle, work first row of lace pattern to within last 3 sts, place marker on needle, k 3. On 2nd row, p first 3 sts, sl marker, work 2nd row of pattern to 2nd marker, sl marker, p 3. Continue in pattern, keeping first and last 3 sts in stockinette st, until piece measures 16″ from beg, or desired length to underarms.

To Shape Armholes (all sizes): Keeping in pattern, bind off 5 [6–7] sts at beg of next 2 rows (75 [79–83] sts). Continuing in pattern as established, work even until armholes measure 6½″ [7″–7½″].

To Shape Shoulders: Bind off 7 [8–8] sts at beg of next 4 rows. Bind off 9 [8–10] sts at beg of next 2 rows. Place remaining 29 [31–31] sts on a st holder for back of neck.

FRONT: Work same as for back until armholes measure 3¼″ [3¾″–4¼″].

To Shape Neck—1st row: Work across 25 [26–28] sts, place next 25 [27–27] sts on a st holder for front neck, attach another ball of yarn and work across remaining 25 [26–28] sts. Continuing in pattern and working on both sections of front with 2 balls yarn, dec 1 st at each neck edge on next row, then every other row once more (23 [24–26] sts on each front section). Work even in pattern until armholes are same length as back armholes.

To Shape Shoulders: Bind off 7 [8–8] sts at beg of next 4 rows. Bind off remaining 9 [8–10] sts on next 2 rows.

SLEEVES: Starting at lower edge with No. 7 [8–8] needles, cast on 48 [54–54] sts. Work in ribbing of k 3, p 3 for 1″. Inc 1 st at end of last row (49 [55–55] sts). Change to No. 8 [9–9] needles. Establish pattern as follows: **1st row:** K 6 [9–9], place marker on needle, work first row of lace pattern over next 37 sts, place marker on needle, k 6 [9–9]. **2nd row:** P 6 [9–9], sl marker, work 2nd row of lace pattern to marker, sl marker, p 6 [9–9]. Continue in pattern, keeping sts before marker at beg of row and sts after marker at end of row in stockinette st. Inc 1 st at beg and end of row on next row, then every ½" 3 [3–4] times more (57 [63–65] sts). Work even in established pattern until sleeve measures 4½" from beg, or desired length to underarm.

To **Shape Cap:** Bind off 5 [6–7] sts at beg of next 2 rows. Dec 1 st at beg and end of every other row 12 [13–14] times. Bind off remaining 23 [25–23] sts.

FINISHING: Sew left shoulder seam. **Neckband:** Attach yarn at right back neck edge. With right side facing you, place the 29 [31–31] sts from back neck holder onto left No. 7 [8–8] needle and k across them; pick up and k 15 [13–13] sts along left side neck edge; place the 25 [27–27] sts from front neck holder onto needle and k across them; pick up and k 15 [13–13] sts along right side neck edge (84 sts). Work in ribbing of k 3, p 3 for 1". Bind off loosely in ribbing. Sew neckband and right shoulder seam. Sew side and sleeve seams. Sew in sleeves.

JACKET

BACK—Hem and Border: Starting at lower edge, cast on 85 [85–97] sts. Work in stockinette st for 1¼", ending with a p row. P next row on right side for hemline. Starting with a p row, continue in stockinette st for 1¼" more, ending with a p row. **Pattern:** Work even in lace pattern until piece measures 20", or desired length to underarms.

To **Shape Armholes:** Keeping in pattern, bind off 5 [5–7] sts at beg of next 2 rows (75 [75–83] sts). Continue in pattern as established until armholes measure 7" [7½"–8"].

To **Shape Shoulders:** Bind off 7 [7–8] sts at beg of next 4 rows. Bind off 9 [9–10] sts at beg of next 2 rows. Place remaining 29 [29–31] sts on a st holder for back of neck.

LEFT FRONT—Hem and Border: Starting at lower edge, cast on 37 [37–49] sts. Work in stockinette st for 1¼", ending with a p row. **Next row:** P next row on right side for hemline, cast 15 [15–9] sts onto right needle for front border (52 [52–58] sts). **Following row:** P across. **Next row:** K to within last 8 [8–5] sts, sl next st (fold line of front border), k 7 [7–4]. Repeat last 2 rows until piece measures 1¼" from hemline, ending with a p row.

Pattern—1st row: Work 37 [37–49] sts in lace pattern, place marker on needle, k 7 [7–4], sl next st, k 7 [7–4]. **2nd row:** P 15 [15–9], sl marker, work across in pattern. Repeat last 2 rows, slipping marker on each row, until piece measures same as back to underarm, ending at side edge.

88

To Shape Armhole: Keeping in pattern, bind off 5 [5–7] sts at beg of next row (47 [47–51] sts). Work even in pattern as established until armhole measures 4″ [4½″–5″], ending at front edge.

To Shape Neck—1st row: Bind off 7 [7–4] sts, p 8 [8–5] sts, sl marker, work 5 [5–11] pattern sts, place all sts just worked onto a st holder for front neck, work across remaining sts to armhole edge. Continuing in lace pattern, dec 1 st at neck edge every other row 4 [4–5] times (23 [23–26] sts). Work even until armhole measures same as back armhole, ending at armhole edge.

To Shape Shoulder: Bind off 7 [7–8] sts at beg of next row, then every other row once more. Bind off remaining 9 [9–10] sts.

RIGHT FRONT—Hem and Border: Work as for left front for 1¼″, ending with a p row. **Next row:** Cast 15 [15–9] sts onto right needle for front border, p across hem sts on right side for hemline (52 [52–58] sts). **Following row:** P across. **Next row:** K 7 [7–4], sl next st, k across. Repeat last 2 rows until piece measures 1¼″ from hemline, ending with a p row. **Pattern—1st row:** K 7 [7–4], sl next st, k 7 [7–4], place marker on needle, work remaining sts in lace pattern. Complete front to correspond to left front, reversing shaping.

SLEEVE—Hem and Border: Starting at lower edge, cast on 39 sts. Work as for back. **Pattern—1st row:** K 1, place marker on needle, work first row of lace pattern across next 37 sts, place marker on needle, k 1. **2nd row:** P 1, sl marker, work 2nd row of pattern, sl marker, p 1. Continue in pattern, keeping sts before marker at beg of row and sts after marker at end of row in stockinette st. Inc 1 st at beg and end of row every 1″ 10 [10–12] times (59 [59–63] sts). Work even until sleeve measures 17″ [17½″–18″] from hemline, or desired length to underarm.

To Shape Cap: Bind off 5 [5–7] sts at beg of next 2 rows. Dec 1 st at beg and end of every other row 7 [7–9] times, then every row 6 [6–4] times. Bind off remaining 23 sts.

FINISHING: Sew shoulders, side and sleeve seams. Sew sleeves in place. Fold borders in half to wrong side on lower edge, front edges and sleeves and whipstitch with yarn. **Neckband:** Attach yarn at right front neck edge. With right side facing you, place the sts from front holder onto left needle and k across them; pick up and k 17 [17–15] sts along right side neck edge; place the sts from back neck holder onto needle and k across them; pick up and k 17 [17–15] sts along left side neck edge; place the sts from left front holder onto needle and k across them (89 [89–93] sts). Work in stockinette st for 1¼″, ending with a p row. P next row on right side for hemline. Starting with a p row, continue in stockinette st for 1¼″ more. Bind off. Fold neckband in half to wrong side and blindstitch.

If desired, sew a few rows of elastic thread through wrong side of neckband to hold its shape. Also, bind shoulder seams with bias tape to prevent stretching.

Surprise Sweater Set

The shawl-collared cardigan (at right) is sleeveless, but for a short, striped cap, and is worn over a long-sleeved V-neck sweater. (Instructions for the Racing Stripes set are on page 98.)

SIZES: Small (8–10) [medium (12–14)—large (16–18)]. Cardigan measures 17″ [19″–21″] across at underarms and 27″ from shoulder to lower edge. Pullover measures 16″ [18″–20″] across at underarms and 25″ from shoulder to lower edge.

MATERIALS: Bucilla Perlette (100% Orlon acrylic, sport yarn weight) 12 [14–15] (1¾ oz.) balls peacock No. 18, 2 balls each sand No. 7, copper No. 14, antique gold No. 5 and rust No. 19 for cardigan and pullover together; knitting needles, 1 pair No. 4 and 1 set (4) dp needles No. 4 (or English needles No.9) **or the size that will give you the correct gauge;** 6 brown buttons ¾″ in diameter; 1 bobbin.

GAUGE: 6 sts = 1″; 8 rows = 1″.

CARDIGAN

BACK: Starting at lower edge with peacock, cast on 106 [118–130] sts. Work in ribbing of k 1, p 1 for 3 rows. Break off peacock; attach sand and k 1 row, p 1 row. Break off sand; attach copper and k 1 row, work in ribbing of k 1, p 1 for 3 rows. Break off copper; attach gold and k 1 row, p 1 row. Break off gold; attach rust and k 1 row, work in ribbing of k 1, p 1 for 3 rows. Break off rust; attach sand and k 1 row, p 1 row. Break off sand; attach peacock and k 1 row; work in ribbing of k 1, p 1 for 3 rows. Break off peacock; attach gold and k 1 row, p 1 row. Break off gold; attach copper and k 1 row; work in ribbing of k 1, p 1 for 3 rows. Break off copper; attach sand and k 1 row, p 1 row. Break off sand; attach rust and k 1 row; work in ribbing of k 1, p 1 for 3 rows. Break off rust; attach gold and k 1 row, p 1 row. Break off gold (12-stripe band completed).

Attach peacock and continue to work even in stockinette st for 2", ending with a p row. **Next row (dec row):** K 2, sl 1, k 1, psso, k to last 4 sts, k 2 tog, k 2 (104 [116–128] sts). Continuing in stockinette st, repeat dec row every 2" once more. Work even on 102 [114–126] sts until piece measures 19" from beg, or desired length to underarms.

To Shape Armholes: Bind off 5 [6–7] sts at beg of next 2 rows. Bind off 4 [4–5] sts at beg of next 2 rows. Bind off 3 [4–4] sts at beg of next 2 rows. Bind off 2 [3–3] sts at beg of next 2 rows. Dec 1 st at beg and end of every row 0 [1–2] times. Work even on 74 [78–84] sts until armholes measure 8¼" [8½"–9"].

To Shape Shoulders: Bind off 8 [9–10] sts at beg of next 4 rows. Place remaining 42 [42–44] sts on a holder for back neck. Break off.

LEFT FRONT: Starting at lower edge with peacock, cast on 58 [64–70] sts. Work in ribbing of k 1, p 1 for 3 rows. Break off peacock; attach sand.

Note: To work front border, wind peacock yarn on a bobbin. When changing colors, twist yarns by bringing new color under yarn you have been working with to avoid holes in work. (See page 35 for bobbin knitting.)

4th row (right side): With sand k across to last 11 sts. Drop sand, do not break off.

Attach peacock bobbin, p 1, (k 1, p 1) 5 times for front border. **5th row:** With peacock k 1, (p 1, k 1) 5 times; drop peacock bobbin; with sand p across row. Mark end of row for side edge.

Working 12-stripe band as for back, continue to work in pattern as established, with peacock rib st border at front edge. When stripes have been completed, break off bobbin. Attach peacock and continue to work in stockinette st, keeping 11 border sts at front edge in ribbing. Work in pattern as established, decreasing 1 st 2 sts in from side edge every 2" twice. Work even on 56 [62–68] sts until piece measures same as back to underarm, ending at side edge.

To Shape Armhole and Neck: Bind off 6 [6–7] sts, k across to within 2 sts of front border, k 2 tog, work front border in ribbing. Work even for 1 row. At armhole edge bind off 4 [5–5], 3 [4–4], 2 [3–3] sts every other row, dec 1 st at same edge every other row 1 [2–4] times,

and at the same time dec 1 st at neck edge inside border every other row 11 times more, then every 4th row 8 [8–9] times (20 [22–24] sts). Work even until armhole measures same as back, ending at armhole edge. **Note:** Front shoulder edge is wider than back shoulder edge, but will be eased in to fit when shoulders are joined.

To Shape Shoulder: Bind off 10 [11–12] sts at beg of next row. Work 1 row even. Bind off remaining 10 [11–12] sts.

With pins, mark front border for placement of 6 buttons, the first one 3″ from lower edge, the rest spaced evenly up to within 1″ of neck shaping.

RIGHT FRONT: Work as for left front, for 3 rib rows. Break off peacock and attach bobbin. **4th row (right side):** With peacock bobbin p 1, (k 1, p 1) 5 times for front border, drop peacock; attach sand and k across. **5th row:** With sand p across to last 11 sts, with peacock bobbin k 1, (p 1, k 1) 5 times. Complete front to correspond to left front, reversing all shaping. Make buttonholes opposite pins on left front as follows: From front edge work 4 sts in ribbing. Bind off next 4 sts. Work to end of row. On following row cast on 4 sts over those bound off.

SHAWL COLLAR: Sew shoulder seams. **1st row (right side of collar):** With wrong side of work facing you, place the 42 [42–44] sts from back neck holder onto left-hand needle, attach peacock and work in ribbing of k 1, p 1 across row; at end of row pick up and k next 3 sts along right front neck edge. **2nd row:** Being careful to work added sts in pattern, work in ribbing across row; at end of row pick up and k next 3 sts along opposite front neck edge. Repeat 2nd row twice more. Break off peacock; attach sand. Work stripe and rib pattern as for back and continue to pick up 3 sts from neck edge at the end of each row, **and at the same time** when collar measures about 1″ from beg, inc 3 sts evenly spaced across back neck section on 2nd row of a gold or sand stripe, then inc 9 sts evenly spaced every inch once more. Bind off in ribbing.

Armhole Ribbing: With right side of work facing you, using peacock, pick up and k 132 [138–144] sts around armhole. Work 3 more rows in ribbing of k 1, p 1. Break off peacock; attach sand and work in stripe and rib pattern as for back, working 2 rows sand, 4 rows copper, 2 rows gold, 4 rows rust, 2 rows sand and 4 rows peacock, **and at the same time** dec 1 st at beg and end of every 6th row twice. Bind off in ribbing.

FINISHING: Sew side seams and armhole ribbing seams. Sew buttons in place.

V-NECK SWEATER

BACK: Starting at lower edge with peacock, cast on 100 [112–124] sts. Then work same as back of cardigan to armholes (96 [108–120] sts).

92

To Shape Armholes: Shape same as back of cardigan. Work even on 66 [70–76] sts until armholes measure 7½" [7¾"–8"].

To Shape Shoulders: Bind off 4 [5–6] sts at beg of next 4 rows. Place remaining 50 [50–52] sts on a holder for back neck. Break off.

FRONT: Work same as for back until piece measures 12" from beg, ending on wrong side.

To Shape Neck and Armholes: Work across 48 [54–60] sts. Place remaining 48 [54–60] sts on a holder. Working on one side only, dec 1 st at neck edge every 4th row 25 [25–26] times; **and at the same time** when piece measures same as back to underarm, shape armholes as follows: at side edge bind off 6 [6–7] sts at beg of next row, then bind off 4 [5–5] sts, 3 [4–4], 2 [3–4] sts at armhole edge every other row, dec 1 st at same edge every other row 0 [1–2] times. Work even on 8 [10–12] sts until armholes measure same as back.

To Shape Shoulder: At arm edge bind off 4 [5–6] sts every other row twice.

Attach yarn at center front and work other side to correspond.

SLEEVES: Starting at lower edge with peacock, cast on 54 [58–62] sts. Work stripe and rib pattern as for back of cardigan. Break off gold; attach peacock and continue in stockinette st, increasing 1 st at beg and end of next row, then at beg and end of every 8th row 11 times more. Work even on 78 [82–86] sts until sleeve measures 16" from beg, or desired length to underarm.

To Shape Cap: Bind off 6 [6–7] sts at beg of next 2 rows. Dec 1 st at beg and end of every other row 14 [16–17] times. Bind off 4 sts at beg of next 6 rows. Bind off remaining 14 sts.

FINISHING: Sew shoulder, side and sleeve seams. Sew sleeves in place. **Neckband:** With dp needles and right side of work facing you, using peacock pick up and k 90 [94–98] sts across left front edge, place marker on needle (at center point of V-neck), pick up and k 90 [94–98] sts across right front edge, pick up and k 52 [52–54] sts from back neck holder (232 [240–250] sts).

Work in stripe and rib pattern as before, until a 7-stripe band has been completed (ending with 4 rnds peacock), decreasing 1 st at each side of marker at center front on each rnd. Bind off in ribbing.

The Reversibles

A sweater set in charcoal gray and winter white. Shown is the square-neck, short- sleeved pullover. Directions are also given for Chanel-type, hip-length, V-neck cardigan that reverses the colors of the pullover.

SIZES: Small (8–10) [medium (12–14)—large (16–18)]. Cardigan measures 17" [19"–21"] across at underarms and 26" from shoulder to lower edge. Pullover measures 15" [17"–19"] across at underarms and 19" from shoulder to lower edge.

MATERIALS: Bucilla Wool and Shetland Wool, 8 [9–10] (2-oz.) balls Oxford gray No. 703, 4 balls winter white No. 205 for cardigan and pullover together, or 7 [8–9] balls gray and 1 ball white for cardigan only; knitting needles, 1 pair No. 6 (or English needles No. 7) **or the size that will give you the correct gauge;** steel crochet hook No. 0; 1 bobbin.

GAUGE: 5 sts = 1"; 7 rows = 1".

CARDIGAN

BACK: Starting at lower edge with gray, cast on 90 [100–110] sts. Work in ribbing of k 1, p 1 for 7 rows. Then starting with a k row, work in stockinette st until piece measures 3" from beg, ending with a p row. **Next row (dec row):** K 2, sl 1, k 1, psso, k across to within last 4 sts, k 2 tog, k 2 (88 [98–108] sts). Continue in stockinette st and repeat dec row every 8th row 5 times more. Work even on 78 [88–98] sts until piece measures 13" from beg, ending with a p row. **Next row (inc row):** K 2, inc 1 st in next st, k to last 3 sts, inc 1 st in next st, k 2 (80

[90–100] sts). Repeat inc row every 8th row 3 times more. Work even in stockinette st on 86 [96–106] sts until piece measures 18″ from beg or desired length to underarm.

To Shape Armholes: Bind off 5 [6–7] sts at beg of next 2 rows. Dec 1 st at beg and end of every other row 5 [6–8] times. Work even on 66 [72–76] sts until armholes measure 7¼″ [7½″–8″].

To Shape Shoulders: Bind off 7 [8–9] sts at beg of next 4 rows. Bind off remaining 38 [40–40] sts.

LEFT FRONT—Note: To work front border, wind white yarn on a bobbin. When changing colors, twist yarns by bringing new color under yarn you have been working with to avoid holes in work. (See page 35 for bobbin knitting.)

Starting at lower edge with gray, cast on 40 [44–48] sts, attach bobbin; with white cast on 7 sts for front border (47 [51–55] sts). Work in ribbing of k 1, p 1 for 7 rows, keeping 7 white border sts in ribbing. **8th row (right side):** With gray k 16 [20–24], p 1, k 8, p 1, k 14, with white p 1 (k 1, p 1) 3 times. **9th row:** With white k 1 (p 1, k 1) 3 times; with gray p 14, k 1, p 8, k 1, p 16 [20–24]. Mark end of row for side edge. Repeating 8th and 9th rows for vertical stripe pattern, work even until piece measures 3″ from beg, ending at side edge. **Next row (dec row):** K 2, sl 1, k 1, psso, work across in pattern as established (46 [50–54] sts). Continue to work in pattern as established and dec 1 st 2 sts in from side edge every 8th row 5 times more. Work even in pattern on 41 [45–49] sts until piece measures 11″ from beg, ending at side edge. Drop gray; attach white and work 2 rows even for first horizontal stripe, keeping vertical stripe pattern and border sts at front edge in ribbing as established. Break off white; pick up gray and work 12 rows even in pattern as before. Drop gray; attach white and work 2 rows even, increasing 1 st 2 sts in from side edge at beg of first row. Continue to work in horizontal stripe pattern as established (2 rows white and 12 rows gray) until 3 white stripes have been completed, and **at the same time** inc 1 st 2 sts in from side edge every 8th row 3 times more. Continue even in vertical pattern on 45 [49–53] sts until piece measures same as back to underarm, ending at side edge.

To Shape Armhole: Bind off 5 [6–7] sts at beg of next row. Dec 1 st at same edge every other row 5 [6–8] times. Work even in pattern on 35 [37–38] sts until armhole measures 3″ [3¼″–3½″], ending at side edge.

To Shape Neck—Next row (dec row): Work across in pattern to within 3 sts of front border; k 2 tog, k 1, work border (34 [36–37] sts). Continue to work in pattern as established, decreasing 1 st at neck edge inside border every other row 13 times more (21 [23–25] sts). Then work even until armhole measures same as back, ending at armhole edge.

To Shape Shoulder: Bind off 7 [8–9] sts at armhole edge on next row. Work 1 row even. Bind off 7 [8–9] sts at beg of next row. Continue to work 7 remaining border sts in ribbing for 3″ more. Bind off in ribbing.

RIGHT FRONT: Starting at lower edge with white bobbin, cast on 7 sts, attach gray and cast on 40 [44–48] sts (47 [51–55] sts). Work in ribbing of k 1, p 1 for 7 rows, keeping 7 border sts in white. **8th row (right side):** With white p 1 (k 1, p 1) 3 times; with gray k 14, p 1, k 8, p 1, k 16 [20–24], mark end of row for side edge. **9th row:** With gray p 16 [20–24], k 1, p 8, k 1, p 14, with white k 1, (p 1, k 1) 3 times. Complete front to correspond to left front, reversing all shaping.

SLEEVES: Starting at lower edge with white, cast on 44 [46–48] sts. Work in ribbing of k 1, p 1 for 1″. Break off white; attach gray. With gray, starting with a k row, work in stockinette st until piece measures 2″ from beg, ending on wrong side. Inc 1 st 2 sts in from edge at beg and end of next row, then inc in same manner at beg and end of every 6th row 15 times more. Work even on 76 [78–80] sts until sleeve measures 16½″ from beg, or desired length to underarm.

To Shape Cap: Bind off 5 sts at beg of next 2 rows. Dec 1 st at beg and end of every other row 12 [13–14] times. Bind off 2 sts at beg of next 2 rows. Bind off 3 sts at beg of next 2 rows. Bind off 4 sts at beg of next 2 rows. Bind off remaining 24 sts.

FINISHING: Sew shoulder, side and sleeve seams. Sew sleeves in place. Sew ends of borders together and sew to back neck edge.

Vertical Sl St Rows: With right side of work facing you and holding white yarn against wrong side of left front, insert crochet hook from front to back through bottom st of a vertical p row and draw up a white loop. Insert hook in next vertical p st and draw a loop through st and through loop on hook (sl st made). Continue to work sl st over each p st to top. Break off. Weave in end. Work along remaining vertical p rows in same manner.

PULLOVER

BACK: Starting at lower edge with gray, cast on 76 [86–96] sts. Work in ribbing of k 1, p 1 for 7 rows. Break off gray; attach white. Starting with a k row, work even in stockinette st until piece measures 11″ from beg, or desired length to armholes, ending with p row.

To Shape Armholes: Bind off 3 [4–5] sts at beg of next 2 rows. Dec 1 st at beg and end of every other row 2 [4–5] times. Work even on 66 [70–76] sts until armholes measure 7¼″ [7½″–8″].

To Shape Shoulders: Bind off 6 [7–8] sts at beg of next 4 rows. Break off white; attach gray and work remaining 42 [42–44] sts in ribbing of k 1, p 1 for 1″. Bind off in ribbing.

FRONT: Work ribbing as for back. Break off gray; attach white. **8th row (right side):** K 15 [20–25], (p 1, k 8) 5 times; p 1, k 15 [20–25]. **9th row:** P 15 [20–25], (k 1, p 8) 5 times; k 1, p 15 [20–25]. Repeat 8th and 9th rows for vertical stripe pattern 10 times more (22 rows in all).

Drop white; attach gray and work 2 rows even for first horizontal stripe. Break off gray; pick up white and work 12 rows in pattern as before. Continue to work in vertical stripe pattern as established, working horizontal stripe pattern (2 rows gray and 12 rows white), until 3 gray stripes have been completed in all. Break off gray; pick up white and work even in vertical stripe pattern until piece measures same as back to underarms.

To Shape Armholes: Bind off 2 [3–5] sts at beg of next 2 rows. Dec 1 st at beg and end of every other row 1 [3–4] times. Work even on 70 [74–78] sts until armholes measure 2½″ [2¾″–3¼″], ending on wrong side.

To Shape Neck—1st row: K 12 [14–16] sts, place center 46 sts on a holder, attach another skein of white and k to end. **2nd row:** P to sts on holder, drop yarn, skip sts on holder, with other skein of yarn p to end. Working on both sides at once in this manner, work even until armholes measure same as back.

To Shape Shoulders: Bind of 6 [7–8] sts at beg (armhole edge) of next 4 rows. Break off.

Neckband: With right side of front facing you, attach gray at left shoulder neck edge, pick up and k 34 [36–38] sts along side neck edge, place 46 sts from holder onto left-hand needle and k across them, pick up and k 34 [36–38] along side neck edge. Work in ribbing of k 1, p 1 for 1″, working k 2 tog in corners on every row. Bind off in ribbing.

Work vertical sl st rows with gray in same manner as for cardigan.

SLEEVES: Starting at lower edge with gray, cast on 76 [78–80] sts. Work in ribbing of k 1, p 1 for 1″. Break off gray; attach white. Starting with a k row, work even in stockinette st until piece measures 2″ from beg, ending with p row.

To Shape Cap: Bind off 5 sts at beg of next 2 rows. Dec 1 st at beg and end of every other row 10 [11–12] times. Bind off 2 sts at beg of next 2 rows. Bind off 3 sts at beg of next 2 rows. Bind off 4 sts at beg of next 2 rows. Bind off remaining 28 sts.

FINISHING: Sew shoulder, neckband, side and sleeve seams. Sew sleeves in place.

Racing Stripes

A long cardigan, shown on page 90, buttons up over a sleeveless turtleneck pullover, both in plain stockinette stitch in an exciting color combination of greens and purples.

SIZES: Small (8–10) [medium (12–14)—large (16–18)]. Cardigan measures 17″ [19″–21″] across at underarms and 24½″ from shoulder to lower edge. Pullover measures 16″ [18″–20″] across at underarms and 17″ from shoulder to lower edge.

MATERIALS: Fleisher's Winsom (100% Orlon acrylic), 8 [9–10] (2-oz.) skeins green mist No. 461, 1 skein each scotch green No. 90, rosy pink No. 442, olive No. 460 and violite No. 466 for cardigan and pullover together; knitting needles, 1 pair No. 6 (or English needles No. 7) **or the size that will give you the correct gauge;** 9 buttons ¾″ in diameter.

GAUGE: 5 sts = 1″; 7 rows = 1″.

CARDIGAN

BACK: Starting at lower edge with green mist, cast on 90 [100–110] sts. Work in ribbing of k 1, p 1 for 7 rows. Starting with a k row, work in stockinette st until piece measures 3″ from beg, ending with a p row. **Next row (dec row):** K 2, sl 1, k 1, psso, k across to within last 4 sts, k 2 tog, k 2 (88 [98–108] sts). Continue in stockinette st and repeat dec row every 12th row 5 times more (78 [88–98] sts). Then inc 1 st in 3rd st from beg of row and 1 st in 3rd st from end of row on next k row. Repeat inc every 6th row twice more.

Work even on 84 [94–104] sts until piece measures 14″ from beg, ending on wrong side. Break off green mist; attach violite and work 4 rows. Break off violite; attach scotch green and work 4 rows. Break off scotch green; attach olive and work 4 rows. Break off olive; attach pink and work 4 rows. Break off pink; attach scotch green and work 8 rows. Break off scotch green; attach green mist and work 2 rows, ending on wrong side.

To Shape Armholes: Bind off 6 [7–8] sts at beg of next 2 rows. Dec 1 st at beg and end of every other row 4 [5–7] times. Work even on 64 [70–74] sts until armholes measure 7¼″ [7½″–8″].

To Shape Shoulders: Bind off 7 [8–9] sts at beg of next 4 rows. Place remaining 36 [38–38] sts on a holder for back neck. Break off.

LEFT FRONT: Starting at lower edge with green mist, cast on 54 [58–62] sts. Work in ribbing of k 1, p 1 for 7 rows. **8th row (right side):** K across to last 9 sts, p 1, (k 1, p 1) 4 times for front border. **9th row:** K 1, (p 1, k 1) 4 times; p across. Mark end of row for side edge. Repeat 8th and 9th rows until piece measures 3″ from beg, ending at side edge. **Next row (dec row):** K 2, sl 1, k 1, psso, work across in pattern. Continue to work in stockinette st with rib st border at front edge and dec 1 st 2 sts in from side edge every 12th row 5 times more (48 [52–56] sts). Then continuing in pattern as before, inc 1 st 2 sts in from side edge on next k row, then every 6th row twice more. Work even in pattern as established on 51 [55–59] sts until piece measures 14″ from beg, ending with a wrong side row. Break off green mist. Work stripe pattern same as back to underarm, ending at side edge.

To Shape Armhole: Bind off 6 [7–8] sts at beg of next row. Dec 1 st at same edge every other row 4 [5–7] times. Work even on 41 [43–44] sts until armhole measures 5″ [5¼″–5½″], ending at front edge.

To Shape Neck: Work across 22 sts and place these sts on a holder for front neck; complete row. Dec 1 st at neck edge every row twice, then every other row 3 [3–2] times (14 [16–18] sts). Work even until armhole measures same as back armhole, ending at armhole edge.

To Shape Shoulder: Bind off 7 [8–9] sts at beg of next row. Work 1 row even. Bind off remaining 7 [9–9] sts.

With pins, mark front border for placement of 8 buttons, the first one about 2¼″ from neck edge, the 7 others evenly spaced along front (a 9th button will be on the neckband).

RIGHT FRONT: Work ribbing as for left front. **8th row (right side):** P 1, (k 1, p 1) 4 times for front border, k across row. Mark end of row for side edge. **9th row:** P across to last 9 sts, k 1, (p 1, k 1) 4 times. Complete front to correspond to left front, reversing all shaping and making buttonholes opposite pins on left front as follows: From front edge work 3 sts in ribbing, bind off next 2 sts. Work to end of row. On following row cast on 2 sts over those bound off.

SLEEVES: Starting at lower edge with green mist, cast on 44 [46–48] sts. Work 4 rows in ribbing of k 1, p 1. Break off green mist; attach violite. Starting with a p row, work in stockinette st for 4 rows each of violite, scotch green, olive and scotch green. Break off scotch green; attach green mist. Continue in stockinette st, increasing 1 st 2 sts in from side edge at beg and end of next k row, then every 6th row 15 times more. Work even on 76 [78–80] sts until sleeve measures 17" from beg, or desired length to underarm.

To Shape Cap: Bind off 5 sts at beg of next 2 rows. Dec 1 st at beg and end of every other row 10 [11–12] times. Bind off 2 sts at beg of next 6 rows. Bind off remaining 34 sts.

FINISHING: Sew shoulder, side and sleeve seams, matching stripes. Sew sleeves in place. Sew on buttons.

Neckband: With right side of work facing you, using green mist, pick up and k 124 [128–128] sts around neck edge, including sts from holders. Work in ribbing of k 1, p 1 for 1 row. **Next row:** Make a buttonhole on right front as before. Work even until neckband measures 1" from beg. Bind off in ribbing.

SLEEVELESS TURTLENECK

BACK: Starting at lower edge with green mist, cast on 80 [90–100] sts. Work in ribbing of k 1, p 1 for 2". Then starting with a k row work in stockinette st until piece measures 7" from beg, ending on wrong side. Break off green mist; attach violite and work stripe pattern same as for cardigan to underarm.

To Shape Armholes: Bind off 6 [7–8] sts at beg of next 2 rows. Dec 1 st at beg and end of every other row 5 [6–8] times. Work even on 58 [66–72] sts until armholes measure 7¼" [7½"–7¾"].

To Shape Shoulders: Bind off 6 [7–8] sts at beg of next 4 rows. Place remaining 34 [38–40] sts on a holder. Break off.

FRONT: Work as for back to underarms, ending with a p row.

To Shape Armholes: Work as for back until armholes measure 5¼" [5½"–5¾"], ending with a p row.

To Shape Neck—1st row: K 16 [18–20] sts. Place center 26 [30–32] sts on a holder, attach another skein of green mist and k to end. **2nd row:** P to sts on holder, skip sts on holder, with other skein p to end. Working on both sides at once in this manner, dec 1 st at each edge of neck every row 4 times (12 [14–16] sts on each side.) Work even until armholes measure same as back armholes.

To Shape Shoulders: Bind off 6 [7—8] sts at beg (armhole edge) of next 4 rows. Break off.

FINISHING: Seam one shoulder. **Turtleneck:** With right side of work facing you, using green mist, pick up and k 104 [108–112] sts around neck edge, including sts from holders. Work even in ribbing of k 1, p 1 for 6". Bind off loosely in ribbing. Sew neck and shoulder seams.

Armhole Ribbing: With right side of work facing you, using green mist, pick up and k 90 [92–96] sts around armhole edge. Work in k 1, p 1 ribbing for 1". Bind off in ribbing. Sew side seams, matching stripes.

Tweedy Sweater Jacket, Vest and Beret

They all work up quickly with four strands of yarn at once, knitted in stockinette stitch with garter-stitch details. The vest mixes two of the four colors of the jacket.

JACKET

SIZES: (8–10) [(12–14)—(16–18)]. Sweater measures 16½" [18½"–20½"] across bust and about 27½" [28½"–29½"] from back of neck to lower edge.

MATERIALS: Bear Brand Winsom Orlon acrylic yarn, 5 [5–6] (2-oz.) skeins each autumn mist (tan) No. 315, green turquoise No. 331. Pompeii (rust) No. 339, rosy pink No. 342; knitting needles, 1 pair No. 13 (or English needles No. 00) **or the size that will give you the correct gauge.**

GAUGE: In stockinette st, 5 sts = 2".

Note: Work with 4 strands yarn held together throughout, using one strand of each color.

BACK: Starting at lower edge, cast on 49 [54–59] sts. Work in garter st (k each row) for 4 rows. Change to stockinette st (p 1 row, k 1 row) and work until piece measures 3" from beg. Dec 1 st at beg and end of next row, then continue in stockinette st and repeat dec row every 3" 3 times more. Work even on 41 [46–51] sts until piece measures 20½" [21"–21½"] from beg.

To Shape Armholes: Bind off 2 [3–3] sts at beg of next 2 rows. Dec 1 st at beg and end of every other row 2 [2–3] times. Work even on 33 [36–39] sts until armholes measure 7″ [7½″–8″].

To Shape Shoulders: Bind off 8 [9–10] sts at beg of next 2 rows. Place remaining 17 [18–19] sts on holder for collar.

LEFT FRONT: Starting at lower edge, cast on 30 [32–35] sts. Work 4 rows in garter st. **Next row (front edge):** K 6 for border, p across. **Following row:** K across. Repeat last 2 rows until piece measures 3″ from beg, ending at side edge. Dec 1 st at beg of next row, then repeat dec at same edge every 3″ 3 times more. Work even in pattern as established on 26 [28–31] sts until piece measures 14½″ [15″–15″] from beg, ending at front edge.

Garter Stitch Block Pattern—1st row: K 6 border sts, p 4, k 7, p remaining sts. **2nd row:** K across. Repeat last 2 rows 5 times more (these 12 rows complete first block). * Keeping first 6 sts at front edge in garter st, work 10 rows even in stockinette st, then repeat 12 rows of garter st block pattern. Repeat from * once more and, **at same time,** when piece measures same as back to underarm, begin armhole shaping as follows: At armhole edge, bind off 2 [3–3] sts at beg of next row, then dec 1 st at armhole edge every other row 2 [2–3] times. After third block is completed, continue in stockinette st and, keeping front border as established, work even on 22 [23–25] sts, if necessary, until armhole measures same as back armhole, ending at arm edge.

To Shape Shoulder: Bind off 8 [9–10] sts at beg of next row, work to end of row. Place remaining 14 [14–15] sts on holder for collar.

RIGHT FRONT: Work as for left front, reversing shaping.

COLLAR: Sew shoulder seams. Place all sts from holders onto needle. Attach yarn at right front neck edge. Work even in garter st on 45 [46–49] sts for 2½″. Bind off.

SLEEVES: Starting at lower edge, cast on 34 [35–36] sts. Work 16 rows in garter st, then change to stockinette st and work even until piece measures 17″ from beg or desired length to underarm.

To Shape Cap: Bind off 2 [3–3] sts at beg of next 2 rows, then dec 1 st at beg of next 10 [12–14] rows. Bind off 2 sts at beg of next 4 rows. Bind off remaining 12 [9–8] sts.

POCKETS (make 2): Cast on 14 sts. Work in garter st for 5″. Bind off.

FINISHING: Sew side and sleeve seams. Sew in sleeves. Following photograph, sew pockets in place.

VEST

SIZES: (8–10) [(12–14)—(16–18)]. Vest measures 15″ [16″–17″] across bust for a snug fit and about 22″ [23″–24″] from back of neck to lower edge.

MATERIALS: Bear Brand Winsom Orlon acrylic yarn, 3 (2-

oz.) skeins each autumn mist (tan) No. 315 and green turquoise No. 331; knitting needles, 1 pair No. 10 (or English needles No. 3) **or the size that will give you the correct gauge.**

GAUGE: In stockinette st, 4 sts = 1".

Note: Work with 2 strands yarn held together throughout, using 1 strand of each color.

BACK: Starting at lower edge, cast on 60 [64–68] sts. Work in garter st (k each row) for 1", then work in stockinette st (p 1 row, k 1 row) until piece measures 13" [13½"–14"] from beg, ending with a k row.

Underarm Border—Next row (wrong side): K 10, p across to within last 10 sts, k 10. **Following row:** K across. Repeat last 2 rows twice more.

To Shape Armholes—1st row (wrong side): Bind off 7 sts, work across row in pattern as established. **2nd row:** Bind off 7 sts, k across. Keeping 3 sts at each armhole edge in garter st, work even on 46 [50–54] sts until armholes measure 7¼" [7¾"–8¼"] from bound-off sts, ending with a k row. **Neck border— Next row (wrong side):** K 3, p 5 [7–8] , k 30 [30–32], p 5 [7–8], k 3. **Following row:** K across. Continue in pattern as established and, **at same time,** shape shoulders as follows:

To Shape Shoulders: Bind off 6 [8–9] sts at beg of next 2 rows, then bind off 6 sts at beg of next 2 rows. Place remaining 22 [22–24] sts on holder for neck.

FRONT: Work same as for back until piece measures 10½" [11"–11½"] from beg, ending with a k row (60 [64–68] sts). Place marker on needle in center of work.

V-Neck Border—Next row (wrong side): P across to within 1 st of marker, k 1, slip marker, k 1, p across remaining sts. **Following row:** K across. **Next row:** P across to within 2 sts of marker, k 2, slip marker, k 2, p across remaining sts. **Following row:** K across. Slipping marker on each row, continue in this manner, working 1 more st on each side of marker in garter st on wrong-side rows until there are 4 sts in garter st on each side, ending with a p row.

To Divide for V-Neck and Shape Armholes—1st row (arm edge): K across to within 2 sts of neck border, sl 1 as if to k, k 1, psso (1 st dec), k 4 sts of border. Remove marker. Place remaining 30 [32–34] sts on holder for other side. Work on one side only from now on. **2nd row:** K 4, p across. Keeping 4 sts at neck edge in garter st, continue to dec 1 st at neck edge in same manner every 4th row 3 times more; then every 6th row 7 [7–6] times and, **at same time,** when piece measures same as back to beg of underarm border, ending at arm edge, work border as follows: **Next row (arm edge):** K 10, continue in pattern across row. **Following row:** work across to within last 10 sts, k 10. Repeat last 2 rows twice more; then shape armholes as follows: At arm edge, bind off 7 sts, work across. Keeping 3 sts at armhole edge in garter st, work even at armhole edge and continue to dec at neck edge until neck shaping is completed. Then work even in pattern on 12 [14–15] sts, if necessary, until armhole measures same as back armhole to beg of shoulder shaping, ending at arm edge.

To Shape Shoulder: Bind off 6 [8–9] sts at beg of next row. Work 1 row even. Bind off remaining 6 sts.

Place 30 [32–34] sts from holder onto needle. With right side facing you, attach yarn at neck edge and work as follows: **1st row:** K 4, k 2 tog, k across. **2nd row (arm edge):** P across to within neck border, k 4. Continuing in this manner, complete to correspond to other side.

Sew shoulder and side seams.

BERET

SIZE: One size fits all.

MATERIALS: Bear Brand Winsom Orlon acrylic yarn, 2 (2-oz.) skeins Pompeii (rust) No. 339; knitting needles, 1 pair each No. 7 and No. 10 (or English needles No. 6 and No. 3) **or the size that will give you the correct gauge.**

GAUGE: In garter stitch, 7 sts = 2".

Note: Work with 2 strands yarn held together throughout.

Starting at lower edge with No. 7 needles, cast on 80 sts. Work in ribbing of k 1, p 1 until piece measures 1½" from beg. Change to No. 10 needles. **1st inc row:** * K 5 sts, inc in next st. Repeat from * across, ending k 2. K even on 93 sts for 2 rows. **2nd inc row:** * K 6, inc in next st. Repeat from * across, ending k 2. Work even in garter st (k each row) on 106 sts until piece measures 4½" from cast-on row.

Dec as follows: **1st dec row:** * K 8, k 2 tog. Repeat from * across, ending k 6 (10 sts dec). K even for 3 rows. **2nd dec row:** * K 7, k 2 tog. Repeat from * across, ending k 6. K even for 3 rows. Working 1 st less between decs, continue to dec 10 sts every 4th row 7 times more (16 sts remain). Break off, leaving 12" end. Thread end through sts, pull up firmly and fasten. Use end to sew center back seam.

Colorful Favorites

Zigzag Smock Top

The black and white chevron pattern is worked in the round from the yoke down. Garter-stitch borders finish it off.

SIZES: (10–12) [(14–16)—(18–20)]. Smock measures 17″ [19″–21″] across at underarms and 23″ from shoulder to lower edge.

MATERIALS: Unger's Roly-Poly (100% acrylic), 1 [1–2] (100-gram, about 3½-oz.) ball each red No. 864, black No. 8767, green No. 8352 and white No. 8001; knitting needles, 1 pair single pointed needles No. 10½, 29″ circular needle No. 10½ (or English needles No.2) **or the size that will give you the correct gauge.**

GAUGE: 4 pattern sts = 1″; 4 rows = 1″.

YOKE: (Note: Front and back yoke is made in one piece without shoulder seams.) Starting at lower front edge with red and single pointed needles, cast on 51 [55–63] sts. Work even in stockinette st until piece measures 4″, ending with a k row.

Neck Border and Shoulders—1st row (wrong side): P 10 [12–15], place marker on needle, k 31 [31–33] for border, place marker on needle, p 10 [12–15]. **2nd row:** K across, slipping markers. Repeat last 2 rows until 7th row is completed (wrong side row).

Color Key

□ white ☐̣ black

To Shape Neck—1st row: K 15 [17–21], bind off center 21 sts, k 15 [17–21]. **2nd row:** P 10 [12–15], sl marker, k 5 [5–6], drop yarn, skip bound-off sts, attach another matching skein, k to marker, sl marker, p to end. **3rd row:** Working on both sides at once, k across. **4th row:** Working on both sides at once, p 10 [12–15], sl marker, k 5 [5–6], drop yarn, pick up other skein and complete row to match. Repeat last 2 rows until piece measures 4″ from neck bind-off.

Next row: Work across in pattern, then cast on 21 sts for back neck. Break off. Pick up other skein and work to end of row (51 [55–63] sts). Work even in stockinette st for 1″, keeping sts between markers in garter st for neck border. Remove markers on last row. Continuing in stockinette st, work even for 4″ more. Bind off.

BODY: With right side of yoke facing you, using circular needle and black, pick up and k 69 [71–77] sts along front yoke edge, cast on 8 [10–12] sts for left armhole (mark center of armhole), pick up and k 69 [71–77] sts along back yoke edge, cast on 8 [10–12] sts for right armhole (154 [162–178] sts). Join sts into circle by knitting the first st, place marker on needle to indicate beg of rnd. Body is worked around and around without seams, with same side (right side) facing you on each rnd. Follow key for colors and chart for design, working in Fair Isle knitting (see page 33).

For sizes (10–12) and (18–20): Starting with first row of chart, work in pattern around, repeating from A to C across chart to within last 4 sts, work from A to B. **For size (14–16) only:** Work chart from A to C around. **For all sizes:** Repeat first through 6th rows of chart for pattern. Work even until body measures 15″ from beg.

Break off white. With black only, k 1 rnd even. Break off black; attach green. With green, k 1 rnd, p 1 rnd. Repeat these last 2 rnds 4 times more. Bind off.

SLEEVES: Starting at armhole edge with red and single pointed needles, cast on 52 [54–54] sts. Work in stockinette st for 3″, ending on right side. Then work 8 rows even in garter st. Bind off.

Sew sleeve seams. Sew sleeves in place.

Deep-V Vest

A vest to make in a jiffy, made up of two striped rectangles, to be folded crosswise, and a ribbed midriff section.

SIZES: Small (10–12) [medium (14–16)].

MATERIALS: Knitting worsted, 4 ounces turquoise (color A), 1 ounce each rose (B), orange (C) and green (D); knitting needles, 1 pair No. 6 (or English needles No. 7), **or the size that will give you the correct gauge.**

GAUGE: 5 sts = 1″; 6 rows = 1″.

FRONT AND BACK SECTIONS (MAKE 2) (Note: These sections are worked vertically.) Beginning at side edge with A, cast on 114 sts. Work in ribbing of k 1, p 1 for 4 rows. Working in stockinette st, work rows of striped pattern as follows: 2 rows A, 2 D, 4 A, 2 B, 4 A, 2 C, 4 A, 2 D, 4 A, 2 B, 4 A, 2 C, 2 A. For medium size only, continue with 2 more rows A, 2 C, 2 A. For both sizes, work 4 rows in ribbing. Bind off in ribbing.

40 Rows

Fold sections in half crosswise with fold at top to form shoulders. Placing sections side by side, lap ribbing of one side over ribbing of other side and baste (center front and back).

FRONT MIDRIFF SECTION: With right side facing you and using A, pick up and k 68 [72] sts along lower edge of front sections. Work in ribbing for 6″. Bind off loosely in ribbing.

46 rows

BACK MIDRIFF SECTION: Work same as for front. Sew side seams of midriff sections.

108

Making Waves

The multicolor striped vest, worked in a wavy openwork pattern, matches up with the cabled cardigan coat shown on page 69 or goes it alone.

SIZES: Small (8–10) [medium (12–14)—large (16–18)]. Zigzag vest fits snugly and will stretch to fit about 33" [36"–40"] at bust.

MATERIALS: Bear Brand Winsom (Orlon acrylic yarn), 1 (2-oz.) skein each coffee No. 376 (color B), tobacco gold No. 340 (G), melon whip No. 359 (M), almond green No. 377 (A), Persian blue No. 321 (P), camel No. 368 (C) and Pompeii (rust) No. 339 (R); knitting needles, **for small size,** 1 pair each No. 3 and No. 5 (or English needles No. 10 and No. 8); **for medium size,** 1 pair each No. 4 and No. 6 (or English needles No. 9 and No. 7); **for large size,** 1 pair each No. 5 and No. 7 (or English needles No. 8 and No. 6) **or the sizes that will give you the correct gauge.**

GAUGE: When stretched. On No. 5 needles, 11 sts = 2". On No. 6 needles, 5 sts = 1". On No. 7 needles, 9 sts = 2".

BACK: Starting at lower edge with No. 3 [No. 4–No. 5] needles and B, cast on 84 sts. Work in ribbing of k 2, p 2 for 4", increasing 6 sts on last row (90 sts). Break off B; attach G. Change to No. 5 [No. 6–No. 7] needles. Work first 4 rows of pattern with G.

Pattern—1st row (right side): K 1, (k 2 tog) twice; * (y o and k 1) 3 times; y o, (k 2 tog) 4 times. Repeat from * across, ending (y o and k 1) 3 times; y o, (k 2 tog) twice; k 1. **2nd row:** P across. **3rd row:** K across. **4th row:** P across. Repeat these 4 rows for pattern and, **at same time,**

work colors as follows: Work 2 rows each M, A, M, A and M; 4 rows G, 2 rows each P, C, P, B, A, B, C, B, A and B; 4 rows R, 2 rows each M, A, M, A and M; 4 rows R, 2 rows each P, C and P; 4 rows G. Back should measure about 12" [13"–14"] from beg.

To Shape Armholes: Being careful to continue in pattern as established, shape armholes (see next paragraph) and, **at same time,** work colors as follows: 2 rows each M, A, M, A and M; 4 rows G, 2 rows each P, C and P; 4 rows R, 2 rows each M, A, M, A and M, 4 rows R, 2 rows each P, C, and P, 4 rows G, 2 rows M.

Bind off 7 sts at beg of first 2 rows. Dec 1 st at beg and end of every other row 4 times, then work even on 68 sts in stripe pattern to shoulder. Armholes should measure about 7½" [8"–8½"].

To Shape Shoulders: Using A, bind off 11 sts at beg of next 2 rows, decreasing 2 sts on last row. Change to No. 3 [No. 4–No. 5] needles and with B work in ribbing of k 2, p 2 on all 44 sts for 4 rows. Bind off all sts in ribbing.

FRONT: Work same as for back until armholes measure 3½" (68 sts on needle).

To Shape Neck: Being careful to keep pattern as established and working colors as for back, work across first 21 sts, place center 26 sts on a holder, place last 21 sts on another holder.

Working on one side only, dec 1 st at neck edge every row 10 times. Work even on 11 sts until armhole is same length as back armhole to shoulder. Bind off all sts.

Place 21 sts for other side on needle. Attach yarn at neck edge and work to correspond to first side.

FINISHING: Use B and No. 3 [No. 4–No. 5] needles for all finishing. **Front Neckband:** With right side of work facing you, pick up and k 76 sts across neck edge (including sts on holder). Work in ribbing of k 2, p 2 for 4 rows. Bind off all sts in ribbing. Sew shoulder and neckband seams. **Armhole Ribbing:** With right side of work facing you, pick up and k 100 sts across entire armhole edge. Work as for front neckband.

Sew side seams and armhole ribbing seams.

The Square Sweater

This sweater consists of eight 8-inch squares; the yoke, cuffs, and waistband are 4-inch wide checkerboard borders.

SIZES: Pullover stretches to fit sizes 8–12.

MATERIALS: Spinnerin Germantown Deluxe (knitted-worsted-weight Orlon acrylic yarn), 2 (4-oz.) skeins each No. 3270 (orange) and No. 3262 (magenta), 1 skein each No. 3258 (gold) and No. 3255 (peach); small amount lightweight yarn for assembling squares; knitting needles, 1 pair No. 4 (or English needles No. 9) **or the size that will give you the correct gauge;** aluminum crochet hook size E (or Canadian hook No. 11) for edging; 1 yard round elastic; tapestry needle.

GAUGE: 5 sts = 1"; 10 rows = 1".

CHANGING COLORS: Never carry the yarn not in use across back of work: Break off at end of each color change and attach yarn again in new place, or leave it hanging until you need it again on the next row. The directions do not specify where to break off or drop old color or where to pick up or attach new one. You will be able to determine this as you work. When color changes are frequent, wind small balls of each color or use bobbins.

Mark right side of work with safety pin. In order to avoid a hole when changing colors, work as follows: Make sure that both colors are hanging on wrong side of work. Drop old color, pick up or attach new color and bring it up from under old color (if wrong side is facing you, then bring new color to right side between points of needles). K next st. Old color will be caught through loop of new color on wrong side.

BODY AND SLEEVES—Square 1 (make 4): Use peach (color A), magenta (B) and orange (C).

Square 2 (make 4): With magenta cast on 25 sts; with peach cast 15 sts onto same needle. **Pattern 1:** Follow directions for Pattern 2 of Square 1 (see instructions, page 113), using peach as color A and magenta as C. **Pattern 2:** Follow directions for Pattern 1 of Square 1, using orange as color B and peach as A. Repeat Patterns 1 and 2 three times more. Bind off in pattern.

Border Strips: Follow directions for 4 ″ knitted border (see instructions on page 113), using orange as color A and gold as B. Working Patterns 1 and 2 four times, make 6 strips, each measuring 16″ long.

Follow directions for 4″ knitted border, using gold as color A and orange as B. Working Patterns 1 and 2 twice, make 2 strips, each measuring 8″ long.

Follow directions for 2″ knitted border, using gold as color A and orange as B. Working Patterns 1 and 2 four times, make 1 strip measuring 8″ long.

ASSEMBLING: Following diagram for layout, pin squares and border strips together. Add right sleeve. With right sides facing, using tapestry needle and lightweight yarn, whipstitch pieces together. Matching front and back at underarms, sew side seams (X) and sleeve seams (Y).

With crochet hook and orange, work 1 rnd sc around lower edge of body, sleeve and neck openings. Weave elastic through seam at waist.

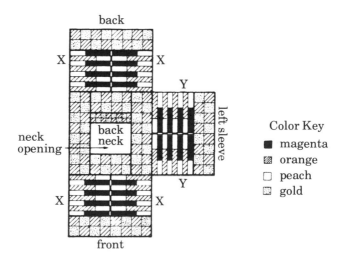

KNITTED BORDERS

Sizes: 2″ [4″] wide.

Starting at narrow end with color A, cast on 5 [10] sts; with B cast 5 [10] sts onto same needle. Knit all sts throughout.

Pattern 1—1st row (right side): Work 5 [10] B, 5 [10] A. **2nd row:** Work 5 [10] A, 5 [10] B. Repeat last 2 rows 4 [8] times more.

Pattern 2—Next row (right side): Work 5 [10] A, 5 [10] B. **Following row:** Work 5 [10] B, 5 [10] A. Repeat last 2 rows 4 [8] times more.

Alternate patterns for desired length.

SQUARE 1 (8″)

With color A, cast on 15 sts; with B cast 25 onto same needle. Knit all sts throughout (garter stitch).

Pattern 1—1st row (right side): Work 25 B, 15 A.
          2nd row: Work 15 A, 25 B.

Repeat last 2 rows 4 times more.

Pattern 2—Next row (right side): Work 15 A, 25 C.
          Following row: Work 25 C, 15 A.

Repeat last 2 rows 4 times more.

Alternate Patterns 1 and 2, 3 times more. Bind off in pattern.

Checks and Stripes Pullover

Checks and stripes update this classic V-neck boy's pullover. The tam picks up stripe detail. Both are worked in stockinette stitch.

SIZES: (8–10) [(12–14)—(16–18)]. Sweater measures 16″ [18″–20″] across back below armholes.

MATERIALS: Bear Brand Winsom (Orlon acrylic yarn), 3 (2-oz.) skeins navy No. 379 (color N), 2 [2–3] skeins each pumpkin No. 302 (P) and brick (orange-red) No. 332 (B), 1 skein Scotch green No. 90 (G). **Knitting Needles—For sweater:** 1 pair each No. 5 and No. 6 (or English needles No. 8 and No. 7); **for tam,** 1 pair each No. 3 and 14″ No. 4 (or English needles No. 10 and No. 9) **or the sizes that will give you the correct gauge.**

PULLOVER

WORKING WITH 2 COLORS: You will be working with 2 colors on each row of the vertical stripes and checkerboard patterns. Attach both colors at beg of first row of pattern and carry the color not in use loosely across back of work. Be careful to keep your tension even and to allow the strands of carried yarns to lie flat across back of work. Do not pull tightly or pattern will pucker and your gauge will not be accurate.

GAUGE: On No. 6 needles, 11 sts = 2″; 7 rows = 1″.

BACK: Starting at lower edge with color N and No. 5 needles, cast on 87 [99–111] sts. Work in ribbing of k 1, p 1 for 3″. Change to No. 6

needles. Break off N and attach P and B. Starting with a k row and continuing in stockinette st throughout, work horizontal stripe pattern as follows: (Work 2 rows P, 2 rows B) 3 times. Break off P and B (horizontal stripe pattern completed). Attach G and work 2 rows for G band. Break off G and attach B and N.

Work vertical stripe pattern as follows: **1st row:** (K 2 N, k 2 B) 21 [24–27] times; k 2 N, k 1 B. **2nd row:** P 1 B, (p 2 N, p 2 B) 21 [24–27] times; p 2 N. Repeat last 2 rows 5 times more (vertical stripe band completed). Break off N and B. Attach G and work G band. Break off G; attach P and B.

Work checkerboard pattern as follows: **1st row:** (K 3 P, k 3 B) 14 [16–18] times; k 3 P. **2nd row:** (P 3 P, p 3 B) 14 [16–18] times; p 3 P. Repeat last 2 rows once more. **5th row:** (K 3 B, k 3 P) 14 [16–18] times; k 3 B. **6th row:** (P 3 B, p 3 P) 14 [16–18] times; p 3 B. Repeat last 2 rows once more. Repeat 1st and 2nd rows 4 times (checkerboard pattern completed). Break off P and B. Attach G and work G band. Break off G.

Repeat patterns of horizontal stripe, G band, vertical stripe, G band, horizontal stripe, G band, checkerboard and G band until piece measures 16″ from beg, or desired length to underarm.

Armholes: Place marker at beg and end of last row to indicate underarms. Work even in patterns until armholes measure 7″ [7¼″–7½″].

To Shape Shoulders: Bind off 10 [12–14] sts at beg of next 2 rows, 8 [10–12] sts at beg of next 4 rows. Place remaining 35 sts on a st holder for back neck.

FRONT: Work as for back until piece measures 14″ from beg, or desired length to start of neck, ending with a p row.

To Shape Neck—1st row: K 36 [42–48] for left front and place on a st holder. Bind off next 15 sts for front neck, k remaining 36 [42–48] sts for right front. Work on right front sts only. Continuing in pattern, dec 1 st at neck edge on next row, then every other row 9 times more and, **at same time,** when front measures same as back to underarm, place marker at side edge to indicate underarm. Continue neck shaping until 26 [32–38] sts remain. Work even until armhole measures same as back armhole, ending at arm edge.

To Shape Shoulder: Bind off 10 [12–14] sts at beg of next row, then 8 [10–12] sts at beg of every other row twice. Break off.

Attach yarn at left front neck edge and place left front sts on needle. Starting with a p row, dec 1 st at neck edge and p across to side edge. Complete to correspond to right front.

SLEEVES: Starting at lower edge with N and no. 5 needles, cast on 55 sts. Work in ribbing of k 1, p 1 for 3″. Change to No. 6 needles. Break off N and attach P and B. Work in patterns of horizontal stripe, G band, vertical stripe, G band, horizontal stripe, G band, checkerboard and G band, increasing 1 st at beg and end of row every 1″ [¾″–¾″] 11 [13–15] times (77 [81–85] sts). Work even until sleeve measures 18" from beg, or desired length. Bind off loosely. Sleeves do not have caps but have slight drop-shouldered effect.

FINISHING: Block matching pieces tog. Sew shoulder, side and sleeve seams. Sew sleeves in place. **Neckband:** Attach N at right back neck edge. Place back neck sts from holder onto left No. 5 needle and k across them. Work in ribbing of k 1, p 1 for 1½". Bind off. Attach N at lower right front edge and, with right side facing you, pick up and k 1 st for each row along right front neck edge. Work in ribbing for 1½". Bind off. Attach N at shoulder edge of left front and repeat border. Sew shoulder border seams. Lap one border end over other at center front and sew along bound-off edge of pullover front.

TAM

GAUGE: On No. 4 needles, 6 sts = 1"; 8 rows = 1".

Starting at lower edge with N and No. 3 needles, cast on 122 sts loosely. Work in ribbing of k 1, p 1 for 1¼". Change to No. 4 needles. Working in stockinette st, inc 10 sts, as evenly spaced as possible, on next row. Inc 10 sts every other row 7 times more, making sure incs are not directly over each other (202 sts). Work even until piece measures 3¾" from beg, ending with a p row. Break off N; attach P and B.

Working in stripe pattern of (2 rows P, 2 rows B) 3 times and 2 rows G, dec every other row as follows, spacing decs as evenly as possible and not directly over each other: Dec 15 sts 4 times (142 sts), 10 sts 7 times (72 sts), 6 sts 5 times (37 sts) and 5 sts 4 times (17 sts). There are 2 complete repeats of stripe pattern and 6 stripes of 3rd repeat. To complete 3rd repeat of pattern, with G work 1 row even. On next row k 2 tog around, k 1 (9 sts). Break off, leaving 18" end. Thread end in needle and run needle through remaining 9 sts. Pull up firmly and fasten; sew tam seam.

Snug Cap-Sleeved Cardigan

Colorful stripes, narrow and wide, are in k 1, p 1 ribbing all the way for a snug fit.

SIZES: (6–8) [(10–12)—(14–16)]. Snug fitting cardigan measures 15″ [17″–19″] across back at underarms, 20½″ [21¾″–23″] from back of neck to lower edge.

MATERIALS: Coats and Clark's Wintuk sport yarn (100% Orlon acrylic), 2 (2-oz.) skeins each royal blue No. 845 (color B), cerise No. 795 (C), apple green No. 648 (G) and yellow No. 230 (Y); knitting needles, 1 pair No. 3 (or English needles No. 10) **or the size that will give you the correct gauge;** 8 ball buttons ½″ in diameter.

GAUGE: 13 sts = 2″, when stretched; 10 rows = 1″.

BACK: Starting at lower edge with B, cast on 98 [112–124] sts. Work in ribbing of k 1, p 1 for 10 rows. Break off B; attach C. **11th row (right side):** With C, k across. Work in ribbing of k 1, p 1 for 9 rows. Break off C. Working as for last 10 rows (k 1 row, rib 9 rows), work in stripe pattern of 10 rows each G, Y, B, C, G, and Y. (Piece should measure about 8″ from beg.) Then working in ribbing of k 1, p 1 every row, work in stripe pattern of 2 rows each B, C, G and Y until piece measures about 13″ [14″–15″] from beg, ending with 2 rows Y.

To Shape Armholes: Working in established pattern, bind off 3 [4–5] sts at beg of next 2 rows, then dec 1 st at beg and end of every row 6 [9–11] times more. Work even in ribbing and stripe pattern on 80 [86–92] sts until armholes measure 7½″ [7¾″–8″] .

To Shape Shoulders: Bind off first 12 [14–16] sts for one shoulder; break off. Place next 56 [58–60] sts on holder for back neck. Attach yarn and bind off remaining 12 [14–16] sts for other shoulder.

LEFT FRONT: Starting at lower edge with B, cast on 58 [64–70] sts. **1st row:** Work in ribbing of k 1, p 1 across. **2nd row:** Working in ribbing with B, work across first 50 [56–62] sts; wind and attach B bobbin (see page 35 for bobbin knitting) and continue in ribbing with B across remaining 8 sts for front band. Keeping 8 band sts in B, work pattern as for back until piece measures same as back to underarm, ending at arm edge with 2 rows Y.

To Shape Armhole: Working in established pattern, bind off 3 sts at beg of next row (armhole edge), work across. Dec 1 st at arm edge every row 7 [9–11] times (48 [52–56] sts). Work even, if necessary, until armhole measures 1½" [1¾"–2"], ending at front edge.

To Shape Neck—1st row: Work across first 31 sts, slip these sts onto holder for front neck; complete row. Dec 1 st at neck edge every row 4 [5–6] times, then every other row 1 [2–3] times more. Work even in pattern on 12 [14–16] sts until front armhole measures same as back to shoulder.

To Shape Shoulder: Bind off 12 [14–16] sts for shoulder.

Mark band for placement of 7 buttons, the first 1" from neck edge, the rest evenly spaced on band. (An 8th button will be added to neckband later.)

RIGHT FRONT: Work to correspond to left front, reversing shaping and working buttonholes opposite markers on left band as follows: **1st row:** Starting at front edge in ribbing, work 2 sts, bind off 4 sts, work across. On next row, cast on 4 sts over bound-off sts.

SLEEVES: Starting at lower edge with B, cast on 122 sts. Working in ribbing of k 1, p 1, work 2 rows each B, C, G and Y. Continuing in pattern as for back, bind off 3 sts at beg of next 2 rows. Dec 1 st at beg and end of every other row 2 [4–6] times, then every row 30 [28–26] times. Bind off 2 sts at beg of next 6 rows. Bind off remaining 40 sts.

FINISHING: Sew side, shoulder and sleeve seams. Sew in sleeves.

Neckband—1st row: With right side of work facing you, with B pick up and k 194 [196–198] sts around neck edge, including sts from holders. Work in ribbing of k 1, p 1 for 7 rows, working 8th buttonhole on neckband. Bind off loosely in ribbing. Sew buttons in place.

Fair Isle Cardigan, Hat and Matching Mittens

Small geometric motifs in brilliant colors, worked in stockinette stitch with knitting worsted. Cable mittens have long, snug cuffs to keep out the cold.

CARDIGAN

SIZES: Small (8–10) [medium (12–14)—large (16–18)]. Cardigan measures 17″ [19″–21″] across bust and about 26″ [26″–26½″] long from lower edge of back neckband.

MATERIALS: Coats and Clark's knitting worsted, 3 (4-oz.) skeins dark gold No. 602 (color A), 1 skein each lilac No. 586 (B), mid rose No. 758 (C), deep rose No. 759 (D), tangerine No. 253 (E), apple green No. 648 (F), burnt orange No. 255 (G), cantaloupe No. 434 (H) and rust No. 282 (I); knitting needles, 1 pair No. 6 (English needles No.7) **or the size that will give you the correct gauge;** steel crochet hook No. 0 for borders and buttons; eight ⅝″ button rings; tapestry needle.

GAUGE: 11 sts = 2″; 5 rows = 1″.

Note: See page 33 for Fair Isle knitting. Be sure to make a swatch to check your gauge and, if you are not familiar with Fair Isle knitting, to practice working with multiple yarns.

Occasionally one color has been substituted for another when working the pattern on different sections of the cardigan. For instance, on the sleeves cantaloupe was substituted for green on the 48th row of the pattern. For clarity, we have kept the colors uniform throughout.

BACK: Starting at lower edge with color A, cast on 93 [105–117] sts. K 1 row, p 1 row. Now, follow Chart 1 for design. **1st row— Small size:** K 2 A, attach B and k 1, (k 7 A, 1 B) 11 times; k 2 A. **Medium size:** Attach B and k 1, (k 7 A, 1 B) 13 times. **Large size:** K 6 A, attach B and k 1, (k 7 A, 1 B) 13 times; k 6 A. **2nd row: Small size:** (P 1 A, 1 B) twice; p 2 A, attach C and p 1, (p 2 A, 1 B, 1 A, 1 B, 2 A, 1 C) 10 times; p 2 A, (p 1 B, 1 A) twice. **Medium size:** P 1 A, 1 B, 2 A, attach C and p 1, (p 2 A, 1 B, 1 A, 1 B, 2 A, 1 C) 12 times; p 2 A, 1 B, 1 A. **Large size:** P 2 A, attach C and p 1, (p 2 A, 1 B, 1 A, 1 B, 2 A, 1 C) 14 times; p 2 A. Continuing in stockinette st and starting with 3rd row of chart, work each row from S [M–L] to Z, then from Y (do not repeat center st) back to S [M–L]. Work until 81st row has been completed.

To Shape Raglan Armholes: Keeping in pattern, bind off 4 [5–5] sts at beg of next 2 rows, then 2 [2–3] sts at beg of following 2 rows, then 1 [2–2] sts at beg of next 2 [2–4] rows. **Small and Medium sizes:** Dec 1 st at beg and end of every other row 20 times (39 [47] sts). **Large size:** Dec 1 st at beg and end of every other row 3 times, ending with first row marked with dot on margin. To add length to armholes, repeat last row once more (added row is omitted from chart in order to keep chart uniform for all sizes). Now work next row of chart. Continue in this manner, following chart and repeating each of the rows marked with dots, as before. Complete chart (55 sts). **All sizes:** With A, work across and dec 9 sts evenly spaced. Place remaining 30 [38–46] sts on a st holder.

RIGHT FRONT: Starting at lower edge with color A, cast on 47 [53–59] sts. K 1 row, p 1 row. Follow Chart 1 for design, working from S [M–L] to Z on k rows and from Z to S [M–L] on p rows. Work until 81st row has been completed.

To Shape Raglan Armhole: Keeping in pattern, bind off 4 [5–5] sts at beg (armhole edge) of next row. Following chart, dec armhole edge, as shown, through row marked with arrow at margin. (**Note:** For large size, add extra rows at dots as for back.)

To Shape Neck: Bind off 6 sts at beg (front neck edge) of next row. Continuing to dec at armhole edge as shown, bind off every other row at neck edge 5 sts 1 [1–4] times, 4 sts 1 [2–0] times, 3 sts 1 [1–0] times and 1 st once. Break off.

LEFT FRONT: Work as for right front, reversing shapings.

SLEEVES: Starting at lower edge with color A, cast on 48 sts. K 1 row, p 1 row. Follow Chart 2 for first section of sleeve (56 sts). Then follow Chart 1, starting with 29th row and work from L to X. Inc 1 st at beg and end of next row, then every 4th row 8 [10–12] times, working added sts in pattern. (**Note:** Sleeve will measure about 16″ from underarm, including ½″ crocheted border. If you wish a longer sleeve, add solid color rows where indicated by a * along margin of chart.) Work even on 74 [78–82] sts through 81st row of chart.

To Shape Cap: Following Chart 1 for pattern but not for shaping, bind off 6 sts at beg of next 2 rows, then dec 1 st at beg and end of every other row 22 times (**Note:** For large size, add extra rows at dots as for back and front). Place remaining 18 [22–26] sts on a holder.

FINISHING: Block pieces (see page 37 for blocking). Sew side and sleeve seams. Sew sleeves in place, carefully matching pattern bands. **Neckband:** Attach A at left front neck edge. With right side facing you, pick up and k 19 sts along shaped front neck edge. Place sts from holders onto needle and k across them, pick up and k 19 sts along shaped right front neck edge (104 [120–136] sts). **2nd row:** P across, decreasing 0 [10–22] sts, evenly spaced (104 [110–114] sts). Work in ribbing of k 1, p 1 for 3″. Bind off in ribbing. Fold band in half to wrong side and sew in place.

Crocheted Border—1st row: With right side facing you and starting at left front neck edge at top of neckband, work row of sc evenly along front edge, work 3 sc in corner, work sc evenly along lower edge, 3 sc in corner, sc evenly along right front edge to top of neckband. Ch 1, turn. **2nd row:** Mark right front edge for 8 buttonholes, evenly spaced. Work sc in each sc to first marker, * ch 4, skip 4 sc, sc in each sc to next marker. Repeat from * 6 times more; ch 4, skip 4 sc, sc in each sc to corner, work 3 sc in corner sc, sc in each sc along lower edge to next corner, 3 sc in corner, sc in each sc to end of row. Ch 1, turn. **3rd row:** Sc in each sc, working 4 sc over each ch-4 loop for buttonholes and 2 sc in each corner sc. Ch 1, turn. **4th row:** Sc in each sc. Break off.

Work 4 rnds of sc around wrist edge of sleeves.

Buttons: With crochet hook and color A, work as many sc around a button ring as will fit. Break off, leaving 12″ end. Thread end in tapestry needle and weave in and out of every other sc around ring. Pull up yarn tightly until sts turn to center of ring. Sew button in place. Make 7 more buttons.

MITTENS

SIZE: One size fits all.

MATERIALS: Brunswick Germantown knitting worsted, 1 (4-oz.) skein curry heather No. 490; knitting needles, 1 pair No. 8 and 1 dp needle No. 8 for cables (or English needles No. 5) **or the size that will give you the correct gauge;** tapestry needle.

GAUGE: 5 sts = 1″ in stockinette st.

RIGHT MITTEN

Cuff: Cast on 36 sts.

Pattern—1st row (wrong side): P 1, k 2, p 2, k 1, p 6, k 1, (p 2, k 2) twice; p 2, k 1, p 6, k 1, p 2, k 2, p 1. **2nd row:** P 1, k 2, p 3, k 6, p 3, k 2, p 2, k 2, p 3, k 6, p 3, k 2, p 1. **3rd row:** K 1, p 2, k 3, p 6, k 3, p 2, k 2, p 2, k 3, p 6, k 3, p 2, k 1. **4th row:** K 1, p 2, k 2, p 1, slip next 3 sts on dp needle and hold in back of work, k 3, then k 3 off dp needle (cable twist made), p 1, (k 2, p 2), twice: k 2, p 1, make cable twist, p 1, k 2, p 2, k 1. **5th row:** Repeat 1st row. **6th row:** Repeat 2nd row. **7th row:** Repeat 3rd row. **8th row:** K 1, p 2, k 2, p 1, k 6, p 1, (k 2, p 2) twice; k 2, p 1, k 6, p 1, k 2, p 2, k 1. Repeat these 8 rows for pattern until cuff measures approximately 4¾″, ending with a 5th pattern row.

Mitten: From now on work mitten in stockinette st but keep first cable pattern on back of mitten. **1st row:** Inc 1 st in first st, k 3, inc 1 st in next st, work p 1, k 6 and p 1 for cable, inc 1 st in next st, k 8, inc 1 st in next st, k 8, inc 1st in next st, k to end (41 sts). **2nd row:** P 26, k 1, p 6, k 1, p 7.

To Shape Thumb Gusset—1st row: Work 21 sts, place marker on needle, inc 1 st in each of next 2 sts, place second marker on needle, k 18 (43 sts). **2nd row:** Work across, slipping markers. **3rd row:** Work to first marker, sl marker, inc 1 st in next st, k 2, inc 1 st in next st, sl second marker, work to end (45 sts). Continue in this manner, increasing in st after first marker and in st before second marker every k row, working 2 more sts between the inc sts 5 times more (55 sts in all). Work 3 more rows even, ending with a p row. **Following row:** Removing markers, work 22 sts and slip them on a holder, k 14 (thumb), slip remaining 19 sts on a holder.

Thumb: Work 14 sts for 13 rows, or desired thumb length, ending with a p row. **Next row:** K 2 tog across row (7 sts). Break off, leaving a 6″ end for sewing seam. Draw end through sts, pull up tightly and fasten.

Hand—Following row: Slip 19 sts from holder onto needle, attach yarn, k across row. **Next row:** P 19, slip 22 sts from other holder onto needle, p 22 (41 sts). Work even for 3½″ from thumb row, or 1″ less than desired length.

To Shape Tip—1st row: K 2 tog, * k 2, k 2 tog. Repeat from * to within last 3 sts, k 1, k 2 tog (30 sts). **2nd row:** P across. **3rd row:** * K 2 tog, k 1. Repeat from * across (20 sts). **4th row:** P across. **5th row:** K 2 tog across (10 sts). Break off, leaving 12″ end for sewing seam. Draw end through sts, pull up tightly and fasten. Sew side and thumb seams.

LEFT MITTEN

Cuff: Work as for right mitten.

Mitten: Reverse shaping as follows and keep 2nd cable for back of mitten: **1st row:** K 4, inc 1 st in next st, k 8, inc 1 st in next st, k 8, inc 1 st in next st, work p 1, k 6 and p 1 for cable panel, inc 1 st in next st, k 3, inc 1 st in last st. **2nd row:** P 7, k 1, p 6, k 1, p 26. **3rd row (thumb gusset):** K 18, place marker, inc 1 st in each of next 2 sts, place marker, k 21. Complete as for right mitten.

HAT

SIZE: Medium.

MATERIALS: Knitting worsted, 1 ounce each of the colors listed for the Fair Isle cardigan, omitting dark gold.

Note: If you are making the cardigan, there should be enough yarn left over for the hat; knitting needles (see cardigan).

GAUGE: 11 sts = 2″; 5 rows = 1″.

Starting at lower edge with color D, cast on 96 sts. Work in ribbing of k 1, p 1 for 1″ for hem. Break off D; attach C. Starting with first row of Chart 3, continue in ribbing for 5 rows, repeating from Y to Z across chart for each row. Starting with 6th row of chart, work in stockinette st, repeating from Y to Z across k rows and from Z to Y across p rows. Complete chart; end with p row.

To Shape Top: Break off B and E; attach G. **1st row:** (K 6, k 2 tog) 12 times (84 sts). **2nd row and all even numbered rows:** P across. **3rd row:** (K 2, k 2 tog) 21 times (63 sts). **5th row:** (K 1, k 2 tog) 21 times (42 sts). **7th row:** K 2 tog across (21 sts). Break off, leaving 18″ end for sewing seam.

FINISHING: Thread end in tapestry needle and run through sts on knitting needle. Remove needle, pull sts tog tightly and fasten. Sew seam, carefully matching pattern bands. Turn hem under and sew in place.

Pompons: Cut 2 cardboard disks 2″ in diameter. Cut out ¼″ hole in center of both disks. Place disks together and cut slit through disks to center. Using 2 or 3 colors for multicolor pompon, slip yarn through slit. Wind yarn to cover disks, working around and around, sliding yarn through slit for each wind, until hole is filled. Slip scissor point between disks and cut all strands at outside edge. Without disturbing clipped strands, carefully slide a strand of yarn between disks and wind several times very tightly around center of clipped strands; knot, leaving ends for attaching pompon. Remove disks. Fluff out pompon and trim any uneven ends. Make another pompon in same manner, then make 2 more 1½″ in diameter. Tie or sew them in a tight bunch to top of hat.

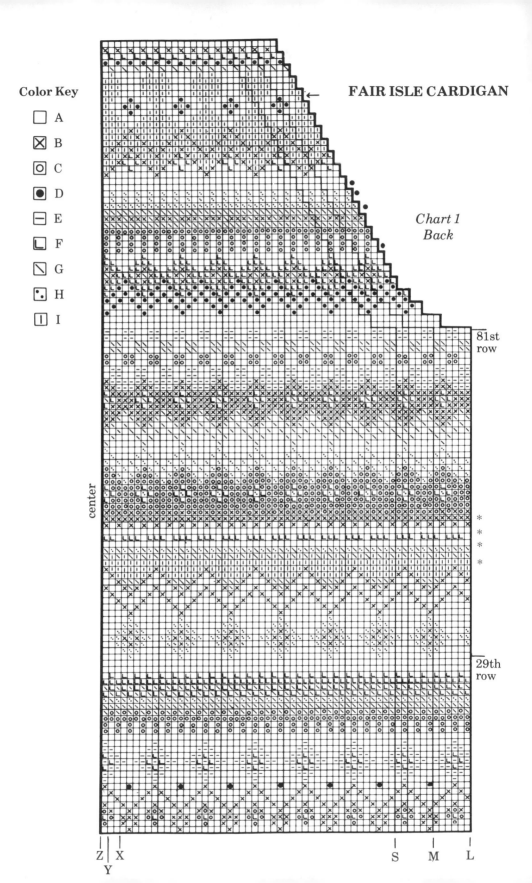

Color Key

- ☐ A
- ☒ B
- ◎ C
- ● D
- ⊟ E
- ⌊ F
- ◺ G
- ∴ H
- ⊞ I

FAIR ISLE CARDIGAN

Chart 1
Back

81st row

29th row

center

Z X
Y

S M L

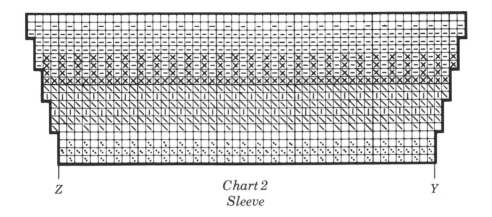

Z   *Chart 2*   Y
        Sleeve

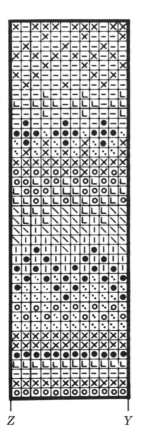

Chart 3
Hat

Z   Y

Mother's Embroidered Cardigan

A pleasing cardigan in a raised diamond pattern with French knots embroidered in the center can be worked for a daughter, too! See page 232 for the smaller version.

SIZES: 10 [12–14–16–18]. Garment width around underarms, about 36½" [38½"–41"–42½"–44½"].

MATERIALS: Sport yarn, 14 [16–16–18–18] ozs. Small amount of colors A, B and C for embroidery. Knitting needles No. 4 and No. 6, **or the size that will give you the correct gauge.** 7 buttons.

GAUGE: 5 sts = 1"; 7 rows = 1".

BEAD STITCH AND PATTERN: See Daughter's Embroidered Cardigan, page 232.

BACK: With No. 4 needles, cast on 92 [98–102–106–112] sts. Work in k 1, p 1 ribbing for 2″, inc 1 st each edge of last row—94 [100–104–108–114] sts. Change to No. 6 needles. Work in stockinette st (k on right side, p on wrong side) keeping first and last 2 sts (edge sts) in k throughout. Work until 16½″ from beg or desired length to underarm.

To Shape Armholes: At each edge bind off 6 [7–7–8–9] sts once, 3 [3–5–5–6] sts 1 [2–1–1–1] times, 2 [2–4–4–4] sts 2 [1–1–1–1] times—68 [70–72–74–76] sts. Work even until 6¾″ [7″–7¼″–7½″–8″] above beg of armhole shaping.

To Shape Neck: Work first 25 [26–27–27–28] sts, join another ball of yarn and bind off center 18 [18–18–20–20] sts, finish row. Working both sides at once, bind off at beg of each neck edge 3 sts once, 2 sts once—20 [21–22–22–23] sts each side. Work even until armholes measure 7¼″ [7½″–7¾″–8″–8¼″] above beg of armhole shaping.

To Shape Shoulders: Bind off at beg of each armhole edge 6 [7–8–8–9] sts once, then 7 sts twice.

RIGHT FRONT: With No. 4 needles, cast on 44 [44–50–50–56] sts. Work in k 1, p 1 ribbing for 2″, inc 1 st at side edge on last row—45 [45–51–51–57] sts. Change to No. 6 needles. **1st row: (right side):** K 1 (front edge st), work next 36 [36–48–48–48] sts in pat; **for sizes 10, 12 and 18** only, bead st, k 6; **for all sizes,** k last 2 sts for side edge. (Keep 1 st at front and 2 sts at side in k throughout.) **2nd row:** K 2, p to last st, k 1. Continue working 1 st at front edge and 2 sts on side edge in k throughout, pat on center 42 [42–48–48–54] sts. Work until same length as back to underarm.

To Shape Armhole: Keeping to pat, bind off at armhole edge 7 [7–7–8–9] sts once, 4 [3–5–5–6] sts 1 [2–1–1–1] times, 2 [2–4–4–4] sts 2 [1–1–1–1] times—30 [30–35–34–38] sts. Work even until 4½″ [4¾″–5″–5¼″–5½″] above beg of armhole.

To Shape Neck: Bind off at beg of front edge 6 [6–7–6–8] sts once, then 1 st 4 [3–6–6–7] times—20 [21–22–22–23] sts. Work even until 7¼″ [7½″–7¾″–8″–8¼″] above beg of armhole shaping.

To Shape Shoulder: At armhole edge bind off 6 [7–8–8–9] sts once, 7 sts twice.

LEFT FRONT: Work to correspond to right front, reversing shaping and pat.

SLEEVES: With No. 4 needles, cast on 48 [50–50–52–54] sts. Work in k 1, p 1 ribbing for 2″, inc 1 st each edge of last row—50 [52–52–54–56] sts. Change to No. 6 needles. Work in stockinette st keeping first and last st in k throughout. Inc 1 st each side after first and before last edge st every 8th row 10 [10–11–12–12] times—70 [72–74–78–80] sts. Work even until 17½″ [18″–18″–18½″–18½″] from beg or desired length to underarm.

To Shape Cap: At each edge bind off 5 [5–6–6–6] sts once, 2 sts 2 [2–2–2–3–3] times. Bind off 1 st at beg of next 24 [26–26–26–28] rows—28 sts. Bind of 2 sts at beg of next 6 rows—16 sts. Bind off.

FINISHING—Left Front Band: With right side facing, using No. 4 needles, pick up and k 1 st in every 3 out of 4 rows on left front. Work in k 1, p 1 ribbing for 7 rows. Bind off loosely in ribbing. Mark position of 7 buttons evenly spaced with the first one ½″ above lower edge, last one to be in neckband.

Right Front Band: Work same as left front edge making buttonholes on Rows 4 and 5 opposite markers, as follows: * Work in established ribbing to next marker, bind off next 2 sts; repeat from * across all markers, finish row. On next row, cast on 2 sts over bound-off sts.

Sew shoulder, side and sleeve seams. Sew in sleeves.

Neckband: With right side facing, using No. 4 needles, pick up and k 94 [96–98–100–102] sts around neck edge including front edges. Work in k 1, p 1 ribbing for 7 rows, working last buttonhole on Rows 4 and 5. Sew on buttons.

Embroidery: See Daughter's Embroidered Cardigan, page 232.

Soft V-Neck Pullover, *page 47*

WOMEN'S SWEATERS

Polo Pullover, *page 48*

Classic Sweater Set, *page 86*

Making Waves, *page 109*

Belted Wrap Jacket, *page 66*

Snug Cap-Sleeved Cardigan, *page 117*

Fair Isle Cardigan, *page 119*

Short Tops, Leg Warmers and Warm Pants, *page 165*

To Shine at Night, *page 146*

Fantastic Fair Isle Sweater Jacket,
page 129

The Strapless Tube, *page 155*

Puff-Sleeved Top, *page 157*

CHILDREN'S SWEATERS

Twin Sweater Set, *page 189*

Child's Cardigan, *page 179*

Tailored Top, *page 184*

Child's Gold Cable
Turtleneck,
page 198
and Man's Traditional
V-Neck Sweater,
page 240

Brightly Colored
Cardigan and
Watch Cap,
page 221

Boy's Cardigan and Cap,
page 218

Turquoise Cardigan,
page 226

Girl's Pullover and Cap,
page 204

Tree of Life Vest,
page 215

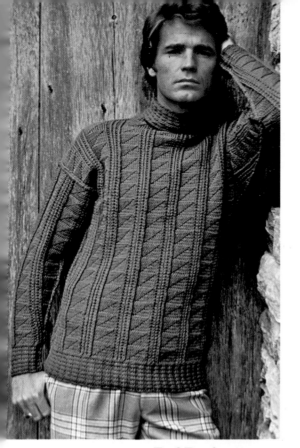

Teal Turtle, *page 238*

MEN'S SWEATERS

Man's V-Neck Pullover,
page 254

New Short-Sleeved Pullover,
page 250

HIS
AND
HERS

Norwegian Snowflake-
Patterned Pullovers,
page 264

Rib and Cable
Pullover and Hat,
page 268

Fantastic Fair Isle Sweater Jacket

Beautiful interlocking stripes make up a sweater jacket for both men and women. Crocheted borders and buttons add the finishing touch.

SIZES: Men's and women's small (34–36) [medium (38–40)—large (42–44)]. Jacket measures about 18½" [20½"–22½"] across back from side seam to side seam. Length from underarm to lower edge (including ¾" crocheted border) is 17¼" [18½"–19¾"].

MATERIALS: American Thread Dawn Sayelle (Orlon acrylic knitting-worsted-weight yarn), 5 (4-oz.) skeins black No. 371 (Color A), 3 [3–4] skeins cardinal No. 327 (B), 2 skeins mulberry No. 324 (C) and 1 skein flame No. 325 (D); knitting needles, 1 pair No. 7 (or English needles No. 6) **or the size that will give you the correct gauge;** steel crochet hook No. 0 for border and buttons; six ¾" button rings; tapestry needle.

GAUGE: 5 sts = 1", 5 rows = 1".

Note: See page 33 for Fair Isle knitting. Be sure to make a swatch to check your gauge and, if you are not familiar with Fair Isle knitting, to practice working with more than one color yarn.

BACK: Starting at lower edge with A, cast on 92 [102–112] sts. **1st row:** With A, k across. **2nd row:** With A, p across. Attach B. **3rd row:** Using colors A and B, continue in stockinette st and, starting design with 3rd row of chart, follow chart, starting at S [M–L] and working to center st, then repeat chart, working from center st to S [M–L].

Note: Before breaking yarn at end of row, check ahead on chart to see which colors will be needed at opposite edge for next row; then carry those colors across back of work, catching them every 2 or 3 stitches. In addition to keeping the texture of the work uniform, it will eliminate some of the extra breaking off of colors.

For small size only: Continue to follow chart until row Y is completed, then repeat pattern from X to Z once (82 rows in all).

For medium size only: Work pattern as for small size, but work 1 extra solid color row at each dot (88 rows in all).

For large size only: Work pattern as for small size, but add 2 extra rows of solid color at each dot (94 rows in all).

For all sizes—To Shape Raglan Armholes: Keeping in pattern, bind off 4 [6–8] sts at beg of next 2 rows. Dec 1 st at beg and end of every other row 19 times (chart completed—46 [52–58] sts).

Continuing in stockinette st with color A only, and carrying one extra strand of A along back of work to keep texture of work uniform, continue to dec every other row 4 [5–6] times more (there are 8 [10–12] rows of color A). **Last row:** With A, work across and dec 2 sts evenly spaced. Place remaining 36 [40–44] sts on a holder.

LEFT FRONT: Starting at lower edge with color A, cast on 46 [51–56] sts. K 1 row, p 1 row. Starting with 3rd row, follow chart for design, working from S [M–L] to center on k rows and from center to S [M–L] on p rows. Work pattern same as on back, adding extra rows on medium and large as for back, until 82nd [88th–94th] row is completed, ending with a p row.

To Shape Raglan Armhole: Keeping in pattern, bind off 4 [6–8] sts at beg (armhole edge) of next row. Dec 1 st at armhole edge every other row 6 times, ending at armhole edge.

Neck and Raglan Armhole Shaping: Continue in pattern and dec 1 st at beg and end of every other row 13 times (chart completed— 10 [13–16] sts).

Working with A only as for back, continue to dec at beg and end of every other row 4 [5–6] times more. Work even on 2 [3–4] sts for 1 row, then bind off.

RIGHT FRONT: Work as for left front, reversing shapings.

SLEEVES—Note: Sleeve will measure about 18½" from underarm to lower edge of ribbed cuff. If you need to adjust this length, change depth to cuff at beg of sleeve.

Cuff: Starting at lower edge with A, cast on 44 sts. Work in ribbing of k 2, p 2 for 1¼". Break off A, attach C. Continue in ribbing and work 1 row each C, B and C. Mark last C row for right side of work. With A, continue in ribbing until cuff is 4½" from beg (see note above), ending with a wrong-side row. K across next row, increasing 12 sts as evenly spaced as possible to 56 sts, then p 1 row.

Starting with 13th row of chart, for design work across entire chart for all sizes, working from 13th row to Y, then repeat from X to Z once

130

and, **at same time,** inc 1 st at beg and end of row every 2″ [1½″–1¼″] 5 [7–9] times, working added sts in pattern. Then work even on 66 [70–74] sts until beg of underarm (Z on chart).

To Shape Raglan Cap: Continue to follow chart for design and, **at same time,** bind off 3 [4–5] sts at beg of next 2 rows, then dec 1 st at beg and end of every other row 19 times (chart completed—22 [24–26] sts).

Working with A only as for back, repeat last 9 [11–13] rows (decreasing every other row as before, then dec 2 sts on last row). Place remaining 12 sts on a holder.

FINISHING: Block pieces lightly. Sew raglan sleeve seams, carefully matching patterns. Sew side seams, leaving a 3″ opening at lower edge for slits. Sew sleeve seams.

COLLAR—1st row: With right side of work facing you, with A, pick up and k 23 sts from beg of neck shaping to first raglan seam along right front neck edge. Place sts from holders for sleeves and back onto another needle and k across them. Then pick up and k 23 sts along left front neck edge to beg of neck shaping. There are 106 [110–114] sts on needle.

Before working next row, put 4 markers on needle: the first one after the 28th st, skip 18 sts, place 2nd marker on needle, skip center 14 [18–22] sts, place 3rd marker on needle, skip 20 sts, place 4th marker on needle (leave 26 sts at end of row).

2nd row: Slipping markers, work in ribbing of k 2, p 2. Slip markers each row until decreases are completed.

3rd row: Being careful to continue in rib pattern, dec 1 st at beg of row, work across to first marker, slip marker and dec 1 st, continue across row, decreasing 1 st before 2nd marker, after 3rd marker, before 4th marker and at end of row (6 sts dec).

Repeat 3rd row three times more, then remove 2nd and 3rd markers. Continue in rib pattern and dec 1 st at beg and end of row and after first marker and before last marker for 4 rows (4 sts dec on each row). Remove both makers.

Work even in rib pattern as established on 66 [70–74] sts until collar measures 7″ [7″–7½″] from beg. Bind off in ribbing.

Crocheted Borders—For Back: Work along slit opening, lower edge and other slit opening as follows: **1st row:** With right side facing you, attach A and crochet 1 row of sc evenly across, working 3 sc in each corner. Break off A; turn.

2nd row: With C, sc across, working in front loop of each sc. Break off C; turn. **3rd row;** With A, sc in back loop of each sc, working 3 sc in each corner. Break off A; do not turn. **4th row:** Attach A at beg of last row and sc in back loop of each sc across. Break off.

For Front and Collar—1st row: With right side facing you, using A, starting at lower corner of right front, work 1 row sc across right front edge, collar and left front edge, increasing at corners of collar; ch 1, turn. **2nd row:** Working in front loops only, sc in each sc

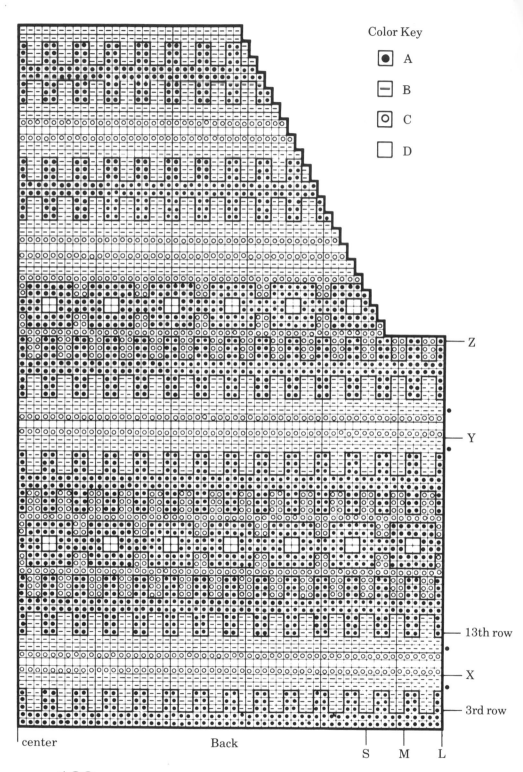

Color Key

⊙	A
⊟	B
⊡	C
☐	D

Z

Y

13th row

X

3rd row

center   Back   S   M   L

across. Break off. **3rd row:** Starting at beg of slit opening on right front, with right side of work facing you, join A and sc along slit opening, inc at corner, sc along lower edge of front, inc at corner; then working through both loops of sts and increasing at corners, sc in each sc of last row to lower left corner, inc at corner; then continue to sc along lower edge of left front, inc at corner, sc along slit opening. Break off. **4th row:** With right side facing you, using B, starting at lower corner of right front, work 1 row sc around right front edge, collar and left front edge. Break off.

Mark border for buttonholes.

Note on Buttonholes: For woman's jacket mark right front edge for 6 buttonholes. For man's jacket mark left front edge. Place first marker about 4″ from lower edge, sixth one about 2″ below beg of neck shaping, the others evenly spaced between.

5th row (buttonhole row): With right side of work facing you, using A, starting at beg of slit opening on right front and increasing at corners, sc in back loop of each sc across slits, lower and front edges, and through both loops around collar, working each buttonhole as follows: Sc in each sc to within 1 sc of marker, sc in both loops of next sc, ch 3, skip 3 sc, sc in both loops of next sc. At end of row, ch 1, turn. **6th row:** Working in front loops only, sc in each sc across, increasing at corners and working 3 sc over each ch-3 loop for buttonholes; ch 1, turn. **7th row:** Working in back loops only, sc in each sc across, increasing at corners. Break off.

Mitre edges of border sts at top of slits and sew in place.

Buttons (make 6): With crochet hook and A, work as many sc around a button ring as will fit. Break off, leaving 12″ end. Thread end in tapestry needle and weave in and out of every other sc around ring. Pull up yarn tightly until sts turn to center of ring. Embroider straight stitches in center of each button, working 2 each with B, C and D. Sew buttons in place, alternating colors.

Special Sweaters

Peacock Jacket

This garter-stitch jacket has a ribbon of openwork on the sleeves. Strands of blue and green yarn are worked as one. The double-button loops, buttons, neck, and edges are finished in crochet.

SIZES: (8–10) [(12–14)—(16–18)]. Sweater measures 16″ [18″–20″] across back at underarms, 20″ [20½″–21″] from back of neck to lower edge. Length is adjustable.

MATERIALS: Brunswick Pomfret sport yarn, 5 [5–6] (2-oz.) skeins each Jamaica green No. 578 and Danish blue No. 584 heathers; 29″ circular knitting needle No. 6 (or English needle No. 7) **or the size that will give you the correct gauge;** 16 button molds ½″ in diameter; aluminum crochet hook size G (or Canadian hook No. 9).

GAUGE: 9 sts = 2″; 9 rows = 1″.

Note: Work with one strand each of green and blue held together throughout. Work back and forth in rows on circular needle.

Starting at lower edge, work individual panels as follows:

Left Front Panel: Cast on 36 [40–44] sts. Work in garter st for 3″. Break off. Push left front panel to back of needle.

Left Side Panel: Cast on 18 [20–22] sts. Work as for left front panel.

Back Panel: Cast on 39 [45–51] sts. Work as for left front panel.

Right Side Panel: Work same as for left side panel.

Right Front Panel: Work same as for left front panel but do not break off. **Next row:** * K across panel to within last st, k tog last st of this panel and the first st of next panel. Repeat from * 3 times more, then k across remaining sts of last panel (143 [161–179] sts). Work even in garter st until piece measures 14″ from beg, or desired length to underarms, ending at right front edge.

To Divide for Raglan Shaping—Next row: K 35 [40–45] sts and place these sts on holder for right front, k next 73 [81–89] sts for back. Place remaining 35 [40–45] sts on holder for left front.

To Shape Back Raglan Armholes: Bind off 2 [3–5] sts at beg of next 2 rows. **3rd row:** K 1, sl 1, k 1, psso, k to within last 3 sts, k 2 tog, k 1. K 2 rows even. Repeat last 3 rows 16 [18–19] times more. Bind off remaining 35 [37–39] sts.

To Shape Left Front Raglan Armhole: Slip 35 [40–45] sts from left front holder onto needle. Attach yarn at underarm. Bind off 1 [2–3] sts at beg of next row, k across. K 2 rows even. **Next row:** K to within last 3 sts, k 2 tog, k 1. K 2 rows even. **Following row:** K 1, sl 1, k 1, psso, k across. K 2 rows even. Repeat last 6 rows 7 [8–9] times more. Bind off remaining 18 [20–22] sts.

To Shape Right Front Raglan Armhole: Slip 35 [40–45] sts from right front holder onto needle. Attach yarn at front edge and k across to underarm. Work to correspond to left front, reversing all shaping.

SLEEVES: Starting at lower edge, cast on 40 [42–44] sts. **1st row (right side):** K 15 [16–17], (y o, k 2 tog) 5 times; k 15 [16–17]. **2nd row:** K across. Repeating first and 2nd rows for pattern, work even until piece measures 6″ from beg. Continuing in established pattern, inc 1 st at beg and end of next row, then every 1½″ [1½″–1″] 5 [6–7] times more. Work even on 52 [56–60] sts until piece measures 16″, or desired length to underarms.

To Shape Raglan Cap: Bind off 2 [2–3] sts at beg of next 2 rows. Work as for back, starting with 3rd row of raglan armhole shaping. Bind off remaining 14 sts.

FINISHING: Sew raglan, side and sleeve seams. **Edging:** With crochet hook and right side facing you, attach yarn to upper right front corner, sc evenly around neck, left front, lower edge and right front, working 3 sc at corners; join. Break off.

Collar—1st row: With right side facing you, skip first 3 sc along right front neck edge, attach yarn and sc in each sc to within 3 sts of left front; ch 1, turn. **2nd row:** * Sc to within 2 sts of next raglan seam, (dec 1 sc in next 2 sts) twice (to dec 1 sc, pull up loop in each of next 2 sc, y o hook and pull through all 3 loops on hook); repeat from * across 3 times more, ending with sc in remaining sc; ch 1, turn. Repeat last row twice more, omitting ch-1 on last row. Break off.

Buttons (make 16): Ch 2. **1st rnd:** Work 6 sc in 2nd ch from hook. (**Note:** Mark beg of rnds and sl marker on each rnd.) **2nd rnd:** Work 2 sc in each sc around. **3rd rnd:** Sc in each sc around. **4th rnd:** (Sc in next sc, work dec over next 2 sc) 4 times. Break off, leaving 12″ end.

Insert button mold and sew opening closed. Sew 8 buttons along each front edge, 1½" in from edge, the first 2" below neck edge, the last 3" from the lower edge, and the others evenly spaced between. **Double Buttonloop (make 8):** Ch 24, sl st in 24th ch from hook to form ring. Work 24 sc in ring; sl st to join. Break off. Twist ring to form figure 8. Tack at center of twist. Slip over buttons.

Square-Necked Pullover

An elegant pure-linen pullover in a multitude of stitches: tiny cables, stockinette, and reverse stockinette stitch.

SIZES: (8–10) [(12–14)—(16–18)]. Sweater measures 16″ [18″–20″] across back at underarms; 21″ [22″–23″] from back of neck to lower edge.

MATERIALS: Frederick J. Fawcett 10/2 linen yarn, 2 [3–3] (8-oz.) tubes bleached (white); knitting needles, 1 pair No. 9 (or English needles No. 4) **or the size that will give you the correct gauge;** steel crochet hook No. 00 for trim.

GAUGE: After washing and blocking, 9 sts = 2″; 5 rows = 1″. Unblocked, 6 sts = 1″; 6 rows = 1″.

Important: In order to insure correct gauge, make a sample swatch as follows: With double yarn, cast on 23 sts. **1st row (right side):** (P 2, k 2) 3 times, p 11. **2nd row:** K 11, (p 2, k 2) 3 times. **3rd row:** (P 2, work 2-st cable—see next paragraph) three times, k 11. **4th row:** P 11, (p 2, k 2) 3 times. Repeat last 4 rows 6 more times. Block (see Blocking Linen, page 141) to measure 5″ wide x 5½″ long, stretching cable vertically. Check gauge.

To make 2-st cable: K into back of 2nd st from point of left needle, k first st, slip both sts from needle.

Note: Work with 2 strands held together throughout.

BACK: Starting at lower edge cast on 70 [78–86] sts. **To Establish Cable Pattern—1st row (right side):** * P 2, k 2. Repeat from * across, ending p 2. **2nd row:** * K 2, p 2. Repeat from * across, ending k 2. **3rd row (1st cable row):** * P 2, work 2-st cable. Repeat from * across, ending p 2. **4th row:** Repeat 2nd row. Repeat 1st through 4th rows 5 [6–7] times more.

To Establish Reverse Stockinette Pattern—1st row: (P 2, k 2) 5 [6–7] times for cable pattern; p 30 for reverse stockinette st pattern; (k 2, p 2) 5 [6–7] times for cable pattern. **2nd row:** (K 2, p 2) 5 [6–7] times; k 30, (p 2, k 2) 5 [6–7] times. **3rd row (7th [8th–9th] cable row):** (P 2, 2-st cable) 5 [6–7] times; k 30, (2-st cable, p 2) 5 [6–7] times. **4th row:** (K 2, p 2) 5 [6–7] times; p 30, (p 2, k 2) 5 [6–7] times. Repeat last 4 rows 9 times more, increasing 1 st at each end of row **following** the 12th [13th–14th] and 16th [17th–18th] cable rows. Continue in established pattern on 74 [82–90] sts for 6 more rows for piece to measure 14″ [15″–16″], or desired length to underarm, when blocked.

To Shape Armholes: Continuing in pattern, starting with 18th [19th–20th] cable row, bind off 5 sts at beg of next 2 rows, then 1 st at beg of following 2 rows. Continue working in pattern on 62 [70–78] sts through the 26th [27th–29th] cable row. Work 1 more row. **For Size (12–14) Only:** Work 2 more rows even in pattern.

For All Sizes—To Shape Shoulders: Bind off 8 [10–12] sts at beg of next 4 rows, then bind off remaining 30 sts.

FRONT: Work same as for back through 19th [20th–21st] cable row, then work 2 more rows in pattern (62 [70–78] sts).

To Shape Neck—Next row (wrong side): (K 2, p 2) 4 [5–6] times; k 1, slip these 17 [21–25] sts onto a holder for right front; bind off next 28 sts, (p 2, k 2) 4 [5–6] times (17 [21–25] sts). Working on left front only, work as follows: **3rd pattern row (20th [21st–22nd] cable row):** (p 2, 2-st cable) 4 [5–6] times; p 1. **4th pattern row:** K 1, (p 2, k 2) 4 [5–6] times. **1st pattern row:** (P 2, k 2) 4 [5–6] times; p 1. **2nd pattern row:** Repeat 4th pattern row. Repeat last 4 rows through 26th [27th–29th] cable row. Work 3 [5–3] rows more in pattern, ending at arm edge.

To Shape Shoulders: Bind off 8 [10–12] sts at beg of next row. Work 1 row even in pattern. Bind off remaining 9 [11–13] sts.

Slip sts from holder onto needle. Attach yarn at neck edge and work right front to correspond to left front, reversing shaping.

SLEEVES: Starting at lower edge, cast on 34 sts. Work in cable pattern as for back for 24 [23–23] rows. **For Sizes (12–14) and (16–18) Only—Next row:** Continuing in pattern, inc 1 st at beg and end of row (36 sts).

For All Sizes: To Establish Reverse Stockinette Pattern—25th row (right side): P 6 [7–7] for reverse stockinette st panel (A on drawing), place marker on needle, (k 2, p 2) 5 times, k 2 for cable panel (B), place marker on needle, p 6 [7–7] for reverse stockinette st panel (C). **(Note:** Slip markers every row.) **26th row (inc row, wrong side):** Inc 1 in first st, k 4 [5–5], inc 1, (p 2, k 2) 5 times; p 2, inc 1, k 4 [5–5], inc 1 in last st (38 [40–40] sts). **27th row (7th cable row):** K 8 [9–9],

(2-st cable, p 2) 5 times; 2-st cable, k 8 [9–9]. **28th row:** P 10 [11–11], (k 2, p 2) 4 times; k 2, p 10 [11–11]. **29th row:** P 8 [9–9], (k 2, p 2) 5 times; k 2, p 8 [9–9]. Continue working in pattern, increasing 1 st at each side edge and 1 st in the first st on each side of center cable panel (4 sts in all) on next row, then once again on next 4th row (46 [48–48] sts). Then inc 1 st at each side edge every 8th row 5 [5–6] times (56 [58–60] sts).

Work even in pattern until piece measures 17½″ [18″–18½″], or desired length to underarm, when blocked.

To Shape Cap: Bind off 5 sts at beg of next 2 rows, then 1 st at beg of following 2 rows. Work even in pattern on 44 [46–48] sts for 16 more rows. Dec 1 st at each end of every other row 6 [7–8] times (32 sts). Bind off 7 sts at beg and end of next row. Bind off remaining 18 sts in pattern.

FINISHING: Sew garment together using 1 strand of yarn and easing sleeve cap to fit armhole. Starting at left shoulder seam and with wrong side facing you, work one rnd sl st around neck, using single strand of yarn.

BLOCKING LINEN: Wash even the newly made sweater thoroughly, as washing will remove some of the sizing and make a softer garment. Squeeze or wring out as much water as possible (linen is a strong fiber and becomes even stronger when wet). Roll sweater briefly in a towel, if desired.

Do not spread sweater flat to block as it takes too long to dry. Hang

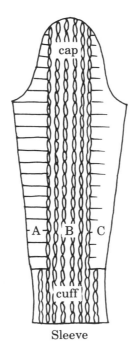

Sleeve

it on a wooden or plastic hanger and shape while still wet by pulling downward and smoothing the stitches with the palm of the hand. Make garment look relatively long and skinny; it will pull up and stretch as needed on the body.

Important: Test all pressing on a swatch first to be sure that the temperature of the iron is correct. Linen can stand a hot iron but you must work quickly to avoid scorching.

When sweater is dry, steam press over a wet cloth. Then remove cloth and quickly go over garment with iron, pressing hard to flatten stitches and to bring out the natural sheen of the linen. Do not press buttons.

Follow these blocking instructions for the newly finished garment before it has been worn, as well as for the soiled garment.

Natural linens last longer and look better if washed rather than dry cleaned. It is best to handwash them, using hot or cool water and soap or detergent. Wash colored linens separately as they may not be completely color-fast when new.

If possible, do not wash garments in humid weather as linens should take no longer than twenty-four hours to dry or they may become musty.

Flare sleeve cuffs slightly when blocking.

Silver and Gold Sparkle Sweater

The cream pullover is in stockinette stitch. The right section of the front is worked vertically with diagonal, the upper edge added on.

SIZES: Small (6–8) [medium (10–12)—large (14–16)]. Sweater measures 15″ [17″–19″] across back at underarms, 19″ [19¾″–20¼″] from back of neck to lower edge.

MATERIALS: Reynolds Classique (100% wool), 6 [7–7] (50 gram—about 1¾ oz.) balls Cachemire No. 2519 (cream-color A); Reynolds Feu d'Artifice (viscose rayon and Lurex metallic), 1 (20 gram—about ⅔ oz.) ball each gold (B) and silver (C); knitting needles, 1 pair each No. 6 and No. 8 (or English needles No. 7 and No.5) **or the size that will give you the correct gauge;** aluminum crochet hook size G (or Canadian hook No. 9).

GAUGE: 9 sts = 2″; 8-row plain stripe = 1″, 8-row sparkle stripe = 1¼″.

Important: You must get the exact stitch and row gauge for this sweater to fit properly. Adjust the size of your knitting needles, if necessary.

BACK: Starting at lower edge with No. 6 needles and A, cast on 64 [73–82] sts. Work in ribbing of k 1, p 1 for 3″, increasing 4 sts as evenly spaced as possible on last row (68 [77–86] sts). Change to No. 8 needles and work even in stockinette st until piece measures 12″ [12¼″–12½″] from beg.

To Shape Armholes: Bind off 3 [4–5] sts at beg of next 2 rows, then dec 1 st at beg and end of every other row 1 [3–5] times. Work even on 60 [63–66] sts until armholes measure 7″ [7½″–8″].

To Shape Shoulders: Bind off 6 sts at beg of next 4 rows, then 5 [6–7] sts at beg of next 2 rows. Bind off remaining 26 [27–28] sts.

FRONT: Work ribbing as for back. Bind off. The first section of front is worked vertically. Stockinette st pattern is as follows: 7 [9–11] rows with A and B together, then a repeat of stripes of 8 rows A, 8 rows A and C, 8 rows A, 8 rows A and B. Starting at right side edge with No. 8 needles and 1 strand each of A and B worked together, cast on 39 [40–41] sts. Work even for 4 [6–8] rows.

To Shape Right Armhole: (Inc 1 st at end of next k row and 1 st at beg of following p row—armhole edge) 1 [2–3] times. K 1 row, then cast on 30 sts for armhole (71 [74–77] sts).

To Shape Right Shoulder: Work 4 [6–8] rows even; inc 1 st at beg (shoulder edge) of next row, then work even on 72 [75–78] sts for 7 more rows, ending at shoulder edge.

To Shape Diagonal Upper Edge: * Dec 1 st at beg (upper edge) of next row, work 1 row even. Repeat from * 44 [47–50] times more until 14 [15–16] stripes have been completed from beg, working last stripe for 6 [8–10] rows. Bind off remaining 27 sts. Piece should measure about 15″ [17″–19″] across.

DIAGONAL YOKE: With right side of front facing you, using A and B together and No. 8 needles, pick up and k 75 [82–89] sts, as evenly spaced as possible, along diagonal upper edge. Work in stockinette st in stripe pattern, shaping as follows:

To Shape Right Shoulder and Neck: At side edge dec 1 st every row 15 [17–19] times and, **at same time,** dec 1 st at shoulder edge every 4th row twice; work 2 rows even. Bind off 16 sts at beg (neck edge) of next row. Continue in stripe pattern, keeping neck edge even and completing side edge shaping (15 [17–19] decs in all at side edge). End at side edge (42 [47–52] sts).

To Shape Left Armhole: Keeping neck edge even, bind off 5 [6–7] sts at beg (armhole edge) of next row, then dec 1 st at same edge every row 20 times (17 [21–25] sts).

To Shape Left Shoulder: Continuing to dec 1 st every row at armhole edge, bind off 4 sts from neck edge every other row 3 times. Bind off remaining 0 [4–8] sts.

SLEEVES: With No. 6 needles and A, cast on 38 [40–42] sts. Work in ribbing of k 1, p 1 for 3″. Change to No. 8 needles and, working in stockinette st, inc 1 st at beg and end of row every 1½″ 7 [8–9] times. Work even on 52 [56–60] sts until piece measures 17½″, or desired length to underarm.

To Shape Cap: Bind off 3 [4–5] sts at beg of next 2 rows. Dec 1 st at beg and end of every other row 13 [15–17] times; then bind off 2 sts at beg of next 4 rows. Bind off remaining 12 [10–8] sts.

FINISHING—Blocking: When pieces are completed, pin them, matching pieces together, wrong side up on a padded surface. Place a damp cloth over them. Then with warm (not hot) iron, holding the weight of the iron in your hand, pat lightly (do not press) so that the pieces are lightly steamed. Remove when dry.

Assembling: Sew ribbing to lower edge of front. Sew shoulder seams, leaving ½″ free at neck edges. Turn free front edges under slightly to form neck facing (tapering to nothing at center front), and sew in place. Sew side and sleeve seams. Sew sleeves in place. With crochet hook and A and B, work 1 row sc around entire neck edge; join. Break off.

To Shine at Night

This silver evening top has a ribbed midriff and crocheted spaghetti straps.

SIZES: Small (6–9) [medium (10–12)]. Garment will stretch to measure 15″ [16″] across bust at underarms.

MATERIALS: 4 (20-gram) balls silver Bucilla Spotlight yarn (polyester/nylon); 1 pair No. 6 knitting needles (or English needles No.7) **or the size that will give you the correct gauge;** steel crochet hook size 0.

GAUGE: 7 sts = 1″; 10 rows = 1″.

Note: In using Spotlight yarn, tie each loose end in a knot to prevent raveling.

BACK: Starting at lower edge with No. 6 needles, cast on 96 [104] sts. Work in ribbing of k 2, p 2 for 5″. Then work in stockinette st until piece measures 9½″ [10″] from beg, or desired length to underarms, ending with a p row.

To Shape Armhole: Bind off 4 [6] sts at beg of next row, k across until there are 26 [28] sts on needle; place remaining 66 [70] sts on holder. Continue to work on sts on needle, decreasing 1 st at beg and

146

end of each row until 2 sts remain; bind off remaining 2 sts, marking last st worked. Break off.

Place 66 [70] sts from holder onto needle. Attach yarn. Bind off 36 sts for neck, then k across remaining sts. Bind off 4 [6] sts at beg (armhole edge) of next row and continue to work as for other side.

FRONT: Work same as for back.

FINISHING: Sew side seams. With right side of piece facing you and with crochet hook, sc evenly around top edge of piece. Break off.

STRAPS: With crochet hook and yarn, sl st in sc directly above marked st. Crochet a chain approximately 12½" long. Sc in 2nd ch from hook and in each ch across. Break off. Work a strap in each sc directly above other 3 marked sts. Weave in all ends. Tie straps on shoulders.

Delicate Blouse

In seed stitch with open-work yoke, cuffs, and separate scarf, the body of the blouse is knitted in one piece without side seams.

SIZES: (8–10) [(12–14)—(16–18)]. Snug fitting blouse measures about 32″ [36″–40″] around bust and about 23″ [23½″–24″] from shoulder to lower edge.

MATERIALS: Frederick J. Fawcett 10/2 linen yarn, 3 [3–4] (8-oz.) tubes rose; knitting needles, 1 pair No. 9 (or English needles No. 4) **or the size that will give you the correct gauge;** steel crochet hook size 00 for edging and buttons; tapestry needle.

GAUGE: Seed st after washing and blocking, 9 sts = 2″; 5 rows = 1″. Unblocked, 5 sts = 1″; 7 rows = 1″.

Important: In order to insure correct gauge, make a sample swatch as follows: With double yarn, cast on 19 sts. **1st row:** * K 1, p 1. Repeat from * across ending with k 1. Repeat this row 19 more times. Block (see blocking directions, page 37) to measure 4″ x 4″ and check gauge.

Note: Work with 2 strands of yarn held together throughout.

BODY: Body of blouse is worked in one piece without side seams (see blouse drawing). Starting at lower edge, cast on 141 [159–177] sts. **1st row:** * K 1, p 1. Repeat from * across, ending k 1. Repeat this row for seed st pattern 75 times more for piece to measure 15″, or desired length to underarm, when blocked.

To Divide for Front and Back—Next row: Work across 38 [42–46] sts for right front. Place next 65 [75–85] sts on holder for back. Place remaining 38 [42–46] sts on another holder for left front. Work on right front sts only as follows:

RIGHT FRONT—To Shape Armhole: Bind off 6 sts at beg of next row. Work 1 row even. Bind off 1 [3–5] sts at beg of next row, work across next 30 sts (31 sts on right-hand needle). **For Sizes (12–14) [(16–18] Only:** Place marker on needle for border, work in pattern across remaining 2 [4] sts. Slipping marker on every row, work 2 [4] rows even on 33 [35] sts, ending at front edge. Keeping 0 [2–4] front border sts in seed st, work as follows on remaining 31 sts.

For All Sizes: To Establish Lace Pattern—1st row (right side): P 1, * y o, k 2 tog, k 1, k 2 tog, y o, p 1. Repeat from * across. **2nd row:** K 1, * p 5, k 1. Repeat from * across. **3rd row:** P 2, * y o, leaving yarn in back sl 1, k 2 tog, psso, y o , p 3. Repeat from * across, ending last repeat with p 2. **4th row:** K 2, * p 3, k 3. Repeat from * across, ending last repeat with k 2.

Repeat these 4 rows for pattern 5 times more, ending at front edge.

To Shape Neck: For Size (8–10) Only—1st row: Bind off 12 sts at beg of row, then repeat from * on 1st row of lace pattern. **For Sizes (12–14) [(16–18)] Only—1st row:** Bind off 12 sts at beg of row, then work 1 [3] sts in seed st for neck border (there are 2 [4] sts on right-hand needle); place marker on needle, p 1, repeat from * on 1st row of lace pattern. Keeping neck border sts in seed st, work as follows on remaining 19 sts:

For All Sizes: Work 1st through 4th rows of lace pattern 8 times, repeat 1st through 4th rows once, then 1st row once more, ending at arm edge. Work in seed st for 2 rows.

To Shape Shoulder: Continuing in seed st, bind off 9 [10–11] sts at beg of next row. Work 1 row even. Bind off remaining 10 [11–12] sts.

BACK: Slip 65 [75–85] sts from back holder onto needle. Attach yarn at right underarm.

To Shape Armholes: Continuing in seed st, bind off 4 [5–6] sts at beg of next 2 rows, then 1 [2–3] sts at beg of following 2 rows (55 [61–67] sts). **For Sizes (12–14) [(16–18)] Only:** Work 2 [4] rows even.

For All Sizes: Work 1st through 4th rows of lace pattern 8 times, then repeat 1st row once more. Work 1 row in seed st.

To Shape Shoulders: Continuing in seed st, bind off 9 [10–11] sts at beg of next 2 rows, then bind off 10 [11–12] sts at beg of following 2 rows. Bind off remaining 17 [19–21] sts for back neck.

LEFT FRONT: Slip 38 [42–46] sts from left front holder onto needle. Attach yarn at underarm and work to correspond to right front, reversing all shaping.

SLEEVES—Cuff: Each cuff is worked in 2 pieces which are joined later. Starting at lower edge, cast on 13 sts for one piece; with another ball of yarn, cast 13 sts for 2nd piece onto same needle. Working on both pieces at once, work 1st through 4th rows of lace pattern 5 times, then repeat 1st and 2nd rows once more. **Next row (joining row):** P 2, * y o, leaving yarn in back sl 1, k 2 tog, psso, y o, p 3. Repeat from * once more, ending repeat with p 2; to join pieces, p 2 tog (last st of 1st group and first st of 2nd group), then continue across the other piece with same ball of yarn, repeating from * (25 sts). Break off other yarn ball at center of work. **Following row (inc row):** K 3, * to inc 1 st work k 1 and p 1 in next y o; p 1, inc 1, k 3. Repeat from * 3 times more, ending last repeat with k 1 (33 sts). **Next row (inc row):** * P 1, y o. Repeat from * across, ending p 1 (65 sts). Work even in seed st for 79 more rows for piece to measure 16″ from top of cuff to underarm, or for desired length to underarm, when blocked.

To Shape Cap: Bind off 6 [5–4] sts at beg of next 2 rows, then 1 st at beg of following 2 rows. Work 14 more rows even on 51 [53–55] sts. Dec 1 st at beg and end of every other row 8 [9–10] times. Bind off 8 sts at beg of next 2 rows. Bind off remaining 19 sts.

SCARF: Scarf is made in 2 pieces. Starting at end of 1 piece, cast on 25 sts. Work 1st through 4th rows of lace pattern 28 times, binding off on last row. Make another piece in same manner. With tapestry needle and single strand, sew pieces together along bound-off edges.

FINISHING: With tapestry needle and single strand of yarn, sew shoulder seams (A to A and B to B on sweater drawing). Sew sleeve seams from X to X on sleeve drawing. Sew in sleeves, easing fullness at shoulders.

Edging: With crochet hook attach single strand of yarn at left front neck edge with sl st. With wrong side facing you, sl st evenly along neck edge to right front; * ch 5 for button loop, skip about ¾″ of front edge, sl st in edge, work 2 more sl sts evenly spaced along edge. Repeat from * 16 times more evenly along right front, ending with last sl st in corner at lower edge (17 button loops). Break off.

Button (make 17): With crochet hook and single strand of yarn, ch 4; join with sl st to form ring. **1st rnd:** Work 8 sc in ring. **2nd rnd:** Sc in each sc around. Repeat 2nd rnd twice more; sl st in next sc. Break off, leaving 1½-yard length. Wind into small ball leaving a 10″ end; stuff ball into crocheted button. Thread end in tapestry needle and sew button closed. Sew in place after sweater has been blocked.

On open cuff seams, work edging and make 4 button loops and 4 buttons as for front.

See blocking instructions, page 37. Sew on buttons.

Scarf may be worn separately or sewn to garment by matching scarf seam to center back neck and tacking to shirt for 3″ along neck edge (between dots on blouse drawing).

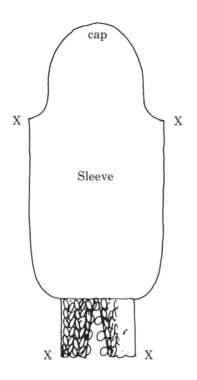

cap

X   X

Sleeve

X   X

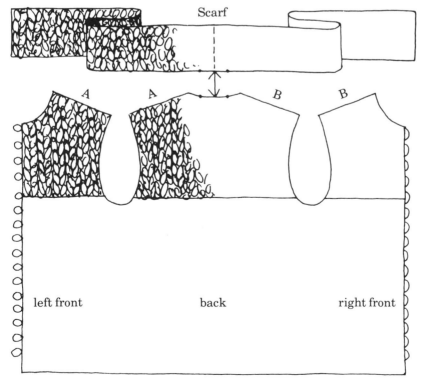

Scarf

A   A   B   B

left front   back   right front

Overblouse

Worked in twisted stockinette stitch, the openwork effect is obtained by using large needles. It buttons at one shoulder.

SIZE: Will stretch to fit sizes 10 through 16.

MATERIALS: Unger's Roly-Poly, 3 (3½-oz.) balls No. 8841 (eggshell); knitting needles, 1 pair each No. 10 and No. 11 (or English needles No. 3 and No. 2) **or the size that will give you the correct gauge;** aluminum crochet hook size G (or Canadian hook No. 9); 4″ neckline zipper; tapestry needle.

GAUGE: Unblocked, 3 sts = 1″; blocked, 11 sts = 4″.

BACK: Starting at lower edge with No. 11 needles, cast on 41 sts. Work border pattern as follows: **1st row (right side):** K 1; * sl 1 y f, p 1. Repeat from * across, ending sl 1 y f, k 1. **2nd row:** K 1, * p 1, sl 1 y b, yarn to front. Repeat from * across, ending p 1, k 1. Repeat these 2 rows once more (border completed). Now work twisted-stockinette-stitch pattern as follows: **1st row:** K across, inserting right-hand needle into back loop of each st. **2nd row:** P across. Repeat these 2 rows for twisted-stockinette pattern. Work even in pattern until piece measures 17″ from beg, or desired length to underarms.

To Shape Armholes: Bind off 3 sts at beg of next 2 rows. Dec 1 st at beg and end of every other row 4 times. Work even on 27 sts until armholes measure 7½″.

To Shape Shoulders: Bind off 3 sts at beg of next 4 rows. **Next row:** Bind off 3 sts at beg of row; work center 9 sts and place these sts on holder for back of neck; complete row. Bind off remaining 3 sts.

FRONT: Work same as back until armholes measure 6½″ (27 sts).

152

To Shape Neck and Shoulders: Work across 11 sts, place center 5 sts on holder for front neck, attach another ball of yarn, complete row. Working both sides at once, dec 1 st at each side of neck every other row twice. Work even on 9 sts on each side until each armhole measures same as back to shoulder.

To Shape Shoulders: At each arm edge bind off 3 sts every other row 3 times. Break off.

SLEEVES: With No. 10 needles cast on 21 sts. Work border pattern same as for back for 6 rows. Change to No. 11 needles. **Next row:** K 1, then inc 1 st in each st across (41 sts). P 1 row. Work even in twisted-stockinette-stitch pattern for 8". Continuing in pattern, dec 1 st at beg and end of every 4th row 7 times. Work even on 27 sts until sleeve measures 16" from beg, or desired length to underarm.

To Shape Cap: Bind off 3 sts at beg of next 2 rows. Dec 1 st at beg and end of every other row 9 times. Bind off remaining 3 sts.

FINISHING: Dampen and block, pinning matching pieces together and stretching to measurements. Sew right shoulder seam. With No. 10 needles pick up and k 39 sts around neck edge, including sts from holders. Starting with 2nd row (wrong side), work border pattern for 10 rows. Bind off all sts. Sew underarm and sleeve seams. Sew sleeves in place. Crochet a row of sc around left shoulder opening. Sew zipper in place in shoulder opening.

Crocheted Buttons (make 4): Ch 2. **1st rnd:** Work 3 sc in 2nd ch from hook. Do not join but work around. **2nd rnd:** Work 2 sc in each sc around (6 sc). **3rd rnd:** Draw up loop in each of next 2 sc, y o and draw through all 3 loops on hook (1 sc dec). Dec 2 more sc. Break off, leaving a 10" end. Thread end in tapestry needle, draw through remaining sc of last rnd, pull up tightly and fasten. Sew buttons evenly spaced along back left shoulder edge.

Button Loops: Crochet four 2" chains. Fold each in half and tack ends in place on front left shoulder edge opposite buttons.

One-Piece Halter Top

A halter in k 2, p 2 ribbing, buttons in front on a neck strap.

SIZE: Knit to fit.

MATERIALS: Kentucky All Purpose (rayon) Yarn, 3 (100-yard) skeins pink No. 731, 1 skein deep rose No. 734; knitting needles, 1 pair No. 5 (or English needles No. 8) **or the size that will give you the correct gauge;** 4 buttons ⅝" in diameter; 2 yards of round elastic (optional).

GAUGE: 8 sts = 1" without stretching; 11 rows = 2".

Starting at center front with pink, work in k 2, p 2 ribbing until piece measures 1" less than desired length, stretched, to fit around bust. Bind off in ribbing.

BORDER AND STRAP: With deep rose, cast on 9 sts. **1st row (right side):** K 2, (p 1, k 1) 3 times; k 1. **2nd row:** K 1, * p 1, k 1. Repeat from * across. Repeat 1st and 2nd rows once more. **5th row (buttonhole row):** Work in pattern across first 3 sts, y o, k 2 tog (for buttonhole), continue in pattern to end of row. Continue in pattern as established, working 3 more buttonholes every 1". Then work even in ribbing pattern until piece measures 30" or desired length to fit from lower edge of one end of tube around neck to lower edge of other end. Bind off in ribbing.

With right sides facing, sew edge of strip with buttonholes along one end of tube and corresponding edge to other end of tube. Sew on buttons. (**Note:** If piece stretches with wear, whipstitch elastic around upper and lower edges of tube.)

The Strapless Tube

Remember them from way back in the forties? This updated version is worked in one piece in k 2, p 2 ribbing, laced with yellow and orange. Buttons are just for show.

SIZES: 6 [8–10–12]. Tube will stretch to fit 32″ [33″–34″–35″] bust measurement. Tube measures 14″ from lower to upper edge.

MATERIALS: Bucilla Perlette (Orlon acrylic), 4 [4–5–5] (1¾-oz.) balls peacock No. 18 (color A), 1 ball each bright yellow No. 11 (B) and burnt orange No. 10 (C); knitting needles, 1 pair No. 4 (or English needles No. 9) **or the size that will give you the correct gauge;** 6 buttons ⅝″ in diameter; 1 bobbin.

GAUGE: 4 sts = 1″ when slightly stretched; 14 rows = 2″.

Note: Tube is worked in one piece without side seams. To prevent gapping, front opening is stitched closed with buttons added. First and last 6 sts of each row form false front borders. When changing colors, twist yarns by bringing new color under old to avoid holes in work. **Use yarn double throughout.**

Starting at lower edge with A, cast on 137 [141–145–149] sts. **1st row:** K 1, * p 1, k 1. Repeat from * across. **2nd row:** K 2, * p 1, k 1. Repeat from * to within last st, k 1. Repeat first and 2nd rows 3 times more, increasing 1st at center of last row (138 [142–146–150] sts).

9th row (right side): (K 1, p 1) 3 times; for stripe, drop A, attach B, k to within last 6 sts, drop B, attach bobbin A for border sts, (p 1, k 1) 3 times. **10th row:** With A, k 2, (p 1, k 1) twice; break off bobbin A; for stripe, pick up B, k to within last 6 sts, break off B, pick up A, (k 1, p 1) twice; k 2. **11th row:** With A, (k 1, p 1) 3 times; k across to within last 6 sts, (p 1, k 1) 3 times. **12th row:** K 2, (p 1, k 1) twice; p 2, * k 2, p 2. Repeat from * to within last 6 sts, (k 1, p 1) twice; k 2. **13th row:** With A, (k 1, p 1) 3 times; k 2, * p 2, k 2. Repeat from * to within last 6 sts, (p 1, k 1) 3 times. Repeat 12th and 13th rows until stripe A measures 2½", ending with 12th row.

Then, working stripe with C, repeat 9th and 10th rows once. Repeat 11th row once, then repeat 12th and 13th rows until stripe A measures 2½", ending with 12th row. Maintaining established pattern, work as follows: work 1 B stripe, 2½" with A, 1 C stripe, 2½" with A, 1 B stripe, decreasing 1 st at center of last row. Repeat first and 2nd rows 4 times. Bind off in ribbing.

Overlap borders and bindstitch. Sew on buttons.

156

Puff-Sleeved Top

*Even beginners can make
this one in simple ribbing,
with little cap sleeves to be
worn on or off the shoulder.*

SIZES: 6 [8–10–12]. Top will stretch to fit 32″ [33″–34″–35″] bust measurement; top measures 13″ from back of neck to lower edge.

MATERIALS: Bucilla Perlette (Orlon acrylic), 4 [4–5–5] (1¾-oz.) balls burnt orange No. 10; knitting needles, 1 pair each No. 4 and No. 8 (or English needles No. 9 and No. 5) **or the size that will give you the correct gauge;** 1 yard elasticized thread.

GAUGE: 4 sts = 1″ on No. 4 needles, when slightly stretched; 14 rows = 2″.

Use yarn double throughout.

BACK: Starting at lower edge with No. 4 needles, cast on 64 [66–68–70] sts. Work in k 1, p 1 ribbing for 6 rows.

To establish rib pattern: K 2 rows, increasing 0 [2–0–2] sts on last row (64 [68–68–72] sts). * Work in k 2, p 2 ribbing for 8 rows. K 2 rows. Repeat from * until piece measures 12½″ from beg, ending with 2 k rows. Work in k 1, p 1 ribbing for 6 rows. Bind off loosely in ribbing.

FRONT: Work same as back.

SLEEVES: Starting at lower edge with No. 4 needles, cast on 50 sts. Work in k 1, p 1 ribbing for 4 rows. **Next row:** * K 1, inc in next st. Repeat from * across (75 sts). Change to No. 8 needles.

To establish puffed pattern—1st row: Insert right-hand needle into first st as if to k, y o needle twice and k st (2 y o's on right-hand needle), * insert right-hand needle into next st as if to k, y o needle twice and k st (2 more y o's on right-hand needle). Repeat from * across. **2nd row:** Insert right-hand needle in first st as if to k, k the st and drop 2nd st (y o) from needle to form long st. * Insert right-hand needle in next st as if to k, k the st and drop next st (y o) from needle to form long st. Repeat from * across. Repeat first and 2nd rows twice more. Change to No. 4 needles. **Next row:** * K 1, p 2 tog. Repeat from * across. Work in k 1, p 1 ribbing for 5 more rows. Bind off loosely in ribbing.

FINISHING: Sew back to front at sides from lower edge to about 4" from upper edge. Sew sleeves to front and back, matching ribbing along upper edges. Weave elasticized thread through last row of ribbing around neck, adjust to fit and fasten off.

A Trio

Long-Sleeved Sweater • Middy • Pullover

Three fun sweaters, to be worn layered or alone. The long-sleeved sweater, in stripes of a different width, to be worn under the middy, with elbow-length sleeves and a white sailor's collar, and to keep adding, there's a blue square-necked pullover, worked in seed stitch with red trim, to top it off.

LONG-SLEEVED SWEATER

SIZES: Small (6–8) [Medium (10–12)]. Sweater measures 15″ [16″] across back at underarms. 19½″ [19¾″] long.

MATERIALS: Bernat's Berella Sportspun, 1 [2] (2-oz.) ball blue (color A), 2 [3] balls each gold (B) and red (C); knitting needles, 1 pair No. 7 (or English needles No. 6), **or the size that will give you the correct gauge.**

GAUGE: 5 sts = 1″; 7 rows = 1″.

BACK: Starting at lower edge with color A, cast on 75 [80] sts. K 3 rows. Starting with a p row, work even in stockinette st (k 1 row, p 1 row) and work stripes as follows: Work 7 more rows A, * work 10 rows B, 10 rows C, 10 rows B, 10 rows A. Repeat from * for stripe pattern throughout. Work even until piece measures 12½″ from beg, or desired length to underarms.

To Shape Armholes: Bind off 3 [4] sts at beg of next 2 rows. Dec 1 st at beg and end of every other row twice (65 [68] sts). Work even until armholes measure 5¾" [6"].

To Shape Neck: Work across first 24 [25] sts, attach another ball of yarn and with new ball, work center 17 [18] sts and place these sts on a holder to be worked later, work across remaining 24 [25] sts. Working both sides at once, at each neck edge bind off 3 sts once, then 2 sts once (19 [20] sts on each side). Work even on each side until armholes measure 7" [7¼"].

To Shape Shoulders: At each arm edge, bind off 6 sts every other row twice, then 7 [8] sts once.

FRONT: Work same as for back until armholes measure 5¼" [5½"]. Shape neck as for back, then work even until armholes measure same as back. Shape shoulders as for back.

SLEEVES: Starting at lower edge with C, cast on 36 [38] sts. Work in ribbing of k 1, p 1 for 4 rows. Now work in stockinette st, alternating 4 rows of B and 4 rows of C throughout. When sleeve measures 2" from beg, inc 1 st at beg and end of next row, then every 8th row 10 [11] times more (58 [62] sts). Work even until sleeve measures 17", or length desired to underarm.

To Shape Cap: Bind off 4 [5] sts at beg of next 2 rows. Dec 1 st at beg and end of every other row 11 [12] times. Bind off 3 sts at beg of next 4 rows. Bind off remaining 16 sts.

FINISHING: Sew one shoulder seam.

Neckband: With C, pick up and k 94 [96] sts, including sts from holders, around neck edge. Work in ribbing of k 1, p 1 for 4 rows. Bind off all sts in ribbing. Sew other shoulder and neckband, side and sleeve seams. Sew sleeves in place.

MIDDY

SIZES: Small (6–8) [Medium (10–12)]. Sweater measures 15½" [16½"] across back at underarms, 16" [16¼"] from shoulder to lower edge.

MATERIALS: Bernat's Berella Sportspun, 5 (2-oz.) balls red (color A), 1 ball white (B); knitting needles, 1 pair each No. 5 and No. 7 (or English needles No. 8 and No. 6), **or the sizes that will give you the correct gauge.**

GAUGE: 5 sts = 1"; 7 rows = 1".

BACK: Starting at lower edge with No. 5 needles and color A, cast on 76 [80] sts. Work in ribbing of k 2, p 2 for 2", increasing 3 sts evenly spaced across last row (79 [83] sts). Change to No. 7 needles and work even in stockinette st until piece measures 9" from beg.

To Shape Armholes: Bind off 3 [4] sts at beg of next 2 rows. Dec 1 st at beg and end of every other row 3 times (67 [69] sts). Work even until armholes measure 7" [7¼"].

160

To Shape Shoulders: Bind off 7 [8] sts at beg of next 2 rows, then 7 sts at beg of next 4 rows. Bind off remaining 25 sts for back neck edge.

FRONT: Work same as for back until armholes measure 1¼″ (67 [69] sts).

To Shape V-Neck: Work across 33 [34] sts, attach another ball of A and with new ball, bind off center st, work to end. Working each side with a separate ball of yarn, dec 1 st at each neck edge on next row, then every 3rd row 11 times (21 [22] sts on each side). Work even until armholes measure same as back.

To Shape Shoulders: At each arm edge bind off 7 [8] sts once, then 7 sts every other row twice.

SLEEVES: Starting at lower edge with No. 5 needles and A, cast on 52 [56] sts. Work in ribbing of k 2, p 2 for 1″. Change to No. 7 needles. Working in stockinette st, work 4 more rows A, 4 rows B, then continuing with A only, inc 1 st at beg and end of row every ¾″ 4 times, then every ½″ 3 times (66 [70] sts). Work even until sleeve measures 8″ from beg.

To Shape Cap: Bind off 4 [5] sts at beg of next 2 rows. Dec 1 st at beg and end of every 3rd row 10 times, then every other row 5 [6] times, then every row 3 times. Bind off remaining 22 sts.

COLLAR: Starting at lower edge of back, with No. 7 needles and B, cast on 63 [65] sts. K 4 rows. **5th row (wrong side):** K 2, p 59 [61], k 2. K 1 row. **7th row:** K 2 B, p 2 B, attach A, p 55 [57] A, attach 2nd ball B, p 2 B, k 2 B. **8th row:** K 4 B, k 55 [57] A, k 4 B. Repeat last 2 rows once more. **9th row:** K 2 B, p 2 B, p 3 A, p 49 [51] B, break off 2nd ball B, attach 2nd ball A, p 3 A, p 2 B, k 2 B. (**Note:** From this point on, ball of B is carried for all B sts.) **10th row:** K 4 B, k 3 A, k 49 [51] B, k 3 A, k 4 B. Repeat last 2 rows until piece measures 9″ from beg. Continuing to keep 7 sts at beg and end in pattern as established, shape neck as follows:

To Shape Neck: Work first 24 [25] sts, attach another ball of B and with new ball, bind off center 15 sts (back neck), work to end. Working on both sides at once, at each neck edge bind off 2 sts once, dec 1 st every other row twice, then every 4th row 8 times, then every other row 12 [13] times.

FINISHING: Sew shoulder, side and sleeve seams. Sew sleeves in place, gathering top of cap to fit armhole. Sew collar in place, joining front ends neatly at point of V-neckline.

PULLOVER

SIZES: Small (6–8) [Medium (10–12)]. Sweater measures 15½″ [16½″] across back at underarms, 22½″ [22¾″] from shoulder to lower edge.

MATERIALS: Bernat's Berella Sportspun, 4 [5] (2-oz.) balls blue (color A), 1 ball red (B); knitting needles, 1 pair each No. 7 and No. 8

(or English needles No. 6 and No. 5), **or the sizes that will give you the correct gauge.**

GAUGE: 4 sts = 1"; 8 rows = 1".

BACK: Starting at hem with No. 8 needles and color A, cast on 67 [71] sts. Work in stockinette st (k 1 row, p 1 row) for 1", ending with a k row. K next row for hemline. Work in seed st as follows: **1st row (right side):** K 1, * p 1, k 1. Repeat from * across. Repeat last row for pattern and dec 1 st at beg and end of row every 3½" 3 times (61 [65] sts). Work even until piece measures 13" from hemline, or desired length to underarms.

To Shape Armholes: Bind off 5 [6] sts at beg of next 2 rows (51 [53] sts). Work even until armholes measure 7" [7¼"].

To Shape Neck: Work across first 12 sts, attach another ball A and with new ball bind off center 27 [29] sts, work to end. Working each side with a separate ball of yarn, work even until armholes measure 9½" [9¾"]. Bind off all sts at shoulders.

FRONT: Work same as for back until armholes measure 2". Now shape neck and complete as for back. Sew shoulder seams.

SLEEVES: With No. 8 needles and A, pick up and k 81 [83] sts along straight edge of one armhole (not across underarm). Work even in seed st for 3", decreasing 1 st on last row (80 [82] sts). Break off A; attach B. Change to No. 7 needles. Work in twisted ribbing as follows: **1st row:** * K 1 in back of st, p 1. Repeat from * across. Repeat last row 5 times more. Bind off all sts in ribbing.

POCKETS (make 2): Starting at top edge with No. 8 needles and A, cast on 15 sts. Work even in seed st until piece measures 2¾" from beg. Bind off all sts.

FINISHING: Sew underarm edges to sleeves. Sew side and sleeve seams. Turn under hem at lower edge and sew in place.

Neckband: With No. 7 needles and B, pick up and k 56 [58] sts along left edge of neck opening. Work in twisted ribbing and dec 1 st at beg and end of every other row 3 times. Bind off remaining 50 [52] sts in ribbing. Repeat along right neck edge. Pick up and k 38 [40] sts along front neck edge and work in same manner. Repeat along back neck edge. Sew neckband together at mitered corners. **Pocket Trim:** With No. 7 needles and B, pick up and k 20 sts across cast-on edge of pocket. Work in twisted ribbing and inc 1 st at beg and end of every other row 3 times. Bind off 26 sts in ribbing. Repeat along opposite long edge. Pick up and k 18 sts across sides and work in same manner, binding off remaining 24 sts. Repeat on other pocket. Sew trim together at corners. Sew a pocket to each side of lower front of sweater (see photograph).

Striped Poncho

In rust, purple, and pink knitting worsted, this poncho has a turtleneck, fringe all around, and a wide garter-stitch edge.

SIZE: Junior petite 7–9.

MATERIALS: Knitting worsted, 7 ounces rust (color A); 3 ounces each purple (B), dusty pink (C), dusty rose (D) and orange (E); knitting needles: For body, 24″ circular needle No. 7 and 1 set (4) dp needles No. 7 (or English needles No. 6), **or the size that will give you the correct gauge;** for ribbed turtleneck, 1 set (4) dp needles No. 6 (or English needles No. 7); 12 markers (plastic rings or paper clips); aluminum crochet hook size H.

GAUGE: On No. 7 needles: 11 sts = 2″; 7 rows = 1″.

Starting at neck edge with dp needles No. 7 and color A, cast on 66 sts. Divide sts evenly on 3 needles and join, being careful not to twist sts. **1st rnd:** K 5, place marker on needle, k 1 (seam st), place marker, * k 10, place marker, k 1 (seam st), place marker. Repeat from * 4 times more; k 5. **2nd rnd:** K to within 1 st of first marker, k in front and back of next st (1 st inc), sl marker, k 1, * sl marker, inc 1 st in next st, k to within 1 st of next marker, inc 1 st in next st, sl marker, k 1. Repeat from * 4 times more; sl marker, inc 1 st in next st, k to end (12 sts inc). **3rd and 4th rnds:** K around, slipping markers. Repeat 2nd, 3rd and 4th rnds 10 times more (198 sts).

Note: Change to circular needle when there are too many sts to work comfortably on dp needles.

Next rnd: * K to next marker, remove marker, k 1, remove marker, k to within 1 st of next marker, inc 1 st in next st, sl marker, k 1 (center seam st), sl marker, inc 1 st in next st, k to next marker, remove marker, k 1, remove marker. Repeat from * once more; k to end of rnd (4 sts inc, 202 sts). Work 3 rnds even, slipping front and back seam markers.

Next rnd: (K to within 1 st of next marker, inc 1 st in next st, sl marker, k 1, sl marker, inc 1 st in next st) twice; k to end of rnd (206 sts). Work 3 rnds even, slipping markers.

Repeat last 4 rnds until piece measures 12″ along a center seam line, ending with an inc rnd.

Continuing to inc every 4th rnd as before, work next 8 rnds in garter st (k 1 rnd, p 1 rnd). Break off A.

To Divide for Side Slits: Attach B and k across half the sts on needle and place them on a piece of yarn as a holder for front, k across remaining sts for back. Work *back and forth* on these sts only.

Increasing every 4th row as before at center back seam, work colors in garter st (k every row) as follows: 12 more rows B, 12 rows C, 8 rows D, 4 rows A, 6 rows E, 16 rows A, 6 rows B, 4 rows C, 8 rows D, 6 rows A, 8 rows E, 4 rows A. Bind off loosely. Work front to correspond.

FINISHING: With A, crochet 1 row sc along slit edges. Make 5-strand tassels (1 strand of each color) 1″ apart along lower edge and side slits. **Turtleneck:** Attach A at neck edge. With dp needles No. 6, pick up 66 sts around neck edge. Divide sts on 3 needles and work in ribbing of k 1, p 1 for 4″. Bind off loosely in ribbing. Turn half of ribbing to wrong side for double turtleneck and sew in place.

Short Tops, Leg Warmers and Warm Pants

Left: A vest with knitted-in reindeer design and long spats in cable and double-seed stitch match mittens, which are the same as those shown on page 119. Right: Short top and knee-warmers are in stockinette stitch with knit-in hearts and flowers. Color-coordinated pants are worked in a fabric-like textured pattern. One size knee-warmers will fit all.

SHORTIE VEST

SIZES: 8 [10–12–14]. Garment measures 15″ [15½″–16″–16¼″] across bust.

MATERIALS: Brunswick Germantown knitting worsted, 2 (4-oz.) skeins brick heather No. 474 (color A), small amount of heather gold

(B) knitting worsted for reindeer; knitting needles, 1 pair each No. 3 and No. 5 (or English needles No. 10 and No. 8) **or the size that will give you the correct gauge;** steel crochet hook No. 0; 5 gold buttons; 1 yard 1½"-wide grosgrain ribbon.

GAUGE: 11 sts = 2"; 7 rows = 1".

BACK: Starting at lower edge with color A and No. 3 needles, cast on 72 [74–78–80] sts. Work in ribbing of k 1, p 1 for 2". Change to No. 5 needles and work in stockinette st for 1". Inc 1 st at beg and end of next row, then every ¾" 4 times more (82 [84–88–90] sts). Work even until piece measures 8½" from beg.

To Shape Armholes: Bind off 5 [6–7–8] sts at beg of next 2 rows. Dec 1 st at beg and end of every other row 6 times. Work even on 60 [60–62–62] sts until armholes measure 8½" [8½"–9"–9"].

To Shape Shoulders: Bind off 7 [7–8–8] sts at beg of next 2 rows. Bind off 8 sts at beg of following 2 rows. Place remaining 30 sts on holder for neck.

LEFT FRONT: Starting at lower edge with A and No. 3 needles, cast on 42 [43–44–45] sts. Work in ribbing of k 1, p 1 for 2". Change to No. 5 needles and k across 31 [32–33–34] sts, slip remaining 11 sts to a holder for front border. P 1 row. Wind a color B bobbin (see page 35 for bobbin knitting). **Next row:** K 3 [4–5–6] A, attach bobbin and k 1 B (first st on chart), k 5 A, 2 B, (2 A, 3 B) twice; 10 A. Continue in pattern, following chart from left to right on p rows and from right to left on k rows, until piece measures 3" from beg. Continuing chart, inc 1 st at side edge on next row, then every ¾" 4 times more (36 [37–38–39] sts). Work even until piece measures 8½" from beg, ending at side edge.

To Shape Armhole: Bind off 5 [6–7–8] sts at beg of next row. Dec 1 st at same edge every other row 6 times (25 sts), ending at front edge.

To Shape Neck: Bind off 3 [3–2–2] sts at beg (front edge) of next row. Dec 1 st at same edge every row 3 times, then every 6th row 4 times. Work even on 15 [15–16–16] sts until armhole measures 8½" [8½"–9"–9"], ending at armhole edge.

To Shape Shoulder: Bind off 7 [7–8–8] sts at beg of next row. Bind off remaining 8 sts.

Border: Slip the 11 sts from holder onto No. 3 needle, attach A and continue in ribbing until border, when slightly stretched, fits front edge to neck. Slip sts to a holder for front neck. Sew border in place and mark for 5 buttons, the first 1" from beg, the 4th 2" below top edge, the remaining 2 evenly spaced between. The 5th button will be on neck ribbing.

RIGHT FRONT: Work to correspond to left front, reversing shaping and reindeer. Make buttonholes opposite markers on front border, as follows. **Buttonhole:** Starting at front edge, work 4 sts, bind off 3, work to end. On next row, cast on 3 sts over bound-off sts.

FINISHING: Block pieces (see blocking directions, page 37). Sew shoulder seams. **Neck Ribbing:** Attach A at right front neck edge.

With right side facing you, using No. 3 needles, pick up and k 150 [152–154–156] sts around neck edge, including sts from holders. Work in ribbing of k 1, p 1 for 6 rows, making last buttonhole on 3rd row. Bind off in ribbing.

first stitch

Armhole Ribbing: With No. 3 needles and A, pick up and k 112 [112–114–114] sts around armhole edge. Work in ribbing for 6 rows. Bind off in ribbing. Sew side seams. With right side facing you, crochet a row of sc with A along front edges. Face front borders with grosgrain ribbon. Cut and finish buttonholes in the ribbon. Sew on buttons.

LONG SPATS

SIZE: One size fits all. Length is adjustable.

MATERIALS: Brunswick Germantown knitting worsted, 2 (4-oz.) skeins No. 474 brick heather; 1 set (4) No. 5 dp knitting needles (or English needles No. 8) **or the size that will give you the correct gauge;** 1 needle to work cable; steel crochet hook No. 0; 6" of 1"-wide black elastic.

GAUGE: 6 sts = 1".

CUFF: Loosely cast on 56 sts and divide them on 3 needles as follows: 16 sts on first needle, 20 sts each on second and third needles. Join, being careful not to twist sts. Work around in ribbing of k 2, p 2, for 3".

PATTERN—1st rnd: * K 2, p 2, k 2, p 1, k 6, p 1. Repeat from * around. **2nd rnd:** * K 2, p 2, k 2, p 1, slip next 3 sts onto cable needle and hold in back of work, k 3, then k 3 off cable needle (cable twist made), p 1. Repeat from * around. **3rd rnd:** P 2, * k 2, p 3, k 6, p 3.

Repeat from * around, ending with p 1 instead of p 3. **4th rnd:** Repeat 3rd rnd. **5th and 6th rnds:** Repeat 1st rnd. **7th and 8th rnds:** Repeat 3rd rnd.

Repeat these 8 rnds for pattern. Work in pattern until piece measures 14½" (or desired length) from beg of cuff, ending on a cable twist rnd. Work in pattern as established for 3 more rnds. Bind off 20 sts (heel), work remaining 36 sts onto one needle (instep). **Instep:** Work in rows from now on. Continue in pattern for 4 more rows ending with a cable twist row. Continue to work back and forth in pattern, decreasing 1 st at beg and end of next 6 rows. Work even on 24 sts for 2" more. Dec 1 st at beg and end of next 6 rows. (**Note:** Omit cable twist on last 1" of pattern so that instep will lie flat.) Bind off remaining 12 sts.

SIDE TABS: Attach yarn and pick up 8 sts along edge of a side cable on instep. Work in stockinette st for 1", then make cable twist on the center 6 sts. Bind off. Work a tab on other side in same manner.

FINISHING: With right side facing you, work a row of sc around heel, instep and tabs. Cut 3" piece of elastic, turn under ends and sew 1 end under each tab. Press lightly.

HEARTS AND FLOWERS TOP

SIZES: 8 [10–12–14]. Garment measures 15" [15½"–16"–16¼"] across bust.

MATERIALS: Brunswick Germantown knitting worsted, 2 (4-oz.) skeins cherry smash No. 420 (color A), small amounts of orange (B) and lavender (C) knitting worsted for design and stripes; knitting needles, 1 pair each No. 7 and No. 9 (or English needles No. 6 and No. 4) **or sizes that will give correct gauge.**

GAUGE: 9 sts = 2"; 6 rows = 1".

BACK: Starting at lower edge with No. 7 needles and color A, cast on 64 [68–68–72] sts. Work in ribbing of k 2, p 2 for 4". K across, increasing 3 [1–3–1] sts evenly spaced across row (67 [69–71–73] sts). Change to No. 9 needles and continue in stockinette st. Work until piece measures 9" from beg.

To Shape Armholes: Bind off 5 sts at beg of next 2 rows. Dec 1 st at beg and end of every other row 4 times. Work even on 49 [51–53–55] sts until armholes measure 5" [5"–5½"–5½"].

To Shape Neck: Work 17 [18–19–20] sts. Slip remaining sts on holder. Working on the 17 [18–19–20] sts on needle, bind off 2 sts at neck edge every other row twice, then dec 1 st every other row at same edge 4 times. Work even on 9 [10–11–12] sts until armhole measures 8½" [8½"–9"–9"], ending at armhole edge.

To Shape Shoulder: At armhole edge, bind off 4 [5–5–6] sts once, then 5 [5–6–6] sts once. Break off. Leave center 15 sts on holder for back neck; slip remaining 17 [18–19–20] sts onto needle and work as for other side, reversing shaping.

168

FRONT: Work same as for back until piece measures 6″ from beg, ending with a p row. Wind a color B bobbin (see page 35 for bobbin knitting), then continue as follows: **Next row:** K 33 [34–35–36], attach bobbin and k 1 (first st on chart), k 33 [34–35–36]. Continue in pattern, following chart until piece measures 9″ from beg.

To Shape Armholes: Continuing to follow chart, work as for back until armholes measure 3″ [3″–3½″–3½″] from beg.

To Shape Neck: Work as for back until 9 [10–11–12] sts are left on needle. Work stripe pattern as follows: 3 rows B, (2 rows A, 1 row C) twice; 2 rows A, 2 rows B, 1 row A, 2 rows B, (2 rows A, 1 row C) twice. Continue with A until armhole measures same as back.

To Shape Shoulder: Work as for back. Break off. Leave 15 center sts on holder for front neck; slip remaining 17 [18–19–20] sts onto needle and work as for other side, reversing shaping.

FINISHING—Neck Ribbing: Attach A at right neck edge of back. With right side facing you, using No. 7 needles, pick up and K 62 sts along back neck edge, including sts from holder. Work in ribbing of k 2, p 2 for 5 rows. Bind off in ribbing. Attach A at left neck edge of front, pick up and k 94 sts along front neck edge and work as for back ribbing. Block pieces (see page 37). Sew shoulder seams. **Armhole Ribbing:** With No. 7 needles and A, pick up and k 104 [104–108–108] sts around armhole edge. Work in ribbing as for neck. Sew side seams.

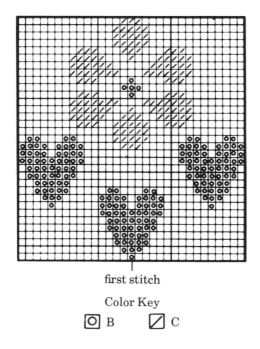

first stitch

Color Key

☑ B   ☑ C

KNEE-WARMERS

SIZE: One size fits all.

MATERIALS: Brunswick Fairhaven 3-ply fingering yarn, 2 (1-oz.) skeins cherry smash No. 1620 (color A), small amounts of orange (B) and lavender (C) fingering yarn for heart and stripes; knitting needles, 1 pair each No. 2 and No. 3 (or English needles No. 11 and No. 10) **or the size that will give you the correct gauge.**

GAUGE: 7 sts = 1"; 9 rows = 1".

Starting at lower edge with No. 2 needles and A, cast on 84 sts. Work in ribbing of k 2, p 2 for 2½". K across, increasing 1 st at center of row (85 sts). Change to No. 3 needles and continue in stockinette st. Work 2 rows A; attach C and work 2 rows C, 2 rows A and 2 rows C. Break off C and continue with A until piece measures 4¾" from beg, ending with a p row.

To Shape Knee: Work short rows as follows: **1st row:** K to within last 22 sts; turn. **2nd row:** Sl 1, p to within last 22 sts; turn. **3rd row:** Sl 1, k to within last 20 sts; turn. **4th row:** Sl 1, p to within last 20 sts; turn. Wind a color B bobbin (see page 35 for bobbin knitting). **5th row:** Sl 1, k until there are 42 sts on right needle; attach bobbin and k 1 (first st on chart), attach 2nd skein of A and k to within last 18 sts; turn.

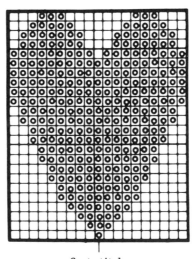

first stitch

Following chart for pattern, continue to work short rows, knitting 2 sts more every row until all sts have been worked. When chart has been completed, continue with A until piece measures 7" from beg, measuring along side edge. Attach C, (work 2 rows C, 2 rows A) twice, decreasing 1 st on last row (84 sts). With same needles, work ribbing of k 2, p 2 for 2½". Bind off loosely in ribbing. Sew back seam.

COLOR-COORDINATED PANTS

SIZES: 8 [10–12–14]. Pants measure 16" [17"–18"–18"] across hips (measured 7" below waistline) and 11" [11½"–12"–12"] across leg at hemline. Pants length is 18½" and is adjustable.

MATERIALS: Brunswick Germantown knitting worsted, 3 (4-oz.) skeins cherry smash No. 420; knitting needles, 1 pair each No. 6 and No. 8 (or English needles No. 7 and No. 5) **or the size that will give you the correct gauge;** 1 yard ¾"-wide elastic.

GAUGE: 5 pattern sts on No. 8 needles = 1"; 7 rows = 1".

LEFT BACK LEG: Starting at lower edge with No. 6 needles, cast on 55 [57–59–59] sts. Starting with a p row, work in stockinette st for 7 rows for facing. **Next row (right side):** P across for hemline. Change to No. 8 needles and work pattern as follows: **1st row (wrong side):** P across. **2nd row:** K 1, * with yarn in back sl 1 as if to p, k 1. Repeat from * across. **3rd row:** P across. **4th row:** K 2, * with yarn in back sl 1 as if to p, k 1. Repeat from * across, ending k 1. Repeat last 4 rows until piece measures 2½" from hemline, ending with a p row.

Inc 1 st at beg (inside leg) of next row, then at same edge every 2" once more (57 [59–61–61] sts). Continue in pattern until piece measures 7½" from hemline, or desired length of leg, ending with a p row.

To Shape Crotch—Next row: Bind off 7 sts (crotch edge), work across in pattern. Dec 1 st at same edge every other row 3 times, then every 4th row 3 times, then every 8th row 4 times (40 [42–44–44] sts). Work even until piece measures 14½" from hemline, or 4" less than desired length, ending with a p row.

Dart—1st row: Work 18 [19–20–20] sts, k 2 tog, place marker on needle, sl 1, k 1, psso, work to end. Continue to dec 1 st each side of marker every 1½" twice more. Work even on remaining 34 [36–38–38] sts for 1", ending with a p row.

Waistband Casing: Change to No. 6 needles and p across right side for hemline. Work in stockinette st for 7 rows. Bind off.

RIGHT BACK LEG: Work as for left back leg, reversing shapings.

RIGHT FRONT LEG: With No. 6 needles cast on 53 [55–57–57] sts. Work facing and hemline as for back leg. Change to No. 8 needles and work in pattern until piece measures same as back to crotch, ending with a p row.

To Shape Crotch—Next row: Bind off 4 sts (crotch edge), work across in pattern. Dec 1 st at same edge every other row twice, then every 4th row twice, then every 8th row 4 times (41 [43–45–45] sts). Work even until piece measures 14½" from hemline, or 4" less than desired length, ending with a p row.

Dart—1st row: Work 19 [20–21–21] sts, k 2 tog, place marker on needle, sl 1, k 1, psso, work to end. Dec 1 st each side of marker every 1½″ twice more (35 [37–39–39] sts). Complete as for back leg.

LEFT FRONT LEG: Work as for right front leg, reversing shapings.

FINISHING: Block pieces (see page 37). Sew side, center front, back and crotch seams. Turn leg facings under and sew in place. Turn waistband casing to wrong side and sew, leaving opening for elastic. Cut elastic to waist measurement, draw through casing and sew ends tog.

CHILDREN'S SWEATERS

Infants' Sweaters

Christening Dress and Bonnet

This exquisite christening dress and bonnet, in wavy feather and fan stitch, will be worn by many generations to come.

SIZE: Infant.
MATERIALS: Baby or Fingering Yarn, 9 (1-oz.) skeins; knitting needles, 1 pair No. 1 and 1 pair No. 2 (or English needles No. 12 and

No. 11) **or the sizes that will give you the correct gauge;** steel crochet hook No. 5; 3 yards ¼"-wide velvet ribbon; 4 small pearl buttons.

GAUGE: Lace pattern: 24 sts (1 pattern repeat) = 2¾"; 10 rows = 1". Seed st: 8 sts = 1"; 14 rows =1".

PATTERN STITCHES

Lace Pattern: (Multiple of 24 sts): **1st row (wrong side):** (K 2 tog) 4 times; * (y o, p 1) 8 times; (k 2 tog) 8 times. Repeat from * across, ending (y o, p 1) 8 times; (k 2 tog) 4 times. **2nd row:** K across. **3rd row:** P across. **4th row:** K across. Repeat these 4 rows for pattern.

Seed Stitch: On an *uneven* number of sts: **1st row:** K 1, * p 1, k 1. Repeat from * across. Repeat this row for pattern. On an *even* number of sts: **1st row:** * K 1, p 1. Repeat from * across. **2nd row:** * P 1, k 1. Repeat from * across. Repeat these 2 rows for pattern.

ROBE

BACK: Starting at lower edge with No. 2 needles, cast on 148 sts. K 6 rows. Establish lace pattern as follows: **1st row:** K 2, work in pattern to within last 2 sts (6 pattern repeats), k 2. **2nd row:** K 2, work in pattern to within last 2 sts, k 2. Always knitting the 2 sts at beg and end of each row, work even in pattern until piece measures 20" from beg, ending with a right side row. **Next row:** K 2, decreasing 51 sts evenly spaced, p across to within last 2 sts, k 2 (97 sts). Change to No. 1 needles and work in seed st for 11 rows. **Next row (beading row):** K 3, * y o, k 2 tog. Repeat from * to within last 2 sts, k 2. Work in seed st for 6 rows.

SLEEVES: Cast on 29 sts at beg of next 2 rows, working added sts in seed st (155 sts). **Next row (back opening):** Work across 77 sts; attach another ball of yarn and bind off 1 st; work across remaining 77 sts. Work even on both sides at once until piece measures 3" from cast-on sleeve sts. At each sleeve edge, bind off 12 sts 5 times; then bind off remaining 17 sts at each neck edge.

FRONT: Work same as for back, omitting back opening, until sleeves measure 2" from cast-on edges. **To Shape Neck:** Work across 65 sts; attach another ball of yarn and bind off 25 sts for front neck; work across remaining 65 sts. Dec 1 st at neck edge every other row 5 times. Work even until piece measures same as back from cast-on sleeve sts. **To Shape Sleeves and Shoulders:** At each sleeve edge, bind off 12 sts 5 times.

FINISHING: Sew shoulders and top sleeve seams. **Sleeve Beading:** With No. 1 needles pick up 53 sts along wrist edge of sleeve. Work in seed st for 3 rows. **4th row:** Work as for beading row on back. Work in seed st for 3 rows. Bind off. **Neck Edging—1st rnd:** Starting at upper left corner of back with right side facing you, use crochet hook and work around neck edge as follows: Sc in first 2 sts, * ch 3, skip 1 st, sc in next 2 sts. Repeat from * around neck. Do not break off, but continue along right back opening edge as follows: (Ch 6 for button loop, skip 4 rows of knitted edge, sc along edge for ¾") 4 times; sc evenly along left back opening edge. Join with sl st at beg of rnd. Break off.

Sew side and under sleeve seams. Sew buttons in place. Thread ribbon through beading at chest and sleeves.

BONNET

Starting at front edge with No. 1 needles, cast on 100 sts. Work in seed st for 6 rows. **Next row (beading row):** K 2, * y o, k 2 tog. Repeat from * to within last 2 sts, k 2. Change to No. 2 needles and establish lace pattern as for back of robe (4 pattern repeats instead of 6). Work until piece measures 4½" from beg. **Back shaping:** Change to No. 1 needles and work in seed st as follows: **First dec row:** Work 15 sts, * k 2 tog, work 15 sts. Repeat from * across (95 sts). Work 3 rows even. **2nd dec row:** Work 5 sts, k 2 tog, * work 10 sts, k 2 tog. Repeat from * to last 4 sts, work last 4 sts (87 sts). Work 1 row even. **3rd dec row:** Work 4 sts, k 2 tog, * work 9 sts, k 2 tog. Repeat from * to within last 4 sts, work last 4 sts (79 sts). Working in established manner, continue to dec 8 sts every other row (1 st less between decreases on each row) until 31 sts remain. Break off. Thread yarn through needle, draw through sts, pull up and fasten.

FINISHING: With right side facing you and using No. 2 needles, pick up 76 sts along neck edge of bonnet. Work in seed st for 4 rows. **Next row (beading row):** Work as for beading row on bonnet front. Work 4 rows in seed st. Bind off.

Thread ribbon through beading on bonnet front and fasten ends. Thread ribbon through beading on bonnet neck edge, leaving 6" ends for ties.

Child's Cardigan

A cardigan for a child in small white design knit-in against a pink background.

SIZES: Child's 1 [2–3]. Cardigan measures about 10″ [10¾″–11½″] across back at underarm and 7½″ [8″–8½″] from lower edge to underarm.

MATERIALS: Fingering-weight yarn, 3 [3–4] ounces pink heather (color P), 1 ounce white (W); knitting needles, 1 pair each No. 2 and No. 3 (or English needles No. 11 and No. 10) **or the size that will give you the correct gauge;** 6 buttons ½″ in diameter; steel crochet hook size 0 for border.

GAUGE: 15 sts = 2″; 10 rows = 1″.

Note: Carry yarn not in use loosely across back of work.

BACK: Starting at lower edge with No. 2 needles and color P, cast on 72 [78–84] sts. Work in ribbing of k 1, p 1 for 1″, increasing 3 sts evenly spaced across last row.

Change to No. 3 needles and work in pattern st on 75 [81–87] sts as follows:

1st through 4th rows: With P, k 1 row, p 1 row, k 1 row, p 1 row. At end of 4th row drop P; attach W. **5th row (right side):** With W, k 3, * holding yarn in back of work sl 3 sts, k next 3 sts. Repeat from * across. **6th row:** With W, p 3, * holding yarn in front of work sl 3 sts, p next 3 sts. Repeat from * across. Drop W; pick up P. **7th row:** With P, k 1, * holding yarn in back of work sl 1, k next 5 sts. Repeat from * across, ending sl 1, k 1. **8th row:** With P, p 1, * with yarn in front sl 1, p 5. Repeat from * across, ending sl 1, p 1. **9th through 12th rows:** With P, k 1 row, p 1 row, k 1 row, p 1 row. Drop P at end of last row. **13th row:** Keeping W in back of work, sl first 3 sts; * with W, k 3, holding yarn in back of work sl 3 sts. Repeat from * across. **14th row:** Sl first 3 sts; * with W, p 3, holding yarn in front of work sl next 3 sts. Repeat from * across. Drop W; pick up P. **15th row:** With P, k 4, then repeat from * on 7th row, ending sl 1, k 4. **16th row:** With P, p 4, then repeat from * on 8th row, ending sl 1, p 4.

Repeat last 16 rows for pattern until back measures 7½" [8"–8½"] from beg, ending with a wrong-side row.

To Shape Raglan Armholes: Being careful to keep pattern as established, bind off 3 sts at beg of next 2 rows. **3rd row (right side):** With P, k first 2 sts, k 2 tog, then work across in pattern as established to within last 4 sts; with P, sl 1, k 1, psso, k last 2 sts. **4th row:** With P, p 3, work across in pattern as established to within last 3 sts; p 3, using P.

Repeat 3rd and 4th rows 20 [21–22] times more. **Last row:** With P only, work across, decreasing 2 [3–4] sts evenly spaced. Bind off 25 [28–31] sts.

LEFT FRONT: Starting at lower edge with No. 2 needles and P, cast on 38 [38–44] sts. Work in ribbing of k 1, p 1 for 1", increasing 1 st on last row.

Change to No. 3 needles and, working as for back, work even in pattern st on 39 [39–45] sts until piece measures same length as back to underarm, ending with a wrong-side row.

To Shape Raglan Armhole: At beg of next row bind off 3 sts, work to end of row. **2nd row:** Work across in pattern to within last 3 sts; p 3, using P. **3rd row (right side):** With P, k 2, k 2 tog, then work across in pattern as established.

Repeat 2nd and 3rd rows 13 [13–15] times more, ending at front edge (22 [22–26] sts).

To Shape Neck and Armhole—Next row: Bind off 9 [9–11] sts at beg of row, work to end of row. Continue to dec 1 st every other row at armhole edge as before and, **at same time,** dec 1 st at neck edge every other row until 1 st remains. Bind off.

RIGHT FRONT: Work to correspond to left front, working as follows for 3rd row of raglan armhole shaping. **3rd row (right side):** Work across in pattern to within last 4 sts; with P, sl 1, k 1, psso, k 2. Complete to correspond to left front.

SLEEVES: Starting at lower edge with No. 2 needles and P, cast on 38 sts. Work in ribbing of k 1, p 1 for 1", increasing 1 st at end of last row.

Change to No. 3 needles. Work in pattern st as for back and, **at same time,** inc 1 st at beg and end of row every ½" 9 [10–11] times, working inc sts in pattern st. Work even on 57 [59–61] sts until sleeve measures 7½″ [8½″–9½″] from beg, ending with a wrong-side row.

To Shape Raglan Armhole: Work same as for back raglan armhole shaping, but dec 2 sts evenly spaced on last row. Bind off remaining 7 sts.

FINISHING: Sew raglan sleeve seams. Sew side and sleeve seams. **Neckband:** With right side of work facing you, using P and No. 2 needles, pick up and k 70 [72–74] sts around neckline. Work in ribbing of k 1, p 1 for 1″. Bind off loosely in ribbing.

Crocheted Borders: For Left Front—1st row: With right side of work facing you, attach P at top of neckband and crochet 1 row sc evenly along front edge; ch 1, turn. **2nd row:** Sc in each sc across; ch 1, turn. Repeat last row 2 [4–2] times more; omit ch 1 at end of last row. Break off. **For Right Front:** Mark right-front edge for 6 buttonholes. Place first marker about ½″ from lower edge, sixth one about ½″ from end of neckband, the others evenly spaced between. Starting at lower edge, repeat first 2 [4–2] rows of left-front border. **Next row:** Work sc in each sc to first marker, * ch 2, skip 2 sc, sc in each sc to next marker. Repeat from * across front edge; ch 1, turn. **Following row:** Sc in each sc, working 2 sc over ch-2 loop for buttonholes. Break off.

Sew buttons in place.

Garter Stitch Poncho and Bootie Set

Two rectangles sewn together,
with booties to match,
have a finishing touch
of pompons added to both.

PONCHO

SIZES: 6 to 12 months.

MATERIALS: Bucilla Lollipop (100% Dupont Orlon acrylic yarn), 2 (1-oz.) balls; knitting needles, 1 pair No. 10 (or English needles No. 3) **or size that will give you the correct gauge;** steel crochet hook No. 00.

GAUGE: 9 sts = 2"; 4 ridges (8 rows) = 1".

Cast on 44 sts loosely. Work in garter st until you have 60 ridges (2 knit rows make one ridge). Piece measures approximately 10" x 15". Bind off but do not break yarn. Working along side of work, pick up and k 2 sts in each of next 4 ridges, * pick up and k 1 st in each of next 2 ridges, 2 sts in next ridge. Repeat from * 8 times more; pick up 1 st in next ridge (45 sts). This leaves 28 ridges free for neck edge. Work in garter st on the 45 sts until you have 60 ridges. Bind off. Garment should look like Diagram 1. Sew edge A (cast-on edge of first piece) to edge B between dots. Garment should look like Diagram 2.

FINISHING: Using yarn double, crochet a chain 32" long. Run chain in and out sts around neck about ½" from edge for ties. Make two pompons 1" in diameter and sew to ends of chain.

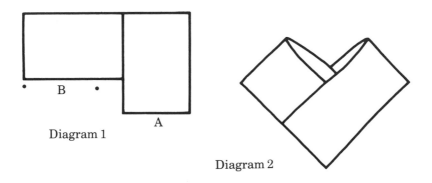

Diagram 1

Diagram 2

BOOTIES

SIZES: 6 to 12 months.

MATERIALS: Bucilla Lollipop, 1 (1-oz.) ball; knitting needles, 1 pair No. 5 (or English needles No. 8) **or the size that will give you the correct gauge;** steel crochet hook No. 00.

GAUGE: 6 sts = 1"; 6 ridges (12 rows) = 1".

LEG: Starting at top edge, cast on 36 sts. Work in garter st until you have 13 ridges (2 knit rows make 1 ridge). **Next row (wrong side):** P across. **Following row (eyelet row):** K 2, * y o, k 2 tog. Repeat from * across. **Next row:** P across. **Following row:** K 12 sts and place these on a holder, k next 12 sts for instep, place last 12 sts on a holder.

INSTEP: Work in garter st on the center 12 sts until you have 11 ridges, ending with a wrong side row. Place these sts on a holder. Break off.

FOOT: With right side facing you, slip 12 sts from a leg holder onto needle. Attach yarn and pick up and k 1 st in each ridge along side of instep (11 sts), k 12 instep sts from holder, pick up and k 1 st in each ridge along other side of instep (11 sts), k 12 sts from other holder with leg sts. **Next row:** K 58 sts. Work in garter st for 6 ridges. **Next row:** K 26 sts, place a marker on needle, k 6 sts, place a marker on needle, k 26. **Following row:** K 1, k 2 tog, k to marker, k 2 tog, k 2, k 2 tog, k to last 3 sts, k 2 tog, k 1 (54 sts). **Next row:** K across. **Following row:** K 1, k 2 tog, k to marker, (k 2 tog) twice; k to last 3 sts, k 2 tog, k 1 (50 sts). Bind off.

FINISHING: Sew back and sole seam. Using yarn double, crochet a chain 16" long. Thread chain through eyelets. Make 2 pompons ¾" in diameter and sew to ends of chain.

Make other bootie in same manner.

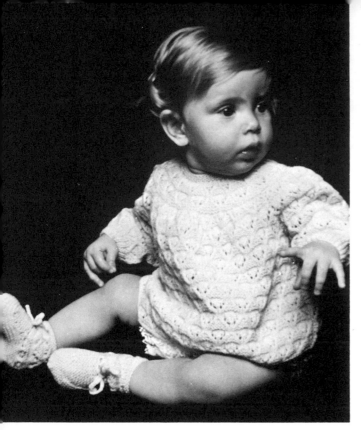

Tailored Top and Dainty Smock Sets

With matching booties and soaker, all in machine-washable nylon and wool baby yarn.

Dainty Smock and Booties

Tailored Top and Soaker

TAILORED TOP AND SOAKER

SIZES: 6 months [1 year].

MATERIALS: Bernat Meadowspun (50% wool, 50% nylon fingering-weight yarn), 5 (1-oz.) skeins horizon blue No. 1162; knitting needles, 1 pair No. 2 [3] (or English No. 11 [10]), **or the size that will give you the correct gauge;** steel crochet hook No. 00; 10 buttons ⅜" in diameter.

GAUGE: 8 [7½] sts = 1"; 13 [12½] rows = 1".

LACY STRIPE PATTERN—Note: Start top with Front directions below and use this 3-stitch pattern as specified. **1st row (right side):** K 3. **2nd row:** P 3. **3rd row:** Y o, sl 1, k 2 tog, psso, y o. **4th row:** P 3. Repeat first through 4th rows for pattern.

TOP—FRONT: Starting at lower edge, cast on 77 sts. Work in ribbing of k 1, p 1 for 8 rows. **Next row (right side):** K 28, place marker on needle, work first row of lacy stripe pattern over next 3 sts, place marker, (k 6, place marker, work first row of lacy stripe pattern over next 3 sts, place marker) twice; k 28. Slipping markers on each row, continue in stockinette st, working 3 lacy stripe patterns as established, until piece measures about 6" [6½"] from beg, ending with a 4th pattern row (wrong side). Place sts on holder.

LEFT BACK: Starting at lower edge, cast on 43 sts. Work in ribbing of k 1, p 1 for 8 rows. **Next row (right side):** (K 1, p 1) 3 times (border), place marker on needle, k remaining 37 sts. Work even in stockinette st, keeping border in ribbing and slipping marker, until piece measures same as front, ending with a 4th pattern row. Place sts on holder.

RIGHT BACK: Starting at lower edge, cast on 43 sts. Work in ribbing of k 1, p 1 for 8 rows. **Next row (right side):** K 37, place marker, (p 1, k 1) 3 times (border). Complete as for left back, working buttonhole in border on 10th row from beg and every following 10th row as follows: **1st row (right side):** K 37, sl marker, p 1, k 1, y o, k 2 tog, p 1, k 1. **2nd row:** P 1, k 1, p 1, k in y o, p 1, k 1, sl marker, p 37.

SLEEVES: Starting at lower edge, cast on 42 sts. Work in ribbing of k 1, p 1 for 8 rows, then p 1 row, increasing 5 sts as evenly spaced as possible (47 sts). **Next row (right side):** K 22, place marker, work first row of lacy stripe pattern over next 3 sts, place marker, k 22. Slipping markers on each row, continue in stockinette st, working 1 lacy stripe pattern as established and increasing 1 st at beg and end of row every ¾" 6 times (59 sts). Then work even until piece measures 7" [7½"] from beg, ending with a 4th pattern row. Place sts on holder.

YOKE: Hold a needle in left hand and, with right sides facing you, slip pieces from holders onto it in the following order, removing markers at the same time: right back, sleeve, front, sleeve, left back (281 sts).

Raglan Shaping—1st row (dec row): (K 1, p 1) 3 times; k 34, k 2 tog, place marker on needle, work first row of lacy stripe pattern over next 3 sts, place marker, sl 1, k 1, psso, work in pattern as established over next 51 sleeve sts; k 2 tog, place marker, work first row of lacy stripe pattern over next 3 sts, place marker, sl 1, k 1, psso, work next 71 sts across front in pattern as established, k 2 tog, place marker, work first row of lacy stripe over next 3 sts, place marker, sl 1, k 1, psso, work in pattern as established over next 51 sleeve sts, k 2 tog, place marker, work first row of lacy stripe pattern over next 3 sts, place marker, sl 1, k 1, psso, k 34, (p 1, k 1) 3 times (273 sts). **2nd row:** (P 1, k 1) 3 times; p to last 6 sts, slipping markers, (k 1, p 1) 3 times. **3rd row (dec row):** (Work to within 2 sts of marker, k 2 tog, sl marker, work lacy stripe pattern over next 3 sts, sl marker, sl 1, k 1, psso) 4 times; work to end (8 sts decreased). Repeat 2nd and 3rd rows 23 times more, then 2nd row again (81 sts); **at same time,** continue working buttonholes every 10th row on right back.

NECKBAND: Work in ribbing of k 1, p 1 for 8 rows, working last buttonhole on 5th ribbing row. Bind off in ribbing.

FINISHING: Sew side and sleeve seams. Sew buttons in place.

SOAKER—BACK: Starting at crotch, cast on 18 sts. Work in stockinette st for 4 rows, casting on 4 sts at end of last row. **5th row:** K 4, sl 1, k 1, psso, k 14, k 2 tog, cast on 4 sts. **6th row:** P 24, cast on 5 sts. **7th row:** K 9, sl 1, k 1, psso, k 12, k 2 tog, k 4; cast on 5 sts. **8th row:** P 32, cast on 5 sts. **9th row:** K 14, sl 1, k 1, psso, k 10, k 2 tog, k 9, cast on 5 sts. **10th row:** P 40, cast on 5 sts. **11th row:** K 19, sl 1, k 1, psso, k 8, k 2 tog, k 14, cast on 5 sts. **12th row:** P 48, cast on 5 sts. **13th row:** K 24, sl 1, k 1, psso, k 6, k 2 tog, k 19, cast on 5 sts. **14th row:** P 56, cast on 5 sts. **15th row:** K 29, sl 1, k 1, psso, k 4, k 2 tog, k 24, cast on 5 sts. **16th row:** P 64, cast on 6 sts. **17th row:** K 70, cast on 6 sts. **18th row:** P 76. **19th row:** K 1, work first row of lacy stripe pattern over next 3 sts, place marker on needle, work in stockinette st over next 68 sts, place marker, work first row of lacy stripe pattern over next 3 sts, k 1. Work even in pattern as established, keeping first and last st of each row in stockinette st, until piece measures 6″ [6½″] from beg.

WAISTBAND: Work 8 rows in ribbing of k 1, p 1. Bind off loosely in ribbing.

FRONT: Work same as back.

FINISHING: Sew side seams. **Cord:** With yarn double, crochet chain 28″ long. Break off. Thread in and out of every 4th p st of ribbing around center of waistband. Knot each end. Tie in bow at front.

LEG BANDS: With right side facing you, pick up and k 75 sts along edge of each leg opening. Work in ribbing of k 1, p 1 for 8 rows. Bind off in ribbing. Sew crotch seam.

DAINTY SMOCK AND BOOTIES

SIZES: 6 months [1 year].

MATERIALS: Bernat Meadowspun (50% wool, 50% nylon, fingering-weight yarn), 4 (1-oz.) skeins orchid No. 1153; knitting needles, 1 pair No. 2 [3] (or English No. 11 [10]), **or the size that will give you the correct gauge;** steel crochet hook No. 00; 2 buttons ⅜" in diameter.

GAUGE: 8 [7½] sts = 1"; 13 [12½] rows = 1".

PATTERN STITCH: Worked on a multiple of 8 sts plus 1 more st. (**Note:** Start smock with Front directions below and use this pattern stitch as specified.) **1st row:** K 2, * p 5, k 3. Repeat from * across, ending last repeat k 2 instead of k 3. **2nd and all even-numbered rows:** P across. **3rd row:** * K 1, y o, sl 1, k 1, psso, p 3, k 2 tog, y o. Repeat from * to last st, k 1. **5th row:** * K 2, y o, sl 1, k 1, psso, p 1, k 2 tog, y o, k 1. Repeat from * to last st, k 1. **7th row:** K across. **9th row:** P 3, * k 3, p 5. Repeat from * across, ending last repeat p 3 instead of p 5. **11th row:** * P 2, k 2 tog, y o, k 1, y o, sl 1, k 1, psso, p 1. Repeat from * to last st, p 1. **13th row:** * P 1, k 2 tog, y o, k 3, y o, sl 1, psso. Repeat from * to last st, p 1. **15th row:** K across. **16th row:** P across. Repeat first row through 16th row for pattern.

SMOCK—FRONT: Starting at lower edge, cast on 97 sts. Work even in pattern until piece measures about 5½" [6"] from beg, ending with a 16th pattern row.

To Shape Underarms: Bind off 2 sts at beg of next 2 rows, then dec 1 st at beg and end of every other row 6 times (81 sts). Work even in pattern for 8 rows more, ending with a 6th pattern row. Place sts on holder.

LEFT BACK: Starting at lower edge, cast on 57 sts. Work even in pattern until piece measures same as front to underarm, ending with a 15th pattern row.

To Shape Underarm: Bind off 2 sts at beg (armhole edge) of next row. Dec 1 st at armhole edge every other row 6 times (49 sts). Work even in pattern for 10 rows more, ending with a 6th pattern row. Place sts on holder.

RIGHT BACK: Work same as for left back until piece measures same as front to underarm, ending with a 16th pattern row.

To Shape Underarm: Bind off 2 sts at beg (armhole edge) of next row. Dec 1 st at armhole edge of every other row 6 times (49 sts). Work even in pattern for 9 rows, ending with a 6th pattern row. Place sts on holder.

SLEEVES: Starting at lower edge, cast on 47 sts. Work in ribbing of k 1, p 1 for ¾", increasing 18 sts as evenly spaced as possible on the last row (65 sts). Work even in pattern until piece measures 6¼" [6¾"] from beg, ending with a 16th pattern row.

To Shape Underarms: Work same as for front. Place remaining 49 sts on holder.

YOKE: Hold a needle in left hand and, with right sides facing you, slip pieces onto it in the following order: right back, sleeve, front, sleeve, left back (277 sts). **Next row (right side):** K across, decreasing 132 sts as evenly spaced as possible (145 sts). K 3 rows even, ending with a wrong side row. Work first through 4th pattern rows. **5th row:** K 2, y o, sl 1, k 1, psso, p 1, k 2 tog, y o, k 1, (k 2, y o, sl 1, k 1, psso, k 3 tog, y o, k 1) 16 times; k 2, y o, sl 1, k 1, psso, p 1, k 2 tog, y o, k 2 (129 sts). **6th row:** P across. **7th row:** K across. **8th row:** P across. **9th row:** P 3, k 3, (p 5, k 2) 16 times; p 5, k 3, p 3. **10th row:** P across. **11th row:** P 2, k 2 tog, y o, k 1, y o, sl 1, k 1, psso, p 1, (p 2, k 2 tog, y o, sl 1, k 1, psso, p 1) 16 times; p 2, k 2 tog, y o, k 1, y o, sl 1, k 1, psso, p 2 (113 sts). **12th row:** P across. **13th row:** P 1, k 2 tog, y o, k 3, y o, sl 1, k 1, psso, (p 1, k 2 tog, y o, k 1, y o, sl 1, k 1, psso) 16 times; p 1, k 2 tog, y o, k 3, y o, sl 1, k 1, psso, p 1 (113 sts). **14th row:** P across. **15th row:** K across. **16th row:** P across. **17th row:** K 12, (k 2 tog) 45 times; k 11 (68 sts). K 6 rows even. Bind off.

FINISHING: Sew side, sleeve, and underarm seams. With right side facing, work 1 row of sc along left back, lower and right back edges. Break off. Starting at upper corner of left back, attach yarn, ch 3 to form buttonloop, skip 2 sc, sc in each sc for 1″, ch 3 to form 2nd buttonloop, skip 2 sc, sc in each sc to lower corner. Break off. Sew buttons along right back edge opposite buttonloops.

BOOTIES—CUFF: Starting at top, cast on 33 sts. K 4 rows, then p 1 row. Work first through 16th rows of pattern once. **Next row:** K across, increasing 2 sts (35 sts). K 3 rows even. **Next row (beading row):** K 1, * y o, k 2 tog. Repeat from * across. K 2 rows.

INSTEP—1st row: K 23, turn. **2nd row:** K 11, turn. Repeat 2nd row 14 times, then dec 1 st at beg and end of every other row twice (7 sts). Place 7 sts on st holder. Break off.

FOOT—1st row: With right side of work facing you, attach yarn at beg of right-hand side of instep. Pick up and k 14 sts along same side of instep, k 7 instep sts, pick up and k 14 sts along left-hand side of instep, k remaining 12 sts from left-hand needle, turn. **2nd row:** K across all sts, including 12 sts on other needle (59 sts). K 14 rows.

SOLE—1st row: K 2 tog, k 25, k 2 tog, k 1, k 2 tog, k 25, k 2 tog (55 sts). **2nd row:** K across. **3rd row:** K 2 tog, k 23, k 2 tog, k 1, k 2 tog, k 23, k 2 tog (51 sts). **4th row:** K across. **5th row:** K 2 tog, k 21, k 2 tog, k 1, k 2 tog, k 21, k 2 tog (47 sts). Bind off.

FINISHING: Sew back and sole seams.

Cord: Crochet chain 16″ long. Sl st in 2nd ch from hook and in each ch across. Break off. Thread through holes in beading row and tie in bow.

Twin Sweater Set

In slip-rib pattern for baby. The pullover has short sleeves and a zipper in the raglan arm seam.

SIZES: Infant's 3 [6–9] months. Garment width around underarms: pullover 19″ [20″–21″]; cardigan 20½″ [21½″–23″].

MATERIALS: Baby or fingering yarn, for pullover: 4 [6–6] ozs.; for cardigan: 6 [6–8] ozs. Knitting needles, 1 pair each No. 2 and No. 3 (or English needles No. 11 and No. 10) **or the size that will give you the correct gauge;** 4″ zipper for pullover and 5 buttons for cardigan.

GAUGE: 15 sts = 2″ (in pattern on No. 3 needles).

PULLOVER

PATTERN—Row 1: K 1, * y o, with yarn in back sl 1 as if to p, k 1, repeat from * across. **Row 2:** K 1, * k next st tog with y o of previous row, y o, with yarn in back sl 1 as if to p, repeat from * across, end k 2 tog, k 1. **Row 3:** K 1, * y o, with yarn in back sl 1 as if to p, k next st tog with y o of previous row, repeat from * across, end y o, sl 1, k 1. Repeat Rows 2 and 3 for pat.

BACK: With No. 2 needles, cast on 73 [77–81] sts. **Row 1:** K 1, * p 1, k 1, repeat from * across. **Row 2:** P 1, * k 1, p 1, repeat from * across. Repeat these 2 rows for ribbing for ¾″. Change to No. 3 needles and pat. Work even until 5″ [5½″–6″] from beg.

To Shape Raglan Armholes: Keeping to pat, bind off 3 sts at each edge once—67 [71–75] sts. Dec 1 st each edge every other row until 25 [27–29] sts remain on needle. Place sts on a holder for back of neck.

FRONT: Work same as back until 35 [37–39] sts remain on needle.

To Shape Neck: Work across 9 sts and place them on a holder, place next 17 [19–21] sts on another holder, join another ball of yarn and work to end of row. Working on last set of sts only, dec 1 st at neck edge every other row; **at the same time,** continue raglan shaping until 1 st remains. Fasten off. Work other side to correspond.

SHORT SLEEVES: With No. 2 needles, cast on 55 [57–59] sts and work in ribbing as on back for ¾". Change to No. 3 needles and pat, inc 1 st each edge on first right-side row—57 [59–61] sts. Work 1 row even.

To Shape Raglan Cap: Keeping to pat, bind off 3 sts at each edge once, then dec 1 st each edge every other row until 9 sts remain. Place sts on a holder.

FINISHING: Steam-press pieces lightly. Sew raglan seams, leaving back left raglan seam open.

Neckband: With No. 2 needles and right side facing, pick up and k 70 [72–74] sts around neck, including sts on holders. Work in k 1, p 1 ribbing for 1½". Bind off loosely in ribbing. Fold neckband double to inside and sew. Sew in zipper in left raglan seam. Sew side and sleeve seams.

CARDIGAN

PATTERN: Same as Pullover.

BACK: With No. 2 needles cast on 73 [77–83] sts. **Row 1:** K 1, * p 1, k 1, repeat from * across. **Row 2:** P 1, * k 1, p 1, repeat from * across. Repeat these 2 rows for ribbing for 1¼". Change to No. 3 needles and pat. Work even until 5½" [6"–6½"] from beg.

To Shape Raglan Armholes: Keeping to pat, bind off 3 sts at each armhole edge once—67 [71–77] sts. Dec 1 st at each armhole edge every other row until 23 [25–27] sts remain. Place remaining sts on a holder for back of neck.

LEFT FRONT: With No. 2 needles, cast on 47 [49–53] sts and work in ribbing as for back for 1¼". Change to No. 3 needles and place 8 sts at front edge on a holder to be worked later. Working remaining sts in pat, work even until 5½" [6"–6½"] from beg.

To Shape Raglan Armhole: Keeping to pat, bind off 3 sts at armhole edge once, then dec 1 st at armhole edge every other row until 22 [23–25] sts remain.

To Shape Neck: Keeping to pat, bind off 7 [8–9] sts at front edge once, then dec 1 st at front edge every other row 6 [6–7] times; **at the same time,** continue raglan shaping until 1 st remains. Fasten off.

190

RIGHT FRONT: Work to correspond to left front, reversing shapings.

SLEEVES: With No. 2 needles, cast on 41 [43–47] sts. Work in ribbing as on back for 1½". Change to No. 3 needles and pat, inc 1 st each edge on first row of pat, then every 5th row until there are 57 [59–63] sts on the needle. Work even until 5½" [6¼"–7¼"] from beg.

To Shape Raglan Cap: Keeping to pat, bind off 3 sts at each edge once, then dec 1 st each edge until 7 sts remain. Place these sts on a holder.

FINISHING: Steam-press pieces lightly. Sew raglan, side, and sleeve seams.

Left Front Border: Work 8 sts from holder in established ribbing, casting on 1 st at end of first row and keeping this st in garter st (k every row) throughout. When border reaches neck edge, bind off the cast-on garter st. Leave remaining sts on needles, or place on a holder, and using garter st as seam allowance, sew front border to front edge of sweater. Mark positions of 4 buttons, evenly spaced, with the first one ½" from lower edge.

Right Front Border: Work to correspond to left front border, making buttonholes opposite markers as follows: Starting at front edge, work across 3 sts, bind off 3 sts, work across; on next row, cast on 3 sts over bound-off sts.

Neckband: With No. 2 needles and right side facing, pick up and k 72 [74–76] sts around neck, including sts on holders. Work with sts from front borders in k 1, p 1 ribbing for 1½", making double buttonhole on right front border on 3rd and 3rd to last rows. Work for 1½". Bind off in ribbing. Fold neckband to inside and sew loosely in place.

Buttonhole stitch around buttonholes. Sew on buttons.

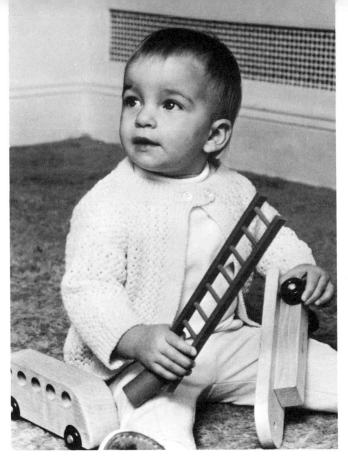

Yellow Jacket

The jacket closes with a two-button tab on a stand-up neckband.

SIZE: 6 to 12 months. Sweater measures 20″ around chest.

MATERIALS: Columbia-Minerva Nantuk fingering yarn (100% Orlon acrylic), 3 (1-oz.) skeins yellow; knitting needles, 1 pair No. 3 (or English needles No. 10) **or the size that will give you the correct gauge;** 2 small buttons.

GAUGE: In pattern stitch: 8 sts = 1″; 12 rows = 1″.

PATTERN STITCH: (Multiple of 6 sts, plus 3). **1st row:** K 3, * y o, sl 1 as if to k, k 2 tog, psso, y o, k 3. Repeat from * across. **2nd row:** Purl. **3rd row:** K 1, k 2 tog, * y o, k 3, y o, sl 1 as if to k, k 2 tog, psso. Repeat from * across to last 6 sts, y o, k 3, y o, k 2 tog, k 1. **4th row:** Purl. Repeat these 4 rows for pattern.

BACK: Starting at lower edge cast on 81 sts. **1st row:** P 1, * k 1, p 1. Repeat from * across. **2nd row (right side):** K 1, * p 1, k 1. Repeat from * across. Repeat these 2 rows for ribbing for 1″, ending with a right side row. P across next row. Change to pattern st and work even until piece measures 7″ from beg. Place a marker at each end of work to mark beg of armholes, then work even in pattern st for 4″ more.

To Shape Shoulders: Bind off 15 sts at beg of next 2 rows. Place remaining 51 sts on a holder.

RIGHT FRONT: Starting at lower edge cast on 41 sts. For ribbed border, repeat first and 2nd rows of back for 1″, ending with a right side

Children's Sweaters

row. **Next row:** P across to last 8 sts, (k 1, p 1) 4 times for front border. Change to pattern st as follows: **1st row:** (K 1, p 1) 4 times for border; then work first row of pattern st. **2nd row:** P across to last 8 sts, (k 1, p 1) 4 times. **3rd row:** (K 1, p 1) 4 times; then work 3rd row of pattern st. **4th row:** Repeat 2nd row. Work even in pattern as established until piece measures 7″ from beg, ending at side edge. Place a marker at this edge to mark beg of armhole, then work even in pattern for 4″ more, ending at marked edge.

To Shape Shoulder: Bind off 15 sts at beg of next row, then work across row. Place remaining 26 sts on a holder.

LEFT FRONT: Work as for right front for 1″, ending with a right side row. **Next row:** (P 1, k 1) 4 times; then p across row. Change to pattern st as follows: **1st row:** Work first row of pattern st across to last 8 sts, (p 1, k 1) 4 times. **2nd row:** (P 1, k 1) 4 times; p across. **3rd row:** Work 3rd row of pattern st across to last 8 sts, (p 1, k 1) 4 times. **4th row:** Repeat 2nd row. Complete as for right front.

SLEEVES: Cast on 51 sts. Work in ribbing as for back for 1″, increasing 6 sts evenly spaced on last row. Change to pattern st and work even on 57 sts until piece measures 7″ from beg, ending with a 4th row of pattern. Bind off all stitches.

FINISHING: Sew shoulder seams. Place bound-off edges of sleeves between markers and sew. Sew underarm and sleeve seams.

Neckband: Starting at left front, slip all sts from holders onto 1 needle (103 sts). Using other needle and yarn, cast on 8 sts; then work in ribbing of k 1, p 1 across 103 sts, casting on 8 sts at end of row (119 sts). Work in ribbing as for back for ½″, ending at right front edge.

Next row: For buttonholes: Work 3 sts, y o, k 2 tog, work 8 sts, y o, k 2 tog; complete row in ribbing. Work even for ½″ more. Bind off in ribbing. Sew on buttons.

Pink Pullover

In this kimono style, with two little pompons at the front neck opening, each sleeve and half the yoke are worked as one, then sewed on.

SIZES: 6 to 12 months [18 to 24 months]. Sweater measures 20″ [22″] around chest.

MATERIALS: Columbia Minerva Nantuk fingering yarn (100% Orlon acrylic), 3 (1-oz.) skeins baby pink; knitting needles, 1 pair No. 3 (or English needles No. 10) **or the size that will give you the correct gauge;** steel crochet hook for finishing only; one small button.

GAUGE: In pattern stitch: 15 sts = 2″; 10 rows = 1″.

Note: Each sleeve and half the yoke are knitted in one piece, then sewed horizontally to front and back. Sweater has one button in back.

PATTERN STITCH: (Multiple of 6 sts, plus 3). **1st row:** P 3, * k 3, p 3. Repeat from * across. **2nd row (right side):** K 3, * p 3, k 3. Repeat from * across. **3rd row:** Repeat first row. **4th row:** K 3, * p 3, y o, sl 1 as if to k, k 2 tog, psso, y o. Repeat from * across to last 6 sts, p 3, k 3. Repeat these 4 rows for pattern.

FRONT: Starting at lower edge, cast on 69 [81] sts. Work even in pattern until piece measures 7″ [7½″] from beg, ending with a 3rd row of pattern. Bind off, knitting the sts.

RIGHT BACK: Starting at lower edge, cast on 41 [47] sts. **1st row:** (P 1, k 1) twice; p 1 (5 sts just worked are for ribbed border), * k 3, p 3. Repeat from * across. **2nd row (right side):** * K 3, p 3. Repeat from * across to last 5 sts, (k 1, p 1) twice; k 1. **3rd row:** Repeat first row. **4th row:** K 3, * p 3, y o, sl 1 as if to k, k 2 tog, psso, y o. Repeat from * across to last 8 sts, p 3, (k 1, p 1) twice; k 1. Repeat these 4 rows until piece measures about 6½" [7"] from beg, ending with 2nd row of pattern.

Next row: Starting at border, p 1, k 1, y o, k 2 tog for buttonhole, p 1, complete row in pattern as established. Work even for 4 rows more. Bind off; ribbing borders and knitting all other sts.

LEFT BACK: Starting at lower edge, cast on 41 [47] sts. **1st row:** * P 3, k 3. Repeat from * across to last 5 sts, (p 1, k 1) twice; p 1. **2nd row (right side):** (K 1, p 1) twice; k 1, * p 3, k 3. Repeat from * across. **3rd row:** Repeat first row. **4th row:** (K 1, p 1) twice; k 1, * p 3, y o, sl 1 as if to k, k 2 tog, psso, y o. Repeat from * across to last 6 sts, then p 3, k 3. Repeat these 4 rows until piece measures 7" [7½"] from beg, ending with a 3rd row of pattern. Bind off, knitting sts.

SLEEVE AND YOKE: Starting at wrist edge of first sleeve, cast on 51 [63] sts. Work even in pattern for 6" [7"]. Place a marker in work at each end of needle to indicate underarm, then continue in pattern for 5" [5½"] more for yoke, ending with 3rd row of pattern. Bind off, knitting sts (neck edge).

Make another piece in same manner for 2nd sleeve and other half of yoke.

FINISHING: Hold yoke-sleeve pieces together, right sides facing and bound-off edges matching. Sew together along bound-off edge for 1" (center front). Sew bound-off edge of sweater front across yoke front from underarm marker on one sleeve to marker on other sleeve. Sew sweater backs across back of yoke in same manner. Sew underarm and sleeve seams. If desired, sew back seam to within 1" of yoke.

Crochet 1 row sc along neck edge, lower edge and sleeves. Sew on button. Make 2 small pompons and sew at center front.

Children's Pullovers

Child's Gold Cable Turtleneck

The center front cable panel and raglan shoulder line are worked on a circular needle for a seamless garment, from the neck down.

SIZES: 4 [6–8–10]. Garment width across back at underarms: 13″ [14″–15″–16″].

MATERIALS: 8 [10–10–12] ounces knitting worsted; knitting needles: For body and sleeves, 1 set 7″ (4) dp needles No. 8 and 16″ circular needle No. 8 (or English needles No. 5), **or the size that will give you the correct gauge;** for ribbing and cable, 1 set (4) 10″ dp needles No. 5 (or English needles No. 8); 11 markers (plastic rings or paper clips).

GAUGE: On No. 8 needles: 5 sts = 1″, 7 rows = 1″.

Start sweater at yoke, which follows directions for center panel pattern.

CENTER PANEL PATTERN: (worked over 18 sts on center front and center back of sweater). **1st row:** P 5, k 8, p 5. **2nd row:** P 4, sl next st on a No. 5 dp needle (or on a toothpick) and hold in back of work, k in back loop of next st, then p st on dp needle (single back cross—sbc—made); k 6, sl next st on dp needle and hold in front of work, p next st, then k in back loop of st on dp needle (single front cross—sfc—made), p 4. **3rd row and all odd-numbered rows:** K the k sts and p the p sts. **4th row:** P 3, sbc, p 1, k 6, p 1, sfc, p 3. **6th row:** P 2, sbc, p 2, sl next 3 sts on dp needle and hold in front of work, k next

3 sts, then k the 3 sts from dp needle (front cross—fc—made), p 2, sfc, p 2. **8th row:** P 1, sbc, p 3, k 6, p 3, sfc, p 1. **10th row:** P 1, sfc, p 3, k 6, p 3, sbc, p 1. **12th row:** P 2, sfc, p 2, fc, p 2, sbc, p 2. **14th row:** P 3, sfc, p 1, k 6, p 1, sbc, p 3. **16th row:** P 4, sfc, k 6, sbc, p 4. Repeat these 16 rows for panel pattern.

YOKE: Starting at neck edge with dp needles No. 8, cast on 76 [80–84–88] sts and divide them on 3 needles. Join, being careful not to twist sts. Work in rnds with same side (right side) facing you on each rnd. **1st rnd:** Starting at back, just before center panel, work first row of center panel pattern across first 18 sts, place marker on needle, k 4 [5–6–7], place marker, k 1 (seam st), place marker, k 10 for sleeve, place marker, k 1 (seam st), place marker, k 4 [5–6–7], place marker, work first row of panel pattern across next 18 sts (center front), place marker, k 4 [5–6–7], place marker, k 1 (seam st), place marker, k 10 for sleeve, place marker, k 1 (seam st), place marker, k remaining 4 sts. **2nd rnd:** Work 2nd row of panel pattern across first 18 sts, sl marker, * k to within 1 st of next marker, k in front and back of next st (1 st inc), sl marker, k 1, sl marker, inc 1 st in next st *. Repeat from * to * once more, k to panel marker, sl marker, work 2nd row of panel pattern across next 18 sts, sl marker. Repeat from * to * twice, k to end (8 sts inc). **3rd rnd:** Slipping markers as you work, p the p sts on center panels and k all other sts.

Repeat last 2 rnds 18 [19–20–21] times more, keeping center panels in pattern (for example, on 4th rnd, work 4th row of panel pattern, on 6th rnd, work 6th row of panel pattern, etc.).

Note: When there are too many sts to handle easily, change to circular needle. End last rnd with 228 [240–252–264] sts.

To Divide Bodice and Sleeves: Work 18 panel sts, sl marker, k to next marker, remove marker, k 1, remove marker, sl next 48 [50–52–54] sts on a holder or piece of yarn for sleeve, cast on 4 sts for underarm, remove marker, k 1, remove marker, k across to next panel marker, sl marker, work 18 panel sts, sl marker, k to next marker, remove marker, k 1, remove marker, sl next 48 [50–52–54] sts on a holder for sleeve, cast on 4 sts for underarm, remove marker, k 1, remove marker, k to end (140 [148–156–164] sts).

Continue to work even, keeping panels in pattern, until piece measures 7½" [8"–8½"–9"] from underarm, or 1½" [1½"–2"–2"] less than desired length. Divide sts on three No. 5 needles. Work in ribbing of k 1, p 1 for 1½" [1½"–2"–2"]. Bind off loosely in ribbing.

SLEEVES: Starting at underarm, divide sts from 1 sleeve holder onto 3 dp needles No. 8. Cast on 2 sts for underarm, k across sleeve sts and cast on 2 sts. K around on 52 [54–56–58] sts for 1". **Next rnd (dec rnd):** K 1, k 2 tog, k around to within last 3 sts, sl 1, k 1, psso, k 1 (2 sts dec).

Repeat dec rnd every inch 6 [6–7–7] times more (38 [40–40–42] sts). K even until sleeve measures 9" [10"–11"–12"] from underarm, or

1½″ [1½″–2″–2″] less than desired length. **Next rnd:** K around, decreasing 4 [4–2–2] sts evenly spaced (34 [36–38–40] sts).

Change to dp needles No. 5 and work in ribbing of k 1, p 1 for 1½″ [1½″–2″–2″]. Bind off loosely in ribbing Work other sleeve in same manner.

TURTLENECK: Starting at center back, pick up 76 [80–84–88] sts around neck edge on three No. 5 needles. Work in ribbing of k 1, p 1 for 4″ [4″–5″–5″]. Bind off loosely in ribbing.

Boy's V-Neck Sweater with Dickey

Boy's V-neck sweater sports green and yellow stripes; a separate dickey tops it off.

SIZES: 6 [8–10]. Sweater measures 12½″ [13½″–14½″] across chest from side seam to side seam.

MATERIALS: Bear Brand Win-knit (100% Dupont Orlon acrylic fiber—knitting worsted weight), 2 (4-oz.) skeins parchment No. 453 (color P), 1 skein each spring green (G) and yellow (Y); 1 pair each No. 5 and No. 8 knitting needles (or English needles No. 8 and No. 5) **or the size that will give you the correct gauge.**

GAUGE: 9 sts = 2″; 11 rows = 2″.

SWEATER

BACK: Starting at lower edge with No. 5 needles and color P, cast on 56 [60–64] sts. Work in ribbing of k 1, p 1 for 1½″. Change to No. 8 needles and k 1 row, then work in stripe pattern as follows:

1st through 3rd rows: With P, p 1 row, k 1 row, p 1 row. Drop P; attach G. **4th row (right side):** With G, * k 1; holding yarn in back of work, sl 1. Repeat from * across. **5th row:** With G, p across. Drop G; attach Y. **6th row:** With Y, * holding yarn in back of work, sl 1, k 1.

Repeat from * across. **7th row:** With Y, p across. Drop Y; pick up P. **8th row:** With P, * k 1; holding yarn in back, sl 1. Repeat from * across.

Repeat last 8 rows for pattern until back measures about 10" [11"–12"] from beg, ending with 3rd row of pattern. Break off G and Y. Continue in stockinette st, working with P only.

To Shape Armholes: Bind off 3 sts at beg of next 2 rows. Dec 1 st at beg and end of every other row 2 [3–4] times. Work even on 46 [48–50] sts until armhole measures 5" [5½"–6"].

To Shape Shoulders: Bind off 5 [6–6] sts at beg of next 2 rows, then 6 sts at beg of next 2 rows. **Last row:** Work across and dec 3 sts evenly spaced. Place remaining 21 [21–23] sts on holder.

FRONT: Work as for back to beg of armhole shaping (56 [60–64] sts).

To Shape Armholes and Neck: Bind off 3 sts at beg of next 2 rows. **To Divide Work—Next row:** Work across first 25 [27–29] sts, place these sts on holder (mark center of work with pin), work to end of row (25 [27–29] sts). Working on one side only, dec 1 st at beg and end of every other row 2 [3–4] times, then continue to dec 1 st at neck edge 10 [9–9] times more. Work even on 11 [12–12] sts, if necessary, until armhole is same length as back armhole to shoulder, ending at armhole edge.

To Shape Shoulder: Bind off 5 [6–6] sts at beg of next row. Work even for 1 row, then bind off 6 sts.

Work other half to correspond.

SLEEVES: Starting at lower edge with No. 5 needles and P, cast on 32 sts. Work in ribbing of k 1, p 1 for 2½"; on last row inc 6 sts evenly across (38 sts).

Change to No. 8 needles and k 1 row, then work even on 38 sts in stripe pattern as for back until 3rd stripe is completed. Break off G and Y. Continue in stockinette st, working with P only; **at same time,** inc 1 st at beg and end of row 1" 3 [4–5] times. Work even on 44 [46–48] sts until sleeve measures 11½" [12½"–13½"] from beg, or desired length to underarm.

To Shape Cap: Bind off 3 sts at beg of next 2 rows. Dec 1 st at beg and end of every other row 8 [9–10] times. Bind off 2 sts at beg of next 6 rows. Bind off remaining 10 sts.

FINISHING—Half of Neckband: With right side of front facing you, using No. 5 needles, attach P at left shoulder. Pick up and k 24 [26–28] sts between shoulder and pin at center of V neck. Work in ribbing of k 1, p 1 for ¾". Bind off loosely in ribbing.

Sew right shoulder seam. Attach P at pin. Pick up and k 24 [26–28] sts between pin and right shoulder seam, then place 21 [21–23] sts from holder onto another needle and k across (45 [47–51] sts). Work as for first half.

Cross both halves of neckband at center front and sew in place.

Sew other shoulder and neckband seams. Sew side and sleeve seams. Sew in sleeves.

DICKEY

FRONT: Use color G and No. 8 needles throughout. Starting at lower edge, cast on 40 sts. K 4 rows. **5th row:** K 2, p across to last 2 sts, k 2. **6th row (right side):** K across. Repeat last 2 rows until piece measures 7" [7½"–8"] from beg.

To Shape Neck: Keeping border as established, work across 12 sts; put these sts on holder. Work center 16 sts; put these sts on another holder. Work to end of row (12 sts). Continue in pattern as established on 12 sts and dec 1 st at neck edge every other row 3 times. Work even on 9 sts for 10 rows more, ending at armhole edge.

To Shape Shoulder: From armhole edge, bind off 4 sts once, then 5 sts.

Work other side to correspond.

BACK: Work as for front until piece measures 4" [4½"–4½"].

To Shape Shoulders: Bind off 4 sts at beg of next 2 rows, then 5 sts at beg of next 2 rows. Place remaining 22 sts on holder.

FINISHING: Sew one shoulder seam.

Turtleneck: Using No. 8 needles, with right side facing you, pick up and k 68 sts (including sts on holders). Work in ribbing of k 1, p 1 for 4" [4½"–4½"]. Bind off loosely in ribbing. Sew other shoulder and neckband seam.

Girl's Pullover and Cap

In this lovely color combination of pink, rose, and apricot, bands of knit-in flowers are separated by striped ribbing.

SIZES: 8 [10–12]. Pullover measures 13″ [14″–15″] across back at underarms, 17″ [17″–17½″] from back of neck to lower edge.

MATERIALS: Bucilla deLuxe knitting worsted, 3 (4-oz.) skeins flamingo pink No. 363 (color A), 1 skein each dusty rose No. 337 (B) and apricot No. 317 (C); knitting needles, 1 pair each No. 4 and No. 5 (or English needles No. 9 and No. 8), 1 set (4) dp needles No. 4 **or the size that will give you the correct gauge;** tapestry needle.

GAUGE: 6 sts = 1″; 7 rows = 1″.

Note: See page 33 for Fair Isle knitting.

PULLOVER

BACK: Starting at lower edge with No. 4 needles and A, cast on 80 [86–92] sts. Work in k 1, p 1 ribbing for 2 rows each of A, B and C. Change to No. 5 needles and with A, working in stockinette st, work even until piece measures 9½″ from beg.

To Shape Armholes: Bind off 3 [4–5] sts at beg of next 2 rows,

204

then dec 1 st at beg and end of every other row 5 [6–7] times. Work even on 64 [66–68] sts until armholes measure 6½″ [6½″–7″].

To Shape Shoulders: Bind off 5 sts at beg of next 4 rows, 5 [6–7] sts at beg of next 2 rows. Place remaining 34 sts on holder for back neck.

FRONT: Starting at lower edge with No. 4 needles and A, cast on 80 [86–92] sts; work ribbing as for back. Change to No. 5 needles. Working in stockinette st, follow Chart 1 from size 8 [10–12] across to Y; repeat from X to Y across 4 times more, ending from size 8 [10–12] to Z. Continue in stockinette st, following chart for design and key for colors. When Chart 1 is completed, * work 2 rows C and 2 rows B in k 1, p 1 ribbing. Work Chart 2 in stockinette st as follows: Work from size 8 [10–12] across to Y; then repeat from X to Y across 9 [9–10] times more, ending from size 8 [10–12] to Z. Complete Chart 2, then work 2 rows B and 2 rows C in k 1, p 1 ribbing. Working in stockinette st, follow Chart 2 once more. * Repeat from * to * for color pattern, and **at same time,** when 4th row of 3rd repeat of Chart 2 is completed, shape armholes. (Piece should measure same as back to armholes).

To Shape Armholes: Work as for back, maintaining established pattern and, **at same time,** when 2nd row of 4th repeat of Chart 2 is completed, shape neck.

To Shape Neck: Continuing in pattern as established, work across first 15 [16–17] sts, place next 34 sts on holder for front neck, attach another ball of yarn and work across remaining 15 [16–17] sts. Working on both sides at once, work even in pattern until armholes measure same as back to shoulders.

To Shape Shoulders: From each arm edge, bind off 5 sts once. Work 1 row even. Repeat last 2 rows once more. Bind off remaining 5 [6–7] sts.

SLEEVES: Starting at lower edge with No. 4 needles and A, cast on 34 [36–38] sts. Work in k 1, p 1 ribbing for 1½″. Change to No. 5 needles and, working in stockinette st, inc 1 st at beg and end of row every ¾″ 13 [15–16] times. Work even on 60 [66–70] sts until piece measures 12½″ [13½″–15″] from beg.

To Shape Cap: Bind off 3 [4–5] sts at beg of next 2 rows, then dec 1 st at beg and end of every other row 13 [14–15] times. Bind off 3 sts at beg of next 6 rows. Bind off remaining 10 [12–12] sts.

FINISHING: Sew shoulder, side and sleeve seams. Sew in sleeves. **Neckband:** Attach A at left neck seam. **1st rnd:** With right side facing you, using No. 4 dp needles, pick up and k sts evenly along left front neck edge, place marker, k 34 sts from front holder, place marker, pick up and k sts evenly along right front neck edge, k 34 sts from back holder. **2nd rnd:** (Work in k 1, p 1 ribbing to within 2 sts of next marker, dec 1 st, slip marker, dec 1 st) twice; complete rnd in ribbing. Maintaining established rib pattern, repeat last rnd 5 times more. Bind off loosely in ribbing.

HAT

Starting at lower edge with No. 4 needles and B, cast on 84 sts. Work in k 1, p 1 ribbing in the following pattern: 2 rows B, 3 rows C, (2 rows each of A, B and C) 3 times. Change to No. 5 needles and, with A, work even in stockinette st until piece measures 6″ from beg.

To Shape Top—1st row: (K 2 tog, k 10) 7 times (77 sts). **2nd row:** P across. **3rd row:** (K 2 tog, k 9) 7 times (70 sts). Continue in this manner decreasing 7 sts every other row 9 times more, working 1 st less between decreases on each dec row (7 sts remain at end of last dec row). P 1 row. Break off, leaving 12″ end. Draw end through sts, pull up firmly and fasten. Use end to sew center back seam.

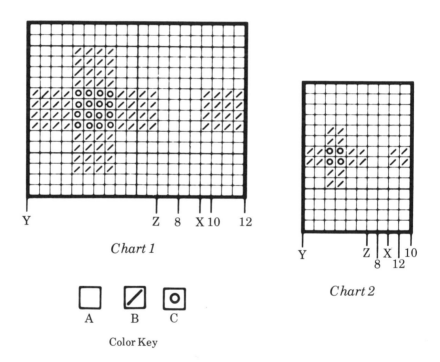

Chart 1

Y   Z   8 X 10   12

Chart 2

Y   Z X 10
              8 12

Color Key

A   B   C

Sungold Sweater

A mock turtle with raglan sleeves, worked in bobble and rib stitches for an outstanding textured pattern.

SIZES: Girls 6 [8–10]. Pullover measures 12″ [13″–14″] across back at underarms, 17″ [17½″–18″] from back of neck to lower edge.

MATERIALS: Spinnerin Germantown Deluxe knitting worsted (100% Orlon acrylic), 3 (4-oz.) skeins sungold No. 3242; knitting needles, 1 pair No. 8 (or English needles No. 7) **or the size that will give you the correct gauge;** 6″ neckline zipper.

GAUGE: 11 sts = 2″; 7 rows = 1″.

BACK: Starting at lower edge, cast on 67 [73–79] sts. Establish popcorn pattern as follows: **1st row (right side):** K 1, * p 2, k 1. Repeat from * across. **2nd row:** P 1, k 2; * for popcorn in next st work k1, y o, k 1, y o and k 1 making 5 sts in one; turn and k these 5 sts, turn and k these 5 sts again (popcorn will be completed on 4th row); k 2, p 1, k 2. Repeat from * to within last 4 sts, work popcorn in next st, k 2, p 1 (11 [12–13] popcorns started). **3rd row:** K 1, p 2, * k 5, p 2, k 1, p 2. Repeat from * to within last 8 sts, k 5, p 2, k 1. **4th row:** P 1, k 2, * to work the 5 popcorn sts tog slip next 5 sts to right-hand needle, then slip the first 4 loops over the 5th loop, slip this remaining st back to left-hand needle and k this st (popcorn completed); k 2, p 1, k 2. Repeat from * to within last 8 sts, work 5 sts tog, k 2, p 1 (11 [12–13] popcorns).

5th row: K 1, * p 2, k 1. Repeat from * across. **6th row:** P 1, k 2, p 1, k 2, * work popcorn in next st, k 2, p 1, k 2. Repeat from * to within last st, p 1. **7th row:** K 1, p 2, k 1, p 2, * k 5, p 2, k 1, p 2. Repeat from * to within last st, k 1. **8th row:** P 1, k 2, p 1, k 2, * work 5 sts tog, k 2, p 1, k 2. Repeat from * to within last st, p 1. Repeat first through 8th rows once more (10 [11–12] popcorns).

Establish rib pattern as follows: **17th row (right side):** K 1, * p 2, k 1. Repeat from * across. **18th row:** P 1, * k 2, p 1. Repeat from * across. Repeat last 2 rows until piece measures 7″ from beg, ending with a wrong side row. Repeat first through 8th rows twice, then repeat 17th and 18th rows until piece measures 11″, or desired length to underarms, ending with a wrong side row.

To Shape Raglan Armholes: Continuing in rib pattern, bind off 3 [4–5] sts at beg of next 2 rows. **3rd row (dec row):** K 1, sl 1 as if to k, k 1, psso, work in pattern to within last 3 sts, k 2 tog, k 1. **4th row:** P 2, work in pattern to within last 2 sts, p 2. Repeat last 2 rows 12 [14–16] times more (35 sts remain). Change to popcorn st pattern as previously established and, **at same time,** continue to dec 8 times more. Slip remaining 19 sts to holder.

FRONT: Work as for back through armhole shaping until 23 sts of popcorn pattern remain.

To Shape Neck—1st row (right side): Continuing in rib pattern as previously established, work 1 st, sl 1, work 1 st, psso, work 3 sts, place next 11 sts on holder for neck, place remaining 6 sts on 2nd holder for neck shaping. **2nd row: (neck edge):** Work 2 sts tog, work 3 sts. **3rd row:** Work 1 st, sl 1, work 2 sts tog, psso. **4th row:** Work 2 sts tog. Bind off remaining st. Attach yarn at neck edge of 6 sts on holder and complete other side of neck shaping to correspond.

SLEEVES: Starting at lower edge, cast on 37 sts. Increasing 1 st at beg and end of row every 1″ [¾″–¾″] 11 [13–15] times, working added sts in pattern, work sleeve as follows: Work as for back for 16 rows. Repeat 17th and 18th rows of rib pattern until piece measures 9″ from beg, ending with a wrong side row. (Completed sleeve will measure 11″. To adjust length, work more or fewer rows of ribbing.) Work first through 8th rows twice more. Work even in rib pattern on 59 [63–67] sts until piece measures same as back from last popcorn st row to underarm.

To Shape Raglan Armholes: Bind off 3 sts at beg of next 2 rows. **3rd row (dec row):** K 1, sl 1 as if to k, k 1, psso, work in pattern to within last 3 sts, k 2 tog, k 1. **4th row:** P 2, work in pattern to within last 2 sts, p 2. Repeat 3rd and 4th rows 12 [14–16] times more (27 sts remain). Change to popcorn st pattern as previously established and, **at same time,** continue to dec as before 8 times more. Place remaining 11 sts on holder for shoulder.

FINISHING: Sew raglan seams, leaving left back seam open about 5″ from neck edge for zipper. **Neckband;** Starting at left back raglan seam, with right side facing you, pick up and k 60 sts along neck edge, including sts from holders. Work in ribbing for 1″. Bind off loosely in ribbing. Sew zipper in place.

Letter Sweater Ensemble

Bold letters lovingly spell Mom and Dad on hat, sweater, and knee warmers in hot pink and scarlet red.

SIZES: 2 [4–6] Sweater measures 11″ [12″–12¾″] across back at underarms and about 13½″ [15″–16″] from back of neck to lower edge.

MATERIALS: Brunswick Windrush Orlon acrylic yarn (knitting-worsted weight), 2 (4-oz.) skeins bright scarlet No. 9025 (color A), 1 skein hot pink No. 9018 (B); knitting needles, 1 pair each No. 6 and No. 8 (or English needles No. 7 and No. 5) **or the sizes that will give you the correct gauge.**

GAUGE: On No. 8 needles, 9 sts = 2″; 13 rows = 2″.

FRONT: Starting at lower edge with No. 6 needles and A, cast on 48 [52–56] sts. Work in k 2, p 2 ribbing for 1″, increasing 2 sts evenly spaced on last row (50 [54–58] sts). Change to No. 8 needles and, working in stockinette st (k 1 row, p 1 row), work even until piece measures 6½″ [7½″–8½″] from beg, or 2½″ less than desired length to underarm, ending with a p row. **Next row:** With A, k 3 [5–7] sts, place marker on needle; following first row of Chart 1 (see page 33 for Fair Isle knitting), k from Y to Z across, place marker on needle and, with A, k 3 [5–7] sts. Slipping markers on each row as you work, continue in stockinette, following Chart 1 between markers and working sts at beg and end of rows with A. Work each right-side row from right to left and each wrong-side row from left to right. When Chart 1 is completed, break off B. With A, work even in stockinette until piece measures 9" [10"–11"] from beg, or desired length to underarms.

To Shape Armholes: Continuing in stockinette, bind off 3 sts at beg of next 2 rows. Dec 1 st at beg and end of every other row 1 [2–3] times. Work even on 42 [44–46] sts until armholes measure 2½" [2¾"–3"] from beg.

To Shape Neck—Next row: Continuing in stockinette, work across first 14 [15–16] sts; place next 14 sts on holder for front neck. Attach another ball of yarn and work across remaining 14 [15–16] sts. Working on both sides at once, at each neck edge dec 1 st every row 5 times. Work even, if necessary, on 9 [10–11] sts on each side until armholes measure 4½" [5"–5¼"].

To Shape Shoulders: From each arm edge, bind off 4 [5–6] sts once. Work 1 row even. Bind off remaining 5 sts.

BACK: Omitting Chart 1, work as for front until armhole shaping is completed. Then work even until armholes measure same as front.

To Shape Shoulders: Bind off 4 [5–6] sts at beg of next 2 rows. Bind off 5 sts at beg of next 2 rows. Place remaining 24 sts on holder for back neck.

NECKBAND: Sew right shoulder seam. Attach A at left front neck edge. With right side facing you, using No. 6 needles, pick up and k 11 [11–13] sts evenly along left front neck edge, k 14 sts from holder, pick up and k 11 [11–13] sts evenly along right front neck edge, k 24 sts from back holder (60 [60–64] sts). Work in k 2, p 2 ribbing for 1". Bind off loosely in ribbing.

SLEEVES: Starting at lower edge with No. 6 needles and A, cast on 28 [32–32] sts. Work in k 2, p 2 ribbing for 1". Change to No. 8 needles and k 1 row, p 1 row. Continue in stockinette st in stripe pattern of 8 rows each B and A and, **at same time,** inc 1 st at beg and end of next row, then every 1½" 5 [5–6] times more. Continuing in established stripe pattern, work even on 40 [44–46] sts until sleeve measures 9½" [10½"–11½"] from beg, or desired length to underarm.

To Shape Cap: Continuing in established stripe pattern, bind off 3 sts at beg of next 2 rows, 2 sts at beg of next 4 rows, then dec 1 st at beg and end of every other row 4 [5–6] times. Bind off 2 sts at beg of next 4 rows. Bind off remaining 10 [12–12] sts.

FINISHING: Sew left shoulder, side and sleeve seams. Sew in sleeves.

CAP

Starting at lower edge with No. 6 needles and B, cast on 76 [80–80] sts. Work in k 2, p 2 ribbing for 1", increasing 2 sts on last row (78

[82–82] sts). Change to No. 8 needles and, starting with a p row, work 3 rows in stockinette. **Next row:** With B, k 17 [19–19] sts, place marker on needle; following Chart 2, k from Y to Z across, place marker on needle and, with B, k 17 [19–19] sts. Continue in stockinette, following Chart 2 between markers and working sts at beg and end of row with B. When chart is completed, starting with a p row, work 3 rows in stockinette, decreasing 0 [4–4] sts evenly spaced on last row (78 sts). Piece should measure about 4″ from beg.

To Shape Top—**1st row:** (K 11, k 2 tog) 6 times (72 sts). **2nd row:** P across. **3rd row:** (K 10, k 2 tog) 6 times (66 sts). Continue in this manner, decreasing 6 sts every other row 10 times more, working 1 st less between decreases on each dec row (6 sts remain at end of last dec row). P 1 row. Break off, leaving 12″ end. Draw end through sts, pull up firmly and fasten. Use end to sew center back seam.

KNEE WARMERS

Starting at lower edge with No. 6 needles and B, cast on 36 sts. Work in k 2, p 2 ribbing for ¾″. Change to No. 8 needles and, starting with a p row, work 3 rows in stockinette st. **Next row:** With B, k 5, place marker on needle; following Chart 1, k from X to Z across, place marker on needle and, with B, k 5. Continue in stockinette, following Chart 1 between markers and working sts at beg and end of row with A. When chart is completed, work 3 rows in stockinette. Change to No. 6 needles and work in ribbing for ¾″. Bind off loosely in ribbing. Break off, leaving 10″ end. Use end to sew center back seam.

Make another knee warmer in same manner, following Chart 2 from X to Z.

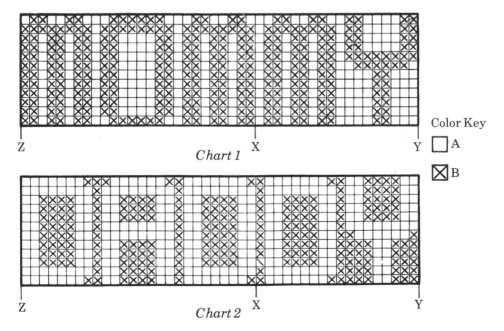

Color Key
☐ A
☒ B

Chart 1
Z   X   Y

Chart 2
Z   X   Y

Little Lambs Ensemble

Little white lambs march in single file on cap, sweater and knee warmers. The lambs are knitted in, yarn ears and felt faces are sewn on.

SIZES: 2 [4–6]. Sweater measures 11″ [12″–12¾″] across back at underarms and about 13½″ [15″–16″] from back of neck to lower edge.

MATERIALS: Brunswick Windrush Orlon acrylic yarn (knitting worsted weight), 2 (4-oz.) skeins medium aqua No. 90392 (color A), 1 skein each shamrock No. 9043 (S) and white No. 9010 (W); knitting needles, 1 pair each No. 6 and No. 8 (or English needles No. 7 and No. 5) **or the sizes that will give you the correct gauge;** scraps of black yarn and pink felt for lambs' faces.

GAUGE: On No. 8 needles, 9 sts = 2″; 13 rows = 2″.

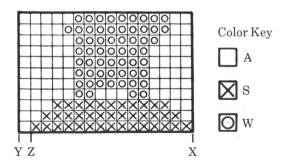

Color Key

☐ A

☒ S

⊡ W

SWEATER

FRONT: Starting at lower edge with No. 6 needles and S, cast on 48 [52–56] sts. Work in k 2, p 2 ribbing for 1″, increasing 1 st on last row (49 [53–57] sts). Change to No. 8 needles and, starting with a k row, work 2 rows in stockinette st (k 1 row, p 1 row). **3rd row:** With S, k 1 [3–5] sts, place marker on needle; following first row of chart (see page 33 for Fair Isle knitting), work from X to Y twice, then from X to Z once; place marker on needle and, with S, k 1 [3–5] sts. Slip markers on each row as you work. Continuing in stockinette, follow chart between markers, working each right side row from X to Y twice and from X to Z once; and each wrong side row from Z to X once and from Y to X twice. Work the 1 [3–5] sts at beg and end of each row with S through 3rd row on chart, and with A for remainder of chart. When chart is completed, break off W. With A, inc 1 st and work even on 50 [54–58] sts in stockinette until piece measures 9″ [10″–11″] from beg.

To Shape Armholes, Neck and Shoulders: Work same as for Letter Sweater, page 209.

BACK: Work same as for front until armhole shaping is completed. Then work even until armholes measure same as front. With A, shape shoulders and work neckband same as for Letter Sweater.

SLEEVES: Starting at lower edge with No. 6 needles and S, cast on 28 [32–32] sts. Work in k 2, p 2 ribbing for 1″, increasing 2 sts on last row (30 [34–34] sts). Change to No. 8 needles and, starting with a k row, work 4 rows in stockinette st. **Next row:** With A, k 7 [9–9] sts, place marker on needle; following chart from 4th row, k from X to Y once, place marker on needle and, with A, k 7 [9–9] sts. Continuing in stockinette st, follow chart between markers, working as for chart for sweater. When chart is completed, with A, inc 1 st at beg and end of next row (32 [36–36] sts), then every 1″ 4 [4–5] times more. Work even on 40 [44–46] sts until sleeve measures 9½″ [10½″–11½″] from beg or desired length to underarm. For cap shaping and finishing, work as for Letter Sweater.

Trimming Lambs: Following photograph, with black yarn, tack small felt circle to head of each lamb. Sew on loop of white yarn for ear.

CAP

Starting at lower edge with No. 6 needles and S, cast on 76 [80–80] sts. Work in k 2, p 2 ribbing for 1″, increasing 3 [1–1] sts on last row (79 [81–81] sts). Change to No. 8 needles and, starting with a k row, work 4 rows in stockinette st. **Next row:** Continuing in stockinette with S, k 8 [9–9] sts, place marker on needle and, following chart, k from X to Y 3 times and from X to Z once; place marker on needle and, with S, k 8 [9–9]. Continuing in stockinette, follow chart between markers and work first and last 7 [9–9] sts with A. When chart is completed, work 2 rows in stockinette, decreasing 1 [3–3] sts on last row (78 sts). Piece should measure about 3½″ from beg. Shape top and complete as for cap matching Letter Sweater. Trim lambs as for sweater.

KNEE WARMERS

Starting at lower edge with No. 6 needles and S, cast on 36 sts. Work in k 2, p 2 ribbing for ¾″. Change to No. 8 needles and work in stockinette for 4 rows, ending with a p row. **Next row:** With A, k 10, place marker on needle; starting with 4th row of chart, k from X to Y once, place marker on needle, with A, k 10. Continuing in stockinette, follow chart between markers and work first and last 10 sts with A. When chart is completed, work ¾″ in stockinette with A; change to No. 6 needles and work in ribbing for ¾″. Bind off loosely in ribbing. Break off, leaving 10″ end. Use end to sew center back seam. Trim lamb as for sweater.

Tree of Life Vest

An enchanting vest for boy or girl alike, in bold, bright colors, worked in stockinette stitch with garter-stitch border and ribbed waistband.

SIZES: 2 [4–6]. Bib area measures 9″ [9½″–10″] across; length is 11½″ [12″–12½″] and is adjustable.

MATERIALS: Knitting worsted, 4 ounces each lime green and sky blue, 1 ounce each dark green and dark brown, a few yards each beige, orange and rust; knitting needles, 1 pair No. 9 (or English needles No. 4) **or the size that will give you the correct gauge.**

GAUGE: 9 sts = 2″; 6 rows = 1″.

Note: See page 35 for bobbin knitting.

BACK: Starting at lower edge with lime green, cast on 52 [56–60] sts. Work in ribbing of k 1, p 1 for 2½″ [3″–3½″]. Bind off 6 [7–8] sts in ribbing at beg of next 2 rows and work remaining sts in ribbing (40 [42–44] sts). Break off green; attach blue. **Next row (wrong side):** K 5 [6–7] sts, p 30, k 5 [6–7]. K 1 row. Repeat last 2 rows until piece measures 8½″ [9″–9½″] from beg, or 3″ less than desired length to shoulder, ending with a right side row. K next 4 [6–8] rows for garter st border.

To Shape Neck and Shoulder Straps—Next row (wrong side): K 8 sts for left shoulder strap, attach another ball of blue and bind off center 24 [26–28] sts for neck, k 8 for right shoulder strap. Working each strap with a separate ball of yarn, k 10 [12–14] rows or desired length. Bind off.

FRONT: Work as for back until ribbing is completed (40 [42–44] sts). Do not break off green. **Next row:** K 5 [6–7] sts, p 30, k 5 [6–7]. Continuing to work 5 [6–7] sts at each edge in garter st as established, work center 30 sts in stockinette st. Follow chart design and attach bobbins as necessary. Work 5 [6–7] garter sts, follow chart from X to Y on k rows and from Y to X on p rows, work 5 [6–7] garter sts. (**Note:** On vest, green was carried tightly across back of brown sts to puff up tree trunk for 3-dimensional effect). Complete chart (work garter st edge with B starting with 13th row). When chart is completed, work with blue until piece measures same as back to garter st border at top. K 4 [6–8] rows. Shape neck and shoulder straps as for back. Bind off.

FINISHING: Sew side seams on ribbing and shoulder seams.

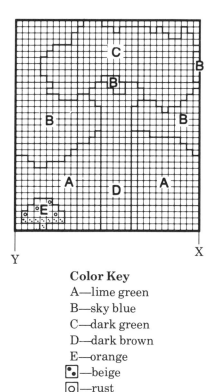

Color Key
A—lime green
B—sky blue
C—dark green
D—dark brown
E—orange
•—beige
○—rust

Children's Buttondowns

Boy's Cardigan and Cap

This charming red, blue, and yellow block-design cardigan and hat are worked in stockinette and slip stitch.

SIZES: 8 [10–12]. Cardigan measures 13″ [14″–15″] across back at underarms, 16½″ [17″–17½″] from back of neck to lower edge.

MATERIALS: Bear Brand Win-Knit (knitting-worsted weight), 2 [3–3] (4-oz.) skeins royale No. 466 (color A), 1 skein each Spanish tile No. 431 (B) and yellow No. 476 (C); knitting needles, 1 pair No. 4 and No. 6 (or English needles No. 9 and No.7) **or the size that will give you the correct gauge;** 4 buttons ½″ in diameter.

GAUGE: 5 sts= 1″; 15 rows = 2″.

CARDIGAN

BACK: Starting at lower edge with No. 4 needles and A, cast on 64 [70–74] sts. Work in k 1, p 1 ribbing for 1½″, increasing 1 [0–1] st on last row (65 [70–75] sts). Change to No. 6 needles and work even in stockinette st until piece measures 11″ [11½″–12″], or desired length to underarm.

To Shape Armholes: Bind off 3 [3–4] sts at beg of next 2 rows. Dec 1 st at beg and end of every other row 3 [4–4] times. Work even on 53 [56–59] sts until armholes measure 5½″ [6″–6½″].

To Shape Shoulders: Bind off 7 [8–8] sts at beg of next 2 rows, 7 [7–8] sts at beg of next 2 rows. Bind off remaining 25 [26–27] sts.

LEFT FRONT: Starting at lower edge with No. 4 needles and A, cast on 32 [34–36] sts. Work in k 1, p 1 ribbing for 1", increasing 1 st on last row (33 [35–37] sts). Change to No. 6 needles. Drop A, attach B and establish pattern as follows: **1st row:** With B, k 1 [2–3], sl 1, (k 5, sl 1) 5 times; k 1 [2–3]. **2nd row:** With B, p 1 [2–3], sl 1, (p 5, sl 1) 5 times; p 1 [2–3]. Repeat first and 2nd rows once more. Drop B, pick up A. **5th row:** With A, k across. **6th row:** With A, p across. Drop A, attach C. **7th row:** With C, k 1 [2–3], sl 1, (k 5, sl 1) 5 times; k 1 [2–3]. **8th row:** With C, p 1 [2–3], sl 1, (p 5, sl 1) 5 times; p 1 [2–3]. Repeat 7th and 8th rows once more. Repeat 5th and 6th rows once. Drop A, pick up B. **13th row:** With B, k 1 [2–3], sl 1, * k 2, sl 1. Repeat from * to within last 1 [2–3] sts, k 1 [2–3]. **14th row:** With B, p 1 [2–3], sl 1, * p 2, sl 1. Repeat from * to within last 1 [2–3] sts, p 1 [2–3]. Repeat 13th and 14th rows once more. Drop B, pick up A. Repeat 5th and 6th rows once. Drop A, pick up C. **19th row:** With C, k 1 [2–3], sl 1, * k 2, sl 1. Repeat from * to within last 1 [2–3] sts, k 1 [2–3]. **20th row:** With C, p 1 [2–3], sl 1, * p 2, sl 1. Repeat from * to within last 1 [2–3] sts, p 1 [2–3]. Repeat 19th and 20th rows once more. Drop C, pick up A. **23rd and 24th rows:** Repeat 5th and 6th rows. Drop A, pick up B.

Repeating first through 24th rows for pattern, work even until piece measures 10" [10½"–11"] or 1" less than desired length to underarm, ending at front edge.

To Shape Neck: Dec 1 st at beg of next row, then dec 1 st at same edge every ½" 12 times more and, **at same time,** when piece measures same as back to underarm, shape armhole as follows, ending with a wrong side row.

To Shape Armhole: Bind off 3 [3–4] sts at beg of next row, then dec 1 st every other row 3 [4–4] times. Work even until armhole measures same as back to shoulder, ending at arm edge.

To Shape Shoulder: Bind off 7 [8–8] sts at beg of next row. Work 1 row even. Bind off remaining 7 [7–8] sts.

RIGHT FRONT: Work to correspond to left front, reversing shapings.

SLEEVES: Starting at lower edge with No. 4 needles and A, cast on 40 sts. Work in k 1, p 1 ribbing for 3". Change to No. 6 needles and, working in stockinette st, inc 1 st at beg and end of row every 1" 5 [7–9] times. Work even on 50 [54–58] sts until sleeve measures 13" [14"–15"], or desired length to underarm.

To Shape Cap: Bind off 3 [3–4] sts at beg of next 2 rows. Dec 1 st at beg and end of every other row 13 [14–15] times. Bind off 2 sts at beg of next 6 rows. Bind off remaining 6 [8–8] sts.

FINISHING: Sew shoulder, side, and sleeve seams. Sew in sleeves.

Front and Neckband: With No. 4 needles and A, cast on 9 sts. **1st row (right side):** K 1, * p 1, k 1. Repeat from * across. **2nd row:** K 2, * p 1, k 1. Repeat from * to within last st, p 1. Repeat these 2 rows until piece is long enough to fit from lower edge, up right front to center of back neck. Mark band for placement of 4 buttons, the first 1″ above lower edge, the 4th at beg of neck shaping, and the others evenly spaced between. Continue in ribbing until piece is long enough to fit around neck and down left front to lower edge, working buttonholes along left front opposite markers on right front, as follows: **1st row (right side):** (K 1, p 1) twice; y o, p 2 tog, k 1, p 1, k 1. **2nd row:** K 2, * p 1, k 1. Repeat from * to within last st, k 1.

Sew band in place. Sew on buttons.

HAT

Starting at lower edge with No. 4 needles and A, cast on 84 sts. Work in k 1, p 1 ribbing for 2½″. Change to No. 6 needles and work in stockinette st until piece measures 5½″ from beg, ending with wrong side row.

Establish pattern as follows: Attach B. **1st row:** With B, * sl 1, k 5. Repeat from * across. **2nd row:** With B, * p 5, sl 1. Repeat from * across. Repeat first and 2nd rows once more. Drop B, pick up A. With A, k 1 row, p 1 row. Attach C. **7th row:** With C, * sl 1, k 5. Repeat from * across. **8th row:** With C, * p 5, sl 1. Repeat from * across. Repeat 7th and 8th rows once more. Drop C, pick up A. With A, k 1 row, p 1 row. Drop A, pick up B. **13th row:** With B, * sl 1, k 2. Repeat from * across. **14th row:** With B, * p 2, sl 1. Repeat from * across. Repeat 13th and 14th rows once more. Break off B and C, pick up A. **15th row:** With A, k across. **16th row:** * P 2 tog. Repeat from * across (42 sts). Repeat 15th and 16th rows once more (21 sts). **19th row:** * K 3 tog. Repeat from * across (7 sts). Break off leaving 30″ end. Thread yarn in tapestry needle. Draw through remaining sts, pull tight, and then sew back seam.

Brightly Colored Cardigan and Watch Cap

A splendid example of Fair Isle knitting, with crocheted borders and buttons, to keep a little one warm in winter.

CARDIGAN

SIZES: 2 [4–6]. Cardigan measures 11″ [12″–13″] across from side seam to side seam and 14½″ [15¼″–16″] long from back neck to lower edge.

MATERIALS: Knitting worsted, 3 ounces turquoise, 2 ounces each white, medium blue and lavender, 1 ounce each yellow, red and royal blue; knitting needles, 1 pair each No. 5 and No. 6 (or English needles No. 8 and No. 7) **or the size that will give you the correct gauge;** steel crochet hook No. 0 for borders and buttons; tapestry needle.

GAUGE: On No. 6 needles: 11 sts = 2″; 5 rows = 1″.

Note: See page 33 for Fair Isle knitting. Be sure to make a swatch to check your gauge and, if you are not familiar with Fair Isle knitting, to practice working with multiple yarns.

BACK: Starting at lower edge above border with No. 6 needles and white, cast on 61 [67–73] sts. K 1 row, p 1 row. Now follow Chart 1 for design. **1st row—Size 2:** K 3 white, attach royal and k 1, (k 5 white, 1 royal) 9 times; k 3 white, **Size 4:** Attach royal and k 1, (k 5 white, 1 royal) 11 times. **Size 6:** K 3 white, attach royal and k 1, (k 5 white, 1 royal) 11 times; k 3 white. **2nd row—Size 2:** P 2 white, (p 1 royal, 1 white, 1 royal, 3 white) 9 times; p 1 royal, 1 white, 1 royal, 2 white. **Size 4:** (P 1 white, 1 royal, 3 white, 1 royal) 11 times, p 1 white. **Size 6:** P 2 white, (p 1 royal, 1 white, 1 royal, 3 white) 11 times; p 1 royal, 1 white, 1 royal, 2 white. Continue in stockinette st and, starting with 3rd row of chart, work each row from 2 [4–6] to Z, then from Y (do not repeat center st) back to 2 [4–6]. Work until first row with * at margin has been completed. To make cardigan longer for sizes 4 and 6, repeat the row with * 0 [1–2] times more, then work next row of chart. Complete chart through 44th row, repeating the * rows as before. (**Note:** This will give you 4 more rows than shown on chart for size 4 and 8 more rows for size 6. Added rows are omitted from chart in order to keep chart uniform for all sizes).

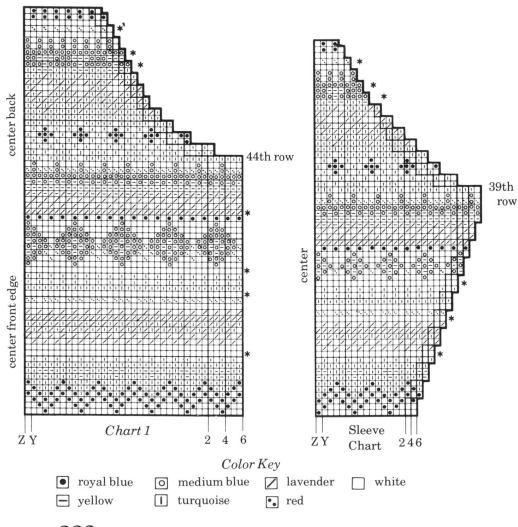

center back

center front edge

Chart 1

Z Y   2 4 6

44th row

center

Sleeve Chart

Z Y   2 4 6

39th row

Color Key

| ⊙ royal blue | ⊙ medium blue | ⊘ lavender | □ white |
| ⊟ yellow | Ⅰ turquoise | ⊡ red | |

To Shape Raglan Armholes: Keeping in pattern, bind off 4 [4–5] sts at beg of next 2 rows. Working extra rows at * rows for sizes 4 and 6 as before, dec as follows: **Size 2:** Bind off 3 sts at beg of next 2 rows, 2 sts at beg of next 4 rows. **Size 4:** Bind off 3 sts at beg of next 4 rows, 2 sts at beg of next 4 rows. **Size 6:** Bind off 4 sts at beg of next 2 rows, 3 sts at beg of next 2 rows, 2 sts at beg of next 4 rows. **All Sizes:** Dec 1 st at beg of every row 18 [16–16] times. With royal, bind off remaining 21 [23–25] sts.

LEFT FRONT: Starting at lower edge with white and No. 6 needles, cast on 31 [34–37] sts. K 1 row, p 1 row. Follow Chart 1 for design, working from 2 [4–6] to Z on k rows and from Z to 2 [4–6] on p rows. Work through 44th row on chart, working extra rows at * rows for sizes 4 and 6 as for back.

To Shape Raglan Armhole: Keeping in pattern, bind off 4 [4–5] sts at beg (armhole edge) of next row. Following chart, dec at armhole edge as shown, working extra rows at * rows for sizes 4 and 6 as before. With royal, bind off remaining 11 [12–13] sts.

RIGHT FRONT: Work as for left front, reversing shaping. Buttonholes will be worked in crocheted border.

SLEEVES: Starting at lower edge with No. 5 needles and white, cast on 24 [26–28] sts. Work in ribbing of k 1, p 1 for 1". K 1 row, increasing 5 sts as evenly spaced as possible across row (29 [31–33] sts). Follow Sleeve Chart, working from 2 [4–6] to Z, then from Y back to 2 [4–6]. Follow chart through 39th row, adding 0 [1–2] extra rows at * rows for a sleeve measuring 9" [9½"–10"] to underarm. For a longer sleeve, add more rows (5 rows = 1"), or for a shorter sleeve add fewer rows. Complete chart, adding rows at * rows at raglan shaping as for back and front. With royal, bind off remaining 7 sts.

FINISHING: Block pieces (see page 37). Sew sleeves in place, matching patterns. Sew side and sleeve seams.

Collar: Attach royal at right front neck edge. **1st row:** With right side facing you and using No. 5 needles, pick up and k 57 [61–65] sts around neck. **2nd row:** P 1, * k 1, p 1. Repeat from * across. **3rd row:** K 1, * p 1, k 1. Repeat from * across. Repeat last 2 rows until collar measures 1¼". Break off royal; attach white and work 1 row. Bind off loosely in ribbing.

Crocheted Border: Attach royal at left front neck edge at collar joining. **1st row:** Working sts evenly spaced and keeping edges smooth and flat, work sc along left front edge, 3 sc in lower corner, sc along lower edge, 3 sc in right lower corner, sc along right front edge to collar, sl st in next st; turn. With pins, mark for 5 buttonholes, evenly spaced, along right front edge for a girl's cardigan or left front edge for a boy's cardigan. **2nd row:** Sl st in first sc, sc in each sc to first pin, (ch 3, skip 3 sc, sc in each sc to next pin) 4 times; ch 3, skip 3 sc, sc in each sc around to last sc, sl st in last sc. Break off. **3rd row:** Attach white in sc at lower right front corner. With right side facing you, sc in each st along front edge, sc evenly along front edge of collar, 2 sc in collar corner, sc evenly across collar edge, 2 sc in corner, sc evenly across other front edge of collar, sc in each st around cardigan; sl st in first st. Break off. With royal work 1 row sc evenly and loosely around each cuff.

Buttons: With royal and crochet hook, ch 4. Join with sl st to form ring. **1st rnd:** Ch 1, work 10 sc in ring. **2nd rnd:** (Sc in next sc, skip next sc) 5 times. Break off, leaving 6″ end. Thread end in tapestry needle and sew up hole in top of button with 2 or 3 sts. Run needle down through center of button and pull thread to other side. Sew button in place. Make 4 more buttons in assorted colors.

WATCH CAP

SIZE: Will fit sizes 2 to 6.

MATERIALS: Knitting worsted, use same colors as for Fair Isle Cardigan, omitting medium blue: 3 ounces white, 1 ounce each royal blue, turquoise, yellow, lavender and red; knitting needles, 1 pair each No. 5 and No. 6 (or English needles No. 8 and No. 7) **or the size that will give you the correct gauge;** tapestry needle.

WATCH CAP

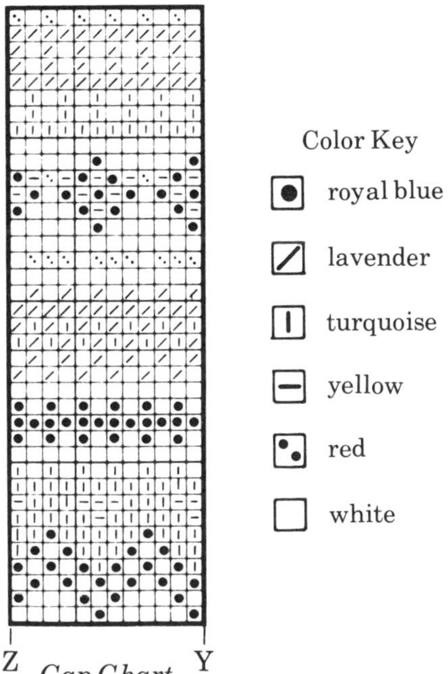

Color Key

●	royal blue
◢	lavender
Ⅰ	turquoise
▬	yellow
•ᵥ	red
☐	white

Z *Cap Chart* Y

GAUGE: 11 sts = 2″, 5 rows = 1″.

Starting at lower edge with white and No. 5 needles, cast on 96 sts. Work in ribbing of k 1, p 1 for 1″ hem. Break off white; attach blue, change to No. 6 needles. Rib 1 row. Attach white and, starting with first row of Cap Chart, work in stockinette st. Repeat from Y to Z across k rows and from Z to Y across p rows. Complete chart, ending with a p row.

To Shape Top: Work with white only. **1st row:** (K 6, k 2 tog) 12 times (84 sts). **2nd row and all even-numbered rows:** P across. **3rd row:** (K 2, k 2 tog) 21 times (63 sts). **5th row:** (K 1, k 2 tog) 21 times (42 sts). **7th row:** K 2 tog across (21 sts). Break off, leaving 18″ end for sewing seam.

FINISHING: Thread end in tapestry needle and run through sts on knitting needle. Remove needle, pull sts tog tightly and fasten. Sew seam, matching pattern bands. Turn hem under and sew in place.

Pompons: Cut 2 cardboard disks 1½″ in diameter. Cut out ¼″ hole in center of both disks. Place disks together and cut slit through disks to center. Using 3 or 4 strands of one color, slip yarn through slit. Wind yarn to cover disks, working around and around, sliding yarn through slit for each wind, until hole is filled. Slip scissor point between disks and cut all strands at outside edge. Without disturbing clipped strands, carefully slide a strand of yarn between disks and wind several times very tightly around center of clipped strands; knot, leaving ends for attaching pompon. Remove disks. Fluff out pompon and trim any uneven edges. Make 2 more pompons in same manner, using 2 other colors. Tie or sew all 3 in a tight bunch to top of cap.

Turquoise Cardigan

This vertical open-work stripe pattern with raglan sleeves is suggested for the more experienced knitter.

SIZE: 18–24 months. Sweater measures 22″ around chest.

MATERIALS: Columbia-Minerva Nantuk fingering yarn (100% Orlon acrylic), 3 (1-oz.) skeins turquoise; knitting needles, 1 pair 14″ No. 4 (or English needles No. 9) **or size that will give you the correct gauge;** steel crochet hook for finishing only; seven ½″ buttons.

GAUGE: In pattern stitch: 8 sts = 1″; 9 rows = 1″.

PATTERN STITCH: (Multiple of 7 sts, plus 2). **1st row:** K 1, * k 2 tog, k 1, (y o, k 1) twice; sl 1 as if to k, k 1, psso. Repeat from * across, ending with k 1. **2nd row and all even-numbered rows:** Purl. Repeat these 2 rows for pattern.

BACK: Starting at lower edge, cast on 79 sts. K 6 rows for border. Work even in pattern until piece measures 7″ from beg, ending with a p row. **Next row:** K 6, y o, k 2 tog. Repeat from * on first row of pattern across to within last 8 sts, k 2 tog, y o, k 6.

To Shape Underarm—Next row: Bind off 6 sts for armhole, p across.

Following row: Bind off 6 sts, k 1, then repeat from * on first row of pattern to last 2 sts, k 2. Break off. Place 67 sts on a holder, being careful not to lose the y o's.

LEFT FRONT: Starting at lower edge, cast on 51 sts. K 6 rows for border. Work pattern as follows: **1st row:** Work across 44 sts in pattern, k last 7 sts. **2nd row:** K 7, p across.

Work even in pattern as established, always knitting 7 sts at front edge, until piece measures 7″, ending with a p row.

To Shape Underarm—Next row: Bind off 6 sts, k 1, then repeat from * on first row of pattern to within last 7 sts, k 7. Break off. Place 45 sts on a holder.

RIGHT FRONT: Starting at lower edge, cast on 51 sts. K 4 rows for border. **Next row:** K 2, k 2 tog, y o (buttonhole made), k across. **Next row:** K across.

Change to pattern as follows: **1st row:** K 7, work across 44 sts in pattern. **2nd row:** P across to within last 7 sts, k 7. Work even in pattern as established, making a buttonhole in front edge every 18th row, until piece measures 7″, ending with a p row.

Next row: K 7, work pattern across to within last 8 sts, k 2 tog, y o, k 6.

To Shape Underarm—Next row: Bind off 6 sts, p across to within last 7 sts, k 7.

Following row: K 7, work in pattern across to last 2 sts, k 2. Break off. Place 45 sts on a holder.

SLEEVES: Starting at lower edge, cast on 58 sts. Work as for back. Break off. Slip 46 sts on a holder. Make another sleeve in same manner.

JOINING: Hold a needle in right hand and slip all 5 pieces from holders onto it in the following order, placing a marker between each piece, being sure that the right side of each piece is facing you: Right front, marker, sleeve, marker, back, marker, sleeve, marker, left front (249 sts). Attach yarn and with wrong side facing you: K 7, p across to within last 7 sts, k 7.

RAGLAN SHAPING: Work as follows and continue to make buttonhole every 18th row. **1st row:** K 7, work across right front in pattern to within 6 sts of first marker, y o, k 4, sl 1, k 1, psso; * sl marker, k 2 tog, k 4, y o, k 1, sl 1, k 1, psso, work in pattern to within 6 sts of next marker, y o, k 4, sl 1, k 1, psso. Repeat from * across back and other sleeve, sl last marker, k 2 tog, k 4, y o, k 1, sl 1, k 1, psso, work in pattern to within last 7 sts, k 7 (241 sts —8 sts decreased). **2nd row and all even-numbered rows:** K 7, p across, slipping all markers to within last 7 sts, k 7. **3rd row:** K 7, work in pattern to within 5 sts of first marker, y o, k 3, sl 1, k 1, psso; * sl marker, k 2 tog, k 3, y o, k 1, sl 1, k 1, psso, work in pattern to within 5 sts of next marker, y o, k 3, k 2 tog. Repeat from * twice more; sl last marker, k 2 tog, k 3, y o, k 1, sl 1, k 1, psso, work in pattern to last 7 sts, k 7. **5th row:** * Work in pattern as established to within 7 sts of marker, k 2 tog, y o, k 3, sl 1, k 1, psso; sl marker, k 2 tog, k 3, y o, sl 1, k 1, psso. Repeat from * across, then work in pattern as established to end of row. **7th row:** * Work in pattern to within 6 sts of marker, k 2 tog, y o, k 2, sl 1, k 1, psso; sl marker, k 2 tog, k 2, y o, k 2 tog. Repeat from * across, then work in pattern to end of row. **9th row:** * Work in pattern to within 5 sts of marker, k 2 tog, y o, k 1, sl 1, k 1, psso; sl marker, k 2 tog, k 1, y o, k 2 tog. Repeat from * across, then work to end of row. **11th row:** * Work in pattern to within 4 sts of marker, k 2, sl 1, k 1, psso; sl marker, k 2 tog, k 2. Repeat from * across, complete row. **13th row:** * Work in pattern to within 3 sts of marker, k 1, sl 1, k 1, psso; sl marker, k 2 tog, k 1. Repeat from * across, complete row. **15th row:** * Work in pattern to within 2 sts of marker, sl 1, k 1, psso; sl marker, k 2 tog. Repeat from * across, complete row. Continue decreasing 8 sts every right-side row 13 times more as follows: Repeat from 2nd row through 15th row once; then repeat from 2nd row through 13th row once. At end of 21st decrease row 81 sts remain. **Next row (wrong side):** K 7, p 2, (p 2 tog, p 7) 7 times; p 2 tog, k 7 (72 sts).

Neckband: K 6 rows. Bind off.

FINISHING: Sew underarm and side seams. Sew buttons in place. Crochet one row sc along each front edge.

Child's Checkerboard Cardigan and Matching Cap

Knit-in patterned squares, with tiny yarn dolls decorating the top of the hat and zipper pull, make up this charming set.

SIZES: 4–6. Cardigan measures 14″ across chest at underarms and about 13½″ from back neck to lower edge.

MATERIALS: Knitting worsted, 8 ounces natural (color N), 4 ounces each red (R), green (G) and royal blue (B); knitting needles, 1 pair each No. 5 and No. 8 (or English needles No. 8 and No. 5), **or the size that will give you the correct gauge;** aluminum crochet hook size E; 14″ separating zipper; 8 bobbins; tapestry needle.

GAUGE: 5 sts = 1″; 7 rows = 1″.

CARDIGAN

CHECKERBOARD PATTERN: Each square is 9 sts wide by 11 rows deep and measures about 1¾″ wide. Color N squares are worked in seed st as follows: **1st row (right side):** K across. **2nd row:** K 1, (p 1, k 1) 4 times. Repeat 2nd row 8 times more. **11th row:** K across. The red snowman (R), green tree (G) and blue snowflake (B) squares are worked in stockinette st, following charts R, G and B from X to Y on each row. Wrap about 7 feet of R, G or B around bobbin for each square. Carry N in back when working these squares, twisting N with colored yarn every 2 sts.

Children's Buttondowns

229

BACK: Starting at lower edge with No. 5 needles and N, cast on 72 sts. Work in ribbing of k 1, p 1 for 1½". Change to No. 8 needles and establish checkerboard pattern as follows: **1st row:** (K 9 R, 9 N, 9 B, 9N) twice. Following Back Chart for placement of squares, work even until 4½ rows of pattern squares have been completed.

To Shape Armholes: Bind off 5 sts at beg of next 2 rows, then dec 1 st at beg and end of every other row 4 times (54 sts). Work even until 7 rows of pattern squares have been completed from lower edge.

To Shape Shoulders: Bind off 9 sts at beg of next 4 rows. Place remaining 18 sts on holder for back neck. Break off.

LEFT FRONT: Starting at lower edge, cast on 36 sts. Work as for back, following half of Back Chart (marked Left Front) until piece measures same as back to underarm, ending at side edge.

To Shape Armhole: Bind off 5 sts at beg of next row, then dec 1 st at side edge every other row 4 times (27 sts). Work even until 6 rows of pattern squares have been completed, ending at front edge.

To Shape Neck: Bind off 5 sts at beg of next row, then dec 1 st at neck edge every other row 4 times (18 sts). Work even until piece measures same as back to shoulder, ending at armhole edge.

To Shape Shoulder: Bind off 9 sts at beg of next row. Work 1 row even. Bind off remaining 9 sts.

RIGHT FRONT: Work as for left front, following half of chart marked Right Front and reversing all shapings.

SLEEVES: Starting at lower edge with No. 5 needles and N, cast on 36 sts. Work in ribbing of k 1, p 1 for 1½". Change to No. 8 needles and, following Sleeve Chart, inc 1 st at beg and end of every 4th row 9 times (54 sts). Work even until 6 rows of pattern squares have been completed from beg.

To Shape Cap: Bind off 3 sts at beg of next 2 rows, then dec 1 st at beg and end of every other row 5 times. Bind off remaining 38 sts.

FINISHING: Sew shoulder seams.

Neckband: With N and No. 5 needles, pick up and k 21 sts along right neck edge, k 18 sts from holder, pick up and k 21 sts along left neck edge (60 sts). Work in ribbing of k 1, p 1 for 6 rows. K next row on wrong side to form turning ridge. Work 6 more rows in ribbing. Bind off loosely.

Sew side and sleeve seams. Sew in sleeves. Crochet 2 rows of N sc evenly along each front edge. Sew in zipper. Turn neck ribbing to inside along turning ridge and sew in place.

YARN-DOLL ZIPPER PULL: Cut a piece of cardboard 3" long. Wind N around cardboard 30 times. Draw a strand of N under loops at one end and tie knot to form top of head. Break off, leaving 4" end to tie to zipper tab. Slip yarn off cardboard. Wind strand of B around loops ¾" from top to form neck. Cut a 2" piece of cardboard and wind N around it 15 times. Slip strand off board and insert crosswise through middle of body strands to form arms. Secure by tying R around body strands below arms to form waist. Divide body strands in half to form legs. Tie strand of B around each leg ¾" from waist. Tie strand of G around each arm ½" from body. Trim ends to form pompon hands and feet. Embroider B eyes and R mouth with straight sts as shown. Tie to zipper tab.

CAP

Starting at lower edge with No. 5 needles and N, cast on 72 sts. Work in ribbing of k 1, p 1 for 10 rows. Change to No. 8 needles. Work as for back, following Sleeve Chart until 3 rows of squares have been completed. Change to No. 5 needles and, with N only, work in k 1, p 1 ribbing for 6 rows.

To Shape Top—1st dec row: * K 2 tog. Repeat from * across (36 sts). Work 5 rows even in stockinette st. **2nd dec row:** Repeat first dec row (18 sts). **Next row:** P across. Cut 30" end, thread in tapestry needle. Run yarn through remaining sts, pull tight and fasten; then sew center back seam.

DOLL POMPON: Make a doll like zipper-pull doll on jacket with 4½"-long 40-strand body and 3"-long 20-strand arms. Do not make legs but cut loops at bottom to form skirt. Sew doll at waist to top of cap. Fasten R, G and B bow to top of doll's head.

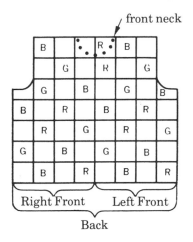

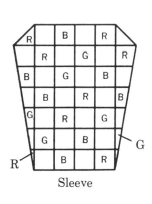

Sleeve

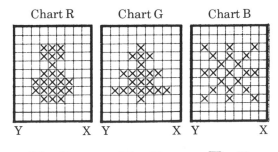

Daughter's Embroidered Cardigan

The little girl's version of Mother's cardigan on page 126 will delight a child for many a season.

SIZES: Child's 6 [8–10–12–14–16]. Garment width around underarms, about 25″ [27″–28″–30″–32½″–35″].

MATERIALS: Sport yarn, 7 [9–9–11–13–13] ozs. Knitting needles No. 4 and No. 6, **or the size that will give you the correct gauge.** 6 buttons.

GAUGE: 5 sts =1″; 7 rows = 1″.

BEAD STITCH: Y o, sl 1, y o; turn, k the sl st and 2 y o's, inserting needle in back loop of the y o's and being careful not to lose a y o when turning; turn, k 3 tog.

PATTERN—Row 1: (right side): * Bead st, k 11, repeat from * across. **Row 2 and all even rows:** Purl. **Row 3:** * K 1, bead st, k 9, bead st, repeat from * across. **Row 5:** * K 2, bead st, k 7, bead st, k 1, repeat from * across. **Row 7:** * K 3, bead st, k 5, bead st, k 2, repeat from * across. **Row 9:** * K 4, bead st, k 3, bead st, k 3, repeat from * across. **Row 11:** * K 5, bead st, k 1, bead st, k 4, repeat from * across. **Row 13:** * K 6, bead st, k 5, repeat from * across. **Row 15:** * K 5, bead st, k 1, bead st, k 4, repeat from * across. **Row 17:** * K 4, bead st, k 3, bead st, k 3, repeat from * across. **Row 19:** * K 3, bead st, k 5, bead st, k 2, repeat from * across. **Row 21:** * K 2, bead st, k 7, bead st, k 1, repeat from * across. **Row 23:** * K 1, bead st, k 9, bead st, repeat from * across. **Row 24:** Purl. Repeat these 24 rows for pat.

BACK: With No. 4 needles, cast on 62 [68–72–78–82–88] sts. Work in k 1, p 1 ribbing for 1½″, inc 1 st each edge of last row—64 [70–74–80–84–90] sts. Change to No. 6 needles. Work in stockinette st (k on right side, p on wrong side), keeping first and last 2 sts (edge sts) in k throughout. Work until 8¾″ [10″–11″–12″–13½″–14½″] from beg or desired length to underarm.

To Shape Armholes: At each armhole edge, bind off 6 sts once, 3 sts once, 2 sts once, 1 st once—40 [46–50–56–60–66] sts. Work even until 4″ [4½″–4¾″–5¼″–5½″–6″] above beg of armhole.

To Shape Neck: Work 12 [14–16–19–20–22] sts, join another ball of yarn and bind off center 16 [18–18–18–20–22] sts, finish row. Working both sides at once, bind off at beg of each neck edge 3 sts once—9 [11–13–16–17–19] sts each side. Work until 4½″ [4¾″–5¼″–5½″–6″–6¼″] above beg of armhole shaping.

To Shape Shoulders: At each armhole edge bind off 4 [5–5–6–5–7] sts once, then 5 [6–4–5–6–6] sts 1 [1–2–2–2–2] times.

RIGHT FRONT: With No. 4 needles, cast on 30 [32–34–38–42–44] sts. Work in k 1, p 1 ribbing for 1½″, inc 1 st at side edge on last row—31 [33–35–39–43–45] sts. Change to No. 6 needles. **Row 1 (right side):** K 1 (edge st), work next 24 [24–24–36–36–36] sts in pat, then work first 4 [6–8–0–4–6] sts of pat on next 4 [6–8–0–4–6] sts, end k 2. **Row 2:** K 2, p to last st, k 1. Continue working 1 st at front edge and 2 sts at side edge in k throughout remaining sts in pat. Work until same length as back to underarm.

To Shape Armhole: Keeping to pat, bind off at armhole edge 6 sts once, 3 sts once, 2 sts once, 1 st once—19 [21–23–27–31–33] sts. Work until 2¼″ [2¾″–3¼″–3½″–3¾″–4″] above beg of armhole.

To Shape Neck: Bind off at front edge 5 [5–5–6–7–7] sts once, 1 st 5 [5–5–5–7–7] times—9 [11–13–16–17–19] sts. Work until 4½″ [4¾″–5¼″–5½″–6″–6¼″] above beg of armhole shaping.

To Shape Shoulder: Bind off at armhole edge 4 [5–5–6–5–7] sts once, then 5 [6–4–5–6–6] sts 1 [1–2–2–2–2] times.

LEFT FRONT: Work to correspond to right front, reversing shaping and pat.

SLEEVES: With No. 4 needles, cast on 34 [38–42–44–46–48] sts. Work in k 1, p 1 ribbing for 1½″, inc 1 st each edge of last row—36 [40–44–46–48–50] sts. Change to No. 6 needles. Work in stockinette st keeping first and last edge sts in k throughout. Inc 1 st each side after first and before last edge st every 8th row 5 [5–6–7–8–8] times—46 [50–56–60–64–66] sts. Work even until 8¾″ [11″–12¼″–13¾″–15″–16″] from beg or desired length to underarm.

To Shape Cap: At each edge, bind off 4 [5–5–6–6–7] sts once, 2 [2–2–3–3–3] sts once, 1 [1–0–2–2–2] sts once. Bind off 1 st at beg of next 8 [10–14–14–16–16] rows—24 [24–24–24–26–26] sts. Bind off 2 sts at beg of next 6 rows—12 [12–12–12–14–14] sts. Bind off.

FINISHING—Left Front Band: With right side facing, using No. 4 needles, pick up and k 1 st in every 3 out of 4 rows on left front. Work in k 1, p 1 ribbing for 5 rows. Bind off loosely in ribbing. Mark position of 6 buttons evenly spaced with the first one ½″ above lower edge, last one to be made in neckband.

Right Front Band: Work same as left front, making buttonholes on Rows 2 and 3 of ribbing opposite markers, as follows: * Work in established ribbing to next marker, bind off next 2 sts; repeat from * across all markers, finish row. On next row, cast on 2 sts over each of bound-off sts. Sew shoulder, side and sleeve seams. Sew in sleeves.

Neckband: With right side facing, using No. 4 needles, pick up and k about 74 [76–78–80–82–84] sts around neck edge including front bands. Work in k 1, p 1 ribbing for 5 rows, working last buttonhole on Rows 2 and 3. Sew on buttons.

Embroidery: Embroider squares using A for squares next to front edge, B for next square, C for next square, then repeat from A again. Embroider 4 French knots in each as shown.

MEN'S SWEATERS

Men's Pullovers

Teal Turtle

This sweater, with dropped shoulders, is patterned with stripes and triangles using knit and purl stitches in an ingenious combination.

SIZES: Small (36–38) [medium (40–42)—large (44–46)].

MATERIALS: Bucilla deLuxe knitting worsted (100% wool), 8 (4-oz.) skeins turquoise No. 312; knitting needles, 1 pair each No. 6 [7–9] and No. 2 (or English needles No. 7 [6–4] and No. 11), 1 set (4) dp needles No. 2, **or the size that will give you the correct gauge.**

GAUGE: With No. 6 needles: 6 sts = 1"; No. 7 needles: 11 sts= 2"; No. 9 needles: 5 sts = 1".

Pattern Stitch for body (multiple of 17 sts)—1st row: * K 1, p 10, (k 1, p 1) 3 times. Repeat from * across. **2nd row (right side):** * K 3, p 1, k 11, p 2. Repeat from * across. **3rd row:** * K 3, p 8, (k 1, p 1) 3 times. Repeat from * across. **4th row:** * K 3, p 1, k 9, p 4. Repeat from * across. **5th row:** * K 5, p 6, (k 1, p 1) 3 times. Repeat from * across. **6th row:** * K 3, p 1, k 7, p 6. Repeat from * across. **7th row:** * K 7, p 4, (k 1, p 1) 3 times. Repeat from * across. **8th row:** * K 3, p 1, k 5, p 8. Repeat from * across. **9th row:** * K 9, p 2, (k 1, p 1) 3 times. Repeat from * across. **10th row:** * K 3, p 1, k 3, p 10. Repeat from * across. Repeat these 10 rows for pattern.

238

Pattern Stitch for waistband and cuffs (multiple of 4 sts)—1st row (right side): * K 2, p 2. Repeat from * across. **2nd row:** * K 2, p 2. Repeat from * across. **3rd row:** K across. **4th row:** P across. Repeat these 4 rows for pattern.

BACK: Starting at lower edge with No. 2 needles, cast on 116 sts. Work in cuff pattern for 3", increasing 3 sts on last pattern row (119 sts). Change to No. 6 [7–9] needles and work in body pattern until piece measures 26" or desired length from beg to shoulder, ending with a 10th pattern row.

To Shape Shoulders: Bind off 35 sts, k 49 sts and place on holder, bind off remaining 35 sts.

FRONT: Work same as back.

SLEEVES: Starting at lower edge with No. 2 needles, cast on 48 sts. Work cuff pattern for 3", increasing 3 sts evenly spaced across last row (51 sts). Change to No. 6 [7–9] needles and work pattern as for back, increasing 1 st at beg and end of every 4th row 28 times, working added sts in pattern, until there are 107 sts. Work even until sleeve measures 19½" or desired length from beg, ending with a 10th pattern row. Bind off.

FINISHING: Sew shoulder seams. Sew sleeves in place. Sew side and sleeve seams.

Collar: Slip sts from holders and divide on 3 dp needles. With wrong side of work facing you, attach yarn and work in rnds as follows: K 1 rnd, p 1 rnd, increasing 2 sts (100 sts). **1st and 2nd rnds:** * K 2, p 2. Repeat from * around. **3rd rnd:** P around. **4th rnd:** K around. Repeat last 4 rnds until collar measures 5½". Bind off loosely.

Traditional V-Neck Sweater

A traditional sweater, with raglan sleeves for a comfortable shoulder line, is worked in stockinette stitch from the neck down without side seams. It has a contrasting neckband, cuffs, and ribbing.

Sizes: 40 [42–44]. Garment width across back at underarms: 21" [22"–23"].

MATERIALS: Knitting worsted, 13 [14–15] ounces green (color A), 2 ounces each apricot (B), natural heather (C) and tan (D); knitting needles: for body and sleeves, 24" circular needle No. 9 and 1 set (4) dp needles No. 9 (or English needles No. 4), **or the size that will give you the correct gauge;** for ribbing, 1 set (4) dp needles No. 7 (or English needles No. 6); 8 markers (plastic rings or paper clips).

GAUGE: 9 sts = 2"; 4 rows = 1".

YOKE: Starting at neck edge with circular needle, cast on 50 sts. Do not join, but work back and forth as follows: **1st row (wrong side):** P 1, place marker on needle, p 1 (seam st), place marker, p 7 for sleeve, place marker, p 1 (seam st), place marker, p 30 for back, place marker, p 1 (seam st), place marker, p 7 for sleeve, place marker, p 1 (seam st), place marker, p 1. **2nd row:** K in front and back of first st (1 st inc), * sl marker, k 1, sl marker, inc 1 st in next st, k to within 1 st of next marker, inc in next st. Repeat from * twice more; sl marker, k 1, sl marker, inc in last st (8 sts inc—58 sts). **3rd row and all odd-numbered rows:** P across, slipping markers. **4th row:** Inc in first st, then inc in next st, sl marker, * k 1, sl marker, inc in next st, k to within 1 st of next marker, inc in next st, sl marker. Repeat from * twice more; k 1, sl marker, inc in each of last 2 sts (10 sts inc, at seams and at neck edges). **6th row:** K to within 1 st of first marker, inc in next st, * sl marker, k 1, sl marker, inc in next st, k to within 1 st of next marker, inc in next st. Repeat from * twice more; sl marker, k 1, sl marker, inc in next st, k to end (8 sts inc, at seams only). **8th row:** Inc in first st, k to within 1 st of first marker, inc in next st, * sl marker, k 1, sl marker, inc in next st, k to within 1 st of next marker, inc in next st. Repeat from * twice more; sl marker, k 1, sl marker, inc in next st, k to last st, inc in last st (10 sts inc, at seams and at neck edges). Repeat 6th row through 9th row 12 times more (302 sts); then repeat 6th and 7th rows once more (310 sts; neck increases completed). Continue by working in rnds with same side (right side) facing you on each rnd. **First rnd:** K to within 1 st of first marker, inc in next st, * sl marker, k 1, sl marker, inc in next st, k to within 1 st of next marker, inc in next st. Repeat from * twice more; sl marker, k 1, sl marker, inc in next st, k to end of rnd (8 sts inc). **2nd rnd:** K around, slipping markers. Repeat last 2 rnds 0 [1–2] times more (318 [326–334] sts).

To Divide Bodice and Sleeves: Removing markers as you work, k 45 [46–47] sts for left front, slip next 69 [71–73] sts on a holder or piece of yarn for sleeve, cast on 4 [5–6] sts for underarm, k 90 [92–94] sts for back, slip next 69 [71–73] sts on a holder for sleeve, cast on 4 [5–6] sts for underarm, k remaining 45 [46–47] sts for right front (188 [194–200] sts). K even in rounds until piece measures 13″ [13½″–13½″] from underarm, or 3″ less than desired length. Break off.

Ribbing: Change to No. 7 dp needles, dividing sts evenly on 3 needles. Work in ribbing of k 1, p 1 as follows, but always k first rnd of each color change: Work 6 rnds B, 5 C, 5 D and 6 B. Bind off loosely in ribbing.

SLEEVES: Starting at underarm, divide sts from a sleeve holder onto 3 dp needles No. 9 and cast on 2 [2–3] sts for underarms; k 69 [71–73], cast on 2 [2–3] sts (73 [75–79] sts). Mark beg of rnds. K even in rnds for 4″. **Next rnd (dec rnd):** K 1, k 2 tog, k around to within last 3 sts, sl 1, k 1, psso, k 1 (2 sts dec). Repeat dec rnd every 1″ 10 times more (51 [53–57] sts). Work even until sleeve measures 14½″ [14½″–15″] from underarm, or 3″ less than desired length. Break off.

Ribbing: Change to No. 7 dp needles and work as for waist ribbing. Work other sleeve in same manner.

FINISHING—Neckband: With right side of work facing you and using dp needles No. 7, starting at shoulder, pick up 48 sts across left front neck edge, place marker on needle, pick up 1 st in center of V, place marker, pick up 48 sts across right front, pick up 8 sts across sleeve, 30 sts across back neck and 8 sts across sleeve (143 sts). Attach B and k 1 rnd even. Keeping center st between markers as k 1 and decreasing 1 st on each side of center st every other rnd, work in ribbing of k 1, p 1 for 2 rnds. Break off. Continuing to dec as before, work 2 rnds each C, D and A. Bind off in ribbing.

Wide-Rib Sweater

The wide ribs are intersected by horizontal colorful bands, which are worked in bobbin knitting.

SIZE: Fits 36"–38" chest. Garment measures 20" across chest at underarms, stretching ribs slightly.

MATERIALS: Bucilla deLuxe knitting worsted, 5 (4 oz.) skeins russet brown No. 380 (color A), 1 skein each cocoa No. 367 (B), tobacco gold No. 391 (C) and copper No. 330 (D); knitting needles, 1 pair each No. 6 and No. 8 (or English needles No. 7 and No. 5), 1 set (4) double-pointed needles No. 6, **or the size that will give you the correct gauge;** 17 bobbins.

GAUGE: 5 sts = 1"; 7 rows = 1".

Note: When changing colors, twist yarns by bringing new color under yarn you have been working to avoid holes in work. Attach another bobbin for each color change. *Never* carry any color yarn across back of work. See page 35 for bobbin knitting.

BACK: Starting at lower edge with No. 6 needles and A, cast on 124 sts. Work in ribbing of k 1, p 1 for 1½". P next row, decreasing 12 sts evenly spaced (112 sts). Change to No. 8 needles and pattern as follows: Wind 9 bobbins with A, 8 with B. **1st row (right side):** K 3 A, (p 8 B, k 6 A) 7 times; p 8 B, k 3 A. **2nd row:** P 3 A, (k 8 B, p 6 A) 7 times; k 8 B, p 3 A. Repeat last 2 rows twice more. Break off B. **7th row:** With A only, k 3, (p 8, k 6) 7 times; p 8, k 3. **8th row:** P 3, (k 8, p 6) 7 times; k 8, p 3. Repeat last 2 rows 4 times more; wind 8 bobbins with C. Repeat first 6 rows, substituting C for B. **23rd–32nd rows:** Repeat 7th through 16th rows. Wind 8 bobbins with D. Repeat first 6 rows, substituting D for B. **39th–48th rows:** Repeat 7th through 16th rows. Repeating first through 48th rows for pattern, work even until piece measures 17″ from beg, or desired length to underarms.

To Shape Armholes: Bind off 6 sts at beg of next 2 rows. Dec 1 st at beg and end of every other row 5 times (90 sts). Work even until armholes measure 8½″.

To Shape Shoulders: Bind off 9 sts at beg of next 6 rows. Place remaining 36 sts on holder for back neck.

FRONT: Work as for back until armholes measure 5½″.

To Shape Neck: Work across first 34 sts. Turn. Bind off 2 sts at beg of next row (neck edge), work across. Dec 1 st at neck edge every other row 5 times (27 sts). Work even until armhole measures same as back armholes, ending at armhole edge.

To Shape Shoulders: Bind off 9 sts at beg of next row. Work 1 row even. Repeat last 2 rows once more. Bind off remaining 9 sts. Place center 22 sts on holder for front neck. Attach yarn to next st and work other side to correspond, reversing all shaping.

SLEEVES: Starting at lower edge with No. 6 needles and A, cast on 48 sts. Work in ribbing of k 1, p 1 for 2½″. P next row, increasing 14 sts evenly spaced (62 sts). Change to No. 8 and pattern as follows: Wind 5 bobbins A, 4 B. **1st row:** K 6 A, (p 8 B, k 6 A) 4 times. Working in established pattern and following color sequence as for back, inc 1 st at beg and end of row every 1¼″ 10 times, working added sts in pattern (82 sts). Work even until sleeve measures 19″ from beg, or desired length to underarm.

To Shape Cap: Bind off 6 sts at beg of next 2 rows. Dec 1 st at beg and end of every row 30 times. Bind off remaining 10 sts.

FINISHING: Sew shoulder seams. **Neckband:** With right side facing you, using double-pointed needles and A, pick up and k 36 sts from back holder, 15 sts along left side of front, 22 sts from front holder and 15 sts along right side of front (88 sts). Work in ribbing of k 1, p 1 for 3½″. Bind off loosely in ribbing. Sew side and sleeve seams. Sew in sleeves. Fold neckband in half to inside and sew in place.

Savvy Striped Pullover

Color and pattern add sparkle to the front of this V-neck sweater, in stockinette stitch in Fair Isle knitting technique.

SIZES: Small (36–38) [medium (40–42)—large (44–46)]. Pullover measures 19″ [21″–23″] across back at underarms, 25½″ [25½″–26″] from back of neck to lower edge.

MATERIALS: Bucilla deLuxe knitting worsted, 4 [4–5] (4-oz.) skeins green No. 80 (color A), 1 skein each scarlet No. 309 (B), turquoise No. 312 (C) and tobacco gold No. 391 (D); knitting needles, 1 pair each No. 4 and No. 5 (or English needles No. 9 and No. 8) **or the size that will give you the correct gauge;** 1 set (4) dp needles No. 4.

GAUGE: 6 sts = 1″; 7 rows = 1″.

BACK: Starting at lower edge with No. 4 needles and A, cast on 114 [126–138] sts. Work in k 1, p 1 ribbing for 2½″. Change to No. 5 needles and work even in stockinette st until piece measures 16½″ from beg, or desired length to underarm.

To Shape Armholes: Bind off 5 [6–7] sts at beg of next 2 rows, 2 [3–3] sts at beg of next 2 rows, then dec 1 st at beg and end of every other row 3 [4–6] times. Work even on 94 [100–106] sts until armholes measure 8½″ [8½″–9″].

To Shape Shoulders: Bind off 9 [10–11] sts at beg of next 6 rows. Place remaining 40 sts on holder for back neck.

FRONT: Work ribbing as for back. Change to No. 5 needles and p 1 row A. Front of sweater is worked in Fair Isle Knitting (see page 33). Working in stockinette st, work Fair Isle pattern as follows: work 2 rows B, 2 rows C, 2 rows D, 2 rows A and 2 rows D. **11th row:** K 2 B, * k 2 A, k 2 B. Repeat from * across. **12th row:** P 2 B, * p 2 A, p 2 B. Repeat from * across. Repeat last 2 rows once more. Work 2 rows D. **17th row:** K 2 B, * k 2 C, k 2 B. Repeat from * across. **18th row:** P 2 B, * p 2 C, p 2 B. Repeat from * across. Repeat last 2 rows once more. Work 2 rows D. Repeating these 22 rows for pattern, work until 1″ less than back to underarm.

To Divide for V-Neck: Keeping in pattern, work across first 57 [63–69] sts. Attach another ball of yarn and work across remaining 57 [63–69] sts. Working on both sides at once, dec 1 st at each neck edge every 3rd row 21 times and, **at same time,** when piece measures same as back to underarm, shape armholes.

To Shape Armholes: Work as for back armhole shaping. When neck shaping is completed, work even until armholes measure same as back to shoulders.

To Shape Shoulders: At each arm edge bind off 9 [10–11] sts. Work 1 row even. Repeat last 2 rows once more. Bind off remaining 9 [10–11] sts.

SLEEVES: Starting at lower edge with No. 4 needles and A, cast on 52 [54–56] sts. Work in k 1, p 1 ribbing for 3″, increasing 6 sts as evenly spaced as possible on last row (58 [60–62] sts). Change to No. 5 needles. Working in stockinette st, inc 1 st at beg and end of row every ¾″ 16 [18–20] times. Work even on 90 [96–102] sts until piece measures 19″ [19¼″–19½″] from beg, or desired length to underarm.

To Shape Cap: Bind off 5 [6–7] sts at beg of next 2 rows, then dec 1 st at beg and end of every other row 19 [20–21] times. Bind off 6 sts at beg of next 6 rows. Bind off remaining 6 [8–10] sts.

FINISHING: Sew shoulder, side and sleeve seams. Sew in sleeves. **Neckband:** With No. 4 dp needles and A, pick up and k 70 [70–72] sts along left front neck edge, place marker on needle (at center point of V-neck), pick up and k 70 [70–72] sts along right front neck edge, then k 40 sts from back holder (180 [180–184] sts). Work in ribbing of k 1, p 1 for 1″, decreasing 1 st at each side of marker at center front on each rnd. Bind off in ribbing.

Bold-Patterned Pullover

Squares and diamonds are worked in Fair Isle technique on the front of this crew-neck pullover. The back and sleeves are plain stockinette stitch.

SIZES: (36–38) [(40–42)—(44–46)]. Pullover measures 18½" [20½"–23"] across back at underarms, 27½" [28"–28½"] from back of neck to lower edge.

MATERIALS: Bucilla deLuxe knitting worsted, 4 [4–5] (4-oz.) skeins natural heather No. 023 (color A), 1 skein each royal blue No. 20 (B) and copper No. 330 (C); knitting needles, 1 pair each No. 4 and No. 6 (or English needles No. 9 and No. 7) **or the size that will give you the correct gauge.**

GAUGE: 11 sts = 2"; 7 rows = 1".

BACK: Starting at lower edge with No. 4 needles and A, cast on 102 [114–126] sts. Work in k 1, p 1 ribbing for 2". Change to No. 6 needles and work even in stockinette st until piece measures 18" from beg.

To Shape Armholes: Bind off 4 [6–7] sts at beg of next 2 rows, then dec 1 st at beg and end of every other row 4 [5–7] times. Work even on 86 [92–98] sts until armholes measure 8½" [9"–9½"].

To Shape Shoulders: Bind off 7 [8–9] sts at beg of next 6 rows (44 sts). Change to No. 4 needles and work in k 1, p 1 ribbing for 1". Bind off loosely in ribbing.

FRONT: Starting at lower edge with No. 4 needles and A, cast on 104 [116–128] sts. Work ribbing as for back. Change to No. 6 needles and, increasing 1 st on first row, work 2 rows A in stockinette st, ending with a p row.

Pattern: Continuing in stockinette st, begin 54-row pattern repeat as follows: Work 2 rows B, 2 rows A, 2 rows C, 4 rows A. **11th row (right side):** K 3 B, * k 3 A, k 3 B. Repeat from * across. **12th row:** P 3 B, * p 3 A, p 3 B. Repeat from * across. **13th row:** Repeat 11th row. **14th row:** P 3 A, * p 3 B, p 3 A. Repeat from * across. **15th row:** K 3 A, * k 3 B, k 3 A. Repeat from * across. **16th row:** Repeat 14th row. **17th row:** K 3 C, * k 3 A, k 3 C. Repeat from * across. **18th row:** P 3 C, * p 3 A, p 3 C. Repeat from * across. **19th row:** Repeat 17th row. **20th row:** P 3 A, * p 3 C, p 3 A. Repeat from * across. **21st row:** K 3 A, * k 3 C, * k 3 A. Repeat from * across. **22nd row:** Repeat 20th row.

Work 4 rows A, 2 rows B, 2 rows A, 2 rows C, 4 rows A, ending with a p row. **37th row:** Continuing in stockinette st and following chart for design, work from S [M–L] to Y, then repeat from X to Y across, ending from Y to S [M–L]. Continue following chart from right to left on each row. When chart has been completed, work 3 rows A. Repeat these 54 rows for pattern and, **at same time,** when 52 rows and 2nd pattern repeat have been completed, start armhole shaping. Piece should measure same as back to armhole.

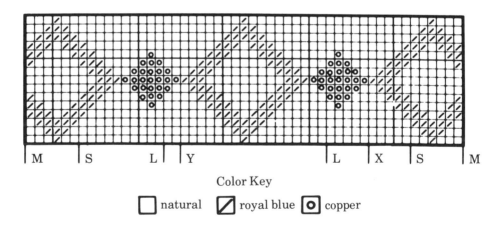

Color Key

□ natural   ▨ royal blue   ☉ copper

To Shape Armholes: Continuing in pattern as established, bind off 5 [7–8] sts at beg of next 2 rows, then dec 1 st at beg and end of every other row 5 [6–7] times more. Work even on 85 [91–99] sts until 48th [51st–54th] row of 3rd pattern repeat has been completed.

To Shape Neck: Continuing in pattern as established, work across first 35 [38–41] sts. Place these sts on holder. Bind off center 15 [15–17] sts; work to end of row. Working on one side only, at neck edge, bind off 2 sts every other row 7 times and, **at same time,** when first C

248

stripe of 4th pattern repeat is complete, work even with A if necessary, until piece measures same as back to shoulders, ending at armhole edge.

To Shape Shoulder: Bind off 7 [8–9] sts at beg of next row, then at beg of every other row twice more. Break off. Place sts from holder on needle. Attach yarn and work to correspond to other side. Break off.

Neckband: Attach A at left front neck edge. With No. 4 needles and with right side facing you, pick up and k 68 [70–72] sts along front neck edge. Work in k 1, p 1 ribbing for 1″. Bind off loosely in ribbing.

SLEEVES: Starting at lower edge with No. 4 needles and A, cast on 52 [54–56] sts. Work in k 1, p 1 ribbing for 3″, increasing 6 sts as evenly spaced as possible on last row (58 [60–62] sts). Change to No. 6 needles. Working in stockinette st, inc 1 st at beg and end of row every 1″ 10 [12–14] times. Work even on 78 [84–90] sts until piece measures 19″ [19¼″–19½″] from beg, or desired length to underarm.

To Shape Cap: Bind off 4 [6–7] sts at beg of next 2 rows, then dec 1 st at beg and end of every other row 19 [20–21] times. Bind off 3 sts at beg of next 6 rows. Bind off remaining 14 [14–16] sts.

FINISHING: Sew shoulder, side and sleeve seams. Sew in sleeves.

New Short-Sleeved Pullover

This handsome geometric design is adapted from an American Indian motif.

SIZES: Men's or women's small—34″ [medium—38″]. Length from back of neck to lower edge, 23″.

MATERIALS: Bucilla deLuxe knitting worsted, 2 (4-oz.) skeins claret No. 13 (color A), 1 skein each tobacco gold No. 391 (B), apricot brandy No. 91 (C), royal blue No. 20 (D), emerald No. 93 (E); knitting needles, 1 pair each No. 5 (for neckband only) and No. 6 (or English needles No. 8 and No. 7), **or the sizes that will give you the correct gauge;** yarn bobbins; tapestry needle.

GAUGE: 5 sts = 1″; 7 rows = 1″ on No. 6 needles.

Note: For this pullover two kinds of pattern knitting are used: Fair Isle and bobbin knitting. If you are not familiar with these techniques, be sure to make a swatch to check your gauge and to practice working with multiple yarns. See pages 33 and 35 for detailed information. Some motifs are embroidered later in duplicate st (see page 33).

BACK: Starting at lower edge with color B, cast on 89 [99] sts. Work in stockinette st for 1″, ending with a k row for hem facing. **Next row:** K across row for turning ridge.

Starting with a k row, work in stockinette st, following charts No. 1, No. 2 and No. 3 on page 252 for design and key for colors.

Chart No. 1 (Fair Isle): For first row, follow chart from S [M] to Y; then repeat from X to Y across. Work until chart is completed (8 rows).

Chart No. 2 (bobbin knitting): Wind 3 [5] D and 4 E bobbins to start. Wind additional bobbins as needed. Follow chart, working each row from S [M] to X, then from Y (do not repeat center st) back to S [M]. Work until chart is completed (15 rows).

Repeat 8 rows of Chart 1. Lower border completed. With A, work even for 4 rows.

Chart No. 3 (bobbin knitting): Wind 6 A, 2 D, 2 E and 1 C bobbins. Follow chart, working each row from S [M] to X, then from Y back to S [M]. Work until chart is completed.

With A only, work until piece measures 15½" from turning ridge.

To Shape Armholes—1st and 2nd rows: Bind off 12 [14] sts at beg of row, work to end of row. Put a marker at beg and end of last row. Work even on 65 [71] sts until armholes measure 7½".

To Shape Shoulders: Bind off 15 [18] sts at beg of next 2 rows. Bind off remaining 35 sts for back of neck.

FRONT: Work same as back until chart No. 3 is completed. With A only, work even until piece measures 14" from turning ridge (or 1½" less than back length to armhole).

To Shape Neck: With A work across first 43 [48] sts. Place remaining 46 [51] sts on a holder. Working on 43 [48] sts, dec 1 st at neck edge every 3rd row 3 times, ending at side edge. Piece should measure 15½" from ridge.

To Shape Armhole: Bind off 12 [14] sts at beg of next row. Continue to work in stockinette st and dec 1 st at neck edge every 3rd row 13 times more.

Work even on 15 [18] sts until armhole measures same as back armhole to shoulder. Bind off all sts.

Place remaining 46 [51] sts onto needle. Attach A at neck edge and bind off 3 sts, mark center st of these 3 sts, work to end of row. Working on 43 [48] sts, work to correspond to other side.

SLEEVE: Sew shoulder seams before starting sleeve. With right side of work facing you and using D, pick up and k 80 sts along armhole edge between markers for one sleeve. With D, p 1 row, k 1 row. Break off D. With C, p 1 row, k 1 row.

Continue in stockinette st, following charts No. 4 and No. 5 for design and key for colors. If desired, instead of knitting the color D sections, they can be embroidered later in duplicate stitch.

Chart No. 4 (bobbin knitting): Wind 5 C and 4 A bobbins to start. Wind additional bobbins as needed.

Starting with 3rd row of chart, work each row from X to Y; then repeat from X to Y across. Work until chart is completed (31 rows for entire chart).

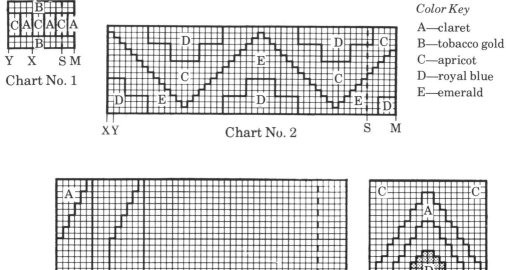

Chart No. 1

Y X S M

Chart No. 2

X Y   Chart No. 2   S   M

Color Key
A—claret
B—tobacco gold
C—apricot
D—royal blue
E—emerald

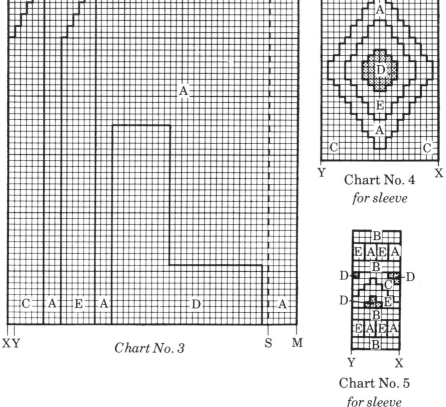

Chart No. 4
for sleeve

Y   X

X Y   *Chart No. 3*   S   M

Chart No. 5
for sleeve

Y   X

Chart No. 5 (Fair Isle and bobbin knitting): For first row, follow chart from X to Y; then repeat from X to Y across. Work until chart is completed. Last row worked is a p row (20 rows). Sleeve should measure about 7½" from beg.

With B, p next row on right side for turning ridge. Starting with a p row, with B work in stockinette st for 1". Bind off.

252

Work other sleeve to correspond.

FINISHING: If color D sections were not knitted on sleeve (charts No. 4 and No. 5), work them in duplicate st as follows: Thread tapestry needle with D and work over the knitted stitches, simulating the stitch. Keep tension even and fairly loose so that entire stitch is covered.

Sew the bound-off 12 [14] sts at armhole to sleeve edge; then sew side and sleeve seams. Turn all hem facings to wrong side and slip-stitch in place.

Front Neckband: With wrong side of work facing you, using No. 5 needles, attach B to right shoulder at neck edge; then pick up and k 49 sts, evenly spaced, between shoulder and marked st; pick up and k one st opposite marked st (mark this st for center st); then pick up and k 49 sts along neck edge between marker and left shoulder (99 sts).

Work facing as follows: **1st row:** P across. **2nd row (dec row):** K to within 1 st of marked center st, sl 1, k 2 tog, psso (2 sts dec), k to end of row. **3rd row:** Repeat last row (95 sts). This row forms a ridge for turning. Mark beg and end of row (facing completed).

1st row (right side—inc row): K across to within marked center st, inc 1 st before center st as follows: insert right-hand needle under horizontal thread before st on left-hand needle and k it without dropping st off left-hand needle, then k the marked st, inc 1 st as before (2 sts inc), k to end of row (97 sts). **2nd row:** P across. Drop B. Attach A and C. **3rd row:** (K 2 A, 2 C) 12 times; with A work as follows: inc 1 st as before in horizontal thread, k center st, then inc 1 st in next horizontal thread; (k 2 A, 2 C) 12 times (99 sts). **4th row:** (P 2 A, 2 C) 12 times; p 3 A for center, (p 2 C, 2 A) 12 times. **5th row:** (K 2 A, 2 C) 12 times; with A k 1, inc as before, k center st, inc as before; then (k 2 C, 2 A) 12 times (101 sts). **6th row:** (P 2 A, 2 C) 12 times; p 2 A, p 1 C for center, p 2 A, (p 2 C, 2A) 12 times. Break off A and C.

7th row: With B, k 1 row, increasing as before. **8th row:** P across. **9th row:** Repeat 7th row (105 sts). **10th row (wrong side):** K across for turning ridge. Bind off loosely.

Back Neckband: With No. 5 needles and B, cast on 8 sts; then with wrong side of back facing you, pick up and k 36 sts evenly across neck edge; then cast on 8 sts (52 sts). P 1 row, k 1 row; then k next row for turning ridge and mark (facing completed).

Starting with a k row, follow chart No. 1. For first row work from X to Y; then repeat from X to Y across. Work until 8 rows of chart are completed. With B, k 2 rows. Last row worked forms turning ridge. Bind off loosely.

Sew each cast-on edge of back neckband to ends of rows of front neckband, matching markers. Turn entire neckband to right side of pullover, folding last turning ridge under neckband; slipstitch in place. Block lightly.

Man's V-Neck Pullover

This handsome pullover is worked in red and navy stockinette stitch pattern with solid-color borders.

SIZES: Small (36–38) [medium (40–42)—large (44–46)]. Sweater measures 19″ [21″–23″] across back at underarms.

MATERIALS: Bear Brand Winsom Orlon acrylic yarn, 3 (2-oz.) skeins each navy No. 379 (color A) and scarlet No. 309 (B); knitting needles, 1 pair each No. 4 and No. 6 (or English needles No. 9 and No. 7) **or the sizes that will give you the correct gauge.**

GAUGE: 6 sts = 1″; 6 rows = 1″.

BACK: Starting at lower edge with A and No. 4 needles, cast on 104 [116–128] sts. Work even in k 1, p 1 ribbing for 8 rows. Break off. Attach B and k 1 row (right side); work in ribbing for 7 rows. Break off. Attach A and k 1 row; work in ribbing for 7 rows, increasing 10 sts evenly spaced on last row (114 [126–138] sts).

To Establish Pattern: Attach B. **1st row (right side):** With No. 6 needles, * k 1 A, k 1 B. Repeat from * across. **2nd row:** * P 1 A, p 1 B. Repeat from * across. Repeating first and 2nd rows for pattern, work until piece measures 17″ [17½″–17½″], or desired length to underarms.

To Shape Armholes: Bind off 6 sts at beg of next 2 rows, then 3 sts at beg of next 2 [4–6] rows. Dec 1 st at beg and end of every other row 6 times. Work even on 84 [90–96] sts until armholes measure 8½″ [9″–9½″], ending with a p row.

To Shape Shoulders: Bind off 11 [12–13] sts at beg of next 4 rows. Place remaining 40 [42–44] sts on holder for back neck.

FRONT: Work as for back until piece measures same as back to underarms.

To Shape V-Neck and Armholes: Place marker on needle between 2 center sts. **1st row:** Bind off first 6 sts, work across to marker, attach 2nd strand each of A and B and work across. **2nd row:** Bind off first 6 sts, work across to marker, pick up first strands of A and B and complete row. Continuing to work on both sides at once, dec 1 st at each neck edge every other row 20 [21–22] times and, **at same time,** bind off 3 sts at arm edge of next 2 [4–6] rows, then dec 1 st at arm edge of every other row 6 times. Work even on 22 [24–26] sts on each side until armholes measure same as back.

To Shape Shoulders: Work as for back.

Neckband: With right side facing you, using No. 4 needles and A, k across 40 [42–44] sts on back holder. Work in ribbing for 8 rows. Bind off in ribbing. With A pick up and k 56 [58–60] sts along left front neck edge; place marker on needle, pick up and k 56 [58–60] sts along right front neck edge. Work in ribbing of k 1, p 1 for 8 rows, decreasing 1 st at each side of marker on each row. Bind off in ribbing.

Sew shoulder seams and ribbing.

Armbands: With right side facing you, with A pick up and k evenly around armhole. Work in k 1, p 1 ribbing for 8 rows. Bind off in ribbing. Sew side seams.

Men's Buttondowns

Double-Breasted Blazer

For the most hard-to-please man, this handsome double-breasted blazer has a moss-stitch patterned front panel and collar.

SIZES: Men's 38 [40–42–44–46]. Garment width around underarms, about 41½″ [43¾″–46″–48″–49½″].

MATERIALS: Knitting worsted, 26 [28–30–30–32] ozs. Knitting needles No. 5 and No. 8, **or the size that will give you the correct gauge.** Aluminum crochet hook size G. 6 buttons.

GAUGE: 5 sts = 1″; 7 rows = 1″ (stockinette st on No. 8 needles).

BACK: With No. 5 needles, cast on 90 [96–100–106–110] sts. Beg on wrong side, work in k 1, p 1 ribbing for 1½″, end wrong side. Change to No. 8 needles and stockinette st (k on right side, p on wrong side). Work even until 5½″ from beg. Inc 1 st each edge on next row, then every 2¾″ 3 times more—98 [104–108–114–118] sts. Work even until 17″ from beg.

To Shape Armholes: At each edge bind off 4 sts once, 2 sts once. Dec 1 st each edge every other row 4 times—78 [84–88–94–98] sts. Work even until 8″ [8¼″–8½″–8¾″–9″] above beg of armhole shaping.

To Shape Shoulders: At each edge, bind off 6 [7–7–8–8] sts 3 times, then 7 [6–8–7–9] sts once—28 [30–30–32–32] sts. Bind off.

RIGHT FRONT: With No. 5 needles, cast on 71 [73–77–79–81] sts. **Row 1 (wrong side):** Work in p 1, k 1 ribbing over 32 [34–38–40–42] sts, place a marker on needle, work moss st over 39 sts to front edge as follows: K 1, * p 1, k 1, repeat from * to end. (**Note:** Sl marker every row.) **Row 2:** K the k sts and p the p sts as they face you. **Row 3:** Work ribbing as established over 32 [34–38–40–42] sts, moss st over 39 sts as follows: P 1, * k 1, p 1, repeat from * to end. **Row 4:** Repeat Row 2. Repeat these 4 rows until ribbing measures same as on back. Change to No. 8 needles. Continue to work moss st front panel as established, working 32 [34–38–40–42] sts at side edge in stockinette st. **At the same time,** at side edge only, inc as on back—75 [77–81–83–85] sts. Work even until same as back to underarm.

To Shape Lapel, Neck and Shoulder: At front edge only, bind off 24 sts once, 3 sts once, 2 sts 4 times, then dec 1 st at same edge every [67–71–73–75] sts. Work even until 4½″ [4¾″–5″–5¼″–5½″] above beg of armhole shaping.

To Shape Lapel, Neck and Shoulder: At front edge only, bind off 24 sts once, 3 sts once, 2 sts 4 times, then dec 1 st at same edge every other row 5 [5–7–7] times—25 [27–29–31–33] sts. Work until armhole is same depth as on back and shape shoulder as on back.

LEFT FRONT: Work to correspond to right front reversing all shaping, establishing pats on Row 1 (wrong side), as follows: Work moss st over 39 sts as on Row 1 of right front, then k 1, p 1 ribbing over remaining 32 [34–38–40–42] sts. Work 3 groups of 2 buttonholes starting 2″ from beg as follows: Beg at front edge, work 6 sts, bind off 4 sts, work until 18 sts beyond bound-off sts, bind off 4 sts, finish row. On next row, cast on 4 sts over each set of bound-off sts. Repeat buttonholes every 7″ twice more.

SLEEVES: With No. 5 needles, cast on 44 [46–48–50–52] sts. Work in k 1, p 1 ribbing for 5″, inc 6 sts evenly spaced across last row— 50 [52–54–56–58] sts. Change to No. 8 needles. Work in stockinette st, inc 1 st each edge every 6 rows 12 [13–13–13–13] times—74 [78–80–82–84] sts. Work even until 20″ from beg, or desired length to underarm.

To Shape Cap: At each edge bind off 4 sts once, 2 sts 9 [10–10–11–11] times, 3 sts twice, 4 [4–5–4–5] sts once—10 sts. Bind off.

COLLAR: With No. 8 needles, cast on 41 [43–45–47–49] sts. Work in moss st, casting on 10 sts at end of each of first 6 rows—101 [103–105–107–109] sts. Work even until 3¼″ [3½″–3¾″–4″–4″] from beg. Bind off in pat.

FINISHING: Sew shoulder seams. Sew cast-on edge of collar to neck and lapel edges; collar will end about 3″ from outer edges of lapels (see photo). Crochet 1 row sc around front edges, lapels and collar. Work buttonhole st around buttonholes. Sew in sleeves. Sew side and sleeve seams. Sew buttons in place.

Camel Vest

This vest is made with knit-in blue stripes; the vertical stripes are crocheted on afterward.

SIZES: Small (36) [medium (38–40)—large (42–44)]. Vest measures 18″ [20″–22″] across at underarms and 21″ [21½″–22″] from shoulder to lower edge.

MATERIALS: Bear Brand Winsom (100% Orlon acrylic), 4 [5–6] (2-oz.) skeins camel No. 368, 1 skein each Persian blue No. 321 and rust No. 339; knitting needles, 1 pair each No. 4 and No. 6 (or English needles No. 9 and No. 7) **or the size that will give you the correct gauge;** steel crochet hook No. 0; 2 bobbins; 4 buttons ¾″ in diameter.

GAUGE: 6 sts = 1″; 8 rows = 1″.

Note: Vertical stripes on front of vest are crocheted in sl st pattern when vest is completed.

BACK: Starting at lower edge with No. 4 needles and camel, cast on 108 [120–132] sts. Work in ribbing of k 1, p 1 for 2½″. Change to No. 6 needles. Starting with a k row, work in stockinette st until piece measures 12″ from beg, or desired length to underarm, ending with a p row.

To Shape Armholes: Bind off 9 [10–11] sts at beg of next 2 rows. Dec 1 st at beg and end of every other row 5 [6–8] times. Work even on 80 [88–94] sts until armholes measure 9″ [9½″–10″].

To Shape Shoulders: Bind off 7 [8–9] sts at beg of next 6 rows. Bind off remaining 38 [40–40] sts.

260

RIGHT FRONT—Note: Wind blue yarn on a bobbin for horizontal stripes (see page 35 for bobbin knitting).

Starting at lower edge with No. 4 needles and camel, cast on 64 [70–76] sts. Work in ribbing of k 1, p 1 for 21 rows. Start horizontal stripe pattern as follows: **1st row (right side):** With camel, (k 1, p 1) 6 times for front border; drop camel; attach blue and k 6 [8–10], (p 1, k 3, p 1, k 12) twice; p 1, k 3, p 1, k 7 [11–15].

2nd row: With blue p 7 [11–15], (k 1, p 3, k 1, p 12) twice; k 1, p 3, k 1, p 6 [8–10]; break off blue; with camel (k 1, p 1) 6 times.

3rd through 14th rows: Working in pattern as established with camel, repeat first and 2nd rows 6 times more.

Repeat first row through 14th row for pattern until piece measures same as back to underarm, ending at side edge.

To Shape Armhole and Neck: Bind off 9 [10–11] sts, work in pattern across to within 2 sts of front border, sl 1, k 1, psso, work front border in ribbing. Work even for 1 row. Dec 1 st at armhole edge every other row 5 [6–8] times and, **at same time,** dec 1 st at neck edge inside border every 4th row 16 [17–17] times more (33 [36–39] sts). Work even in pattern until armhole measures same as back, ending at armhole edge.

To Shape Shoulder: Bind off 7 [8–9] sts at armhole edge on next row, then every other row twice more. Continue to work 12 remaining border sts in k 1, p 1 ribbing for 3½" more for back of neck. Bind off in ribbing.

With pins, mark front border for placement of 4 buttons, the first one 2¼" from lower edge, the rest evenly spaced up to beginning of neck shaping.

LEFT FRONT: Work as for right front for 21 rows. Drop camel; attach blue bobbin. **1st row (right side):** With blue, k 7 [11–15], (p 1, k 3, p 1, k 12) twice; p 1, k 3, p 1, k 6 [8–10], drop blue; attach camel bobbin, (p 1, k 1) 6 times for front border. **2nd row:** With camel bobbin (p 1, k 1) 6 times; with blue bobbin p 6 [8–10], (k 1, p 3, k 1, p 12) twice; k 1, p 3, k 1, p 7 [11–15]. Complete left front to correspond to right front, reversing all shaping and making buttonholes opposite pins on right front as follows: Work 4 sts in ribbing, bind off next 4 sts, rib remaining 4 sts. On following row, cast on 4 sts over those bound off. (**Note:** When working decreases at neck edge inside border, k 2 tog instead of sl 1, k 1, psso.)

FINISHING: Sew shoulder seams. Sew ends of borders together and sew to back neck edge.

Armhole Ribbing: With right side of work facing you, using camel, pick up and k 132 [134–138] sts around armhole edge. Work in k 1, p 1 ribbing for 1". Bind off in ribbing. Sew side seams. Sew on buttons.

Vertical Stripes: With right side of work facing you and holding blue yarn against wrong side of right front, insert crochet hook from front to back through bottom st of first vertical p row and draw up a blue loop. Insert hook in next vertical p st and draw a loop through st and through loop on hook (sl st made). Continue to work sl st over each p st to top. Break off and weave in end. Work along remaining vertical p rows in same manner, alternating blue and rust. Repeat along left front.

HIS AND HERS

Norwegian Snowflake-
Patterned Sweaters

The dark background with the light pattern on the man's sweater reverses on the woman's sweater. It is worked in stockinette stitch in any two-color combination of your choice.

MAN'S SWEATER

SIZES: Men's 40 [42–44–46]. Garment width around underarms, about 43″ [45″–47½″–50″].

MATERIALS: Knitting worsted, 26 [28–30–32] ozs. main color (MC), 6 [6–8–8] ozs. contrasting color (CC). Knitting needles No. 5 and No. 8, **or the size that will give you the correct gauge.**

GAUGE: 5 sts = 1″; 7 rows = 1″.

BACK: With No. 5 needles and MC, cast on 106 [112–118–124] sts. Work in k 1, p 1 ribbing for 2½″, inc 1 st at end of last row—107 [113–119–125] sts. Change to No. 8 needles. Work first 18 rows of chart, beg and ending as indicated by arrows for appropriate size.

Body Pattern—Row 1 (right side): K across 2 MC, * 1 CC, 5 MC, repeat from * to last 3 sts, 1 CC, 2 MC. **Rows 2 and 3:** With MC p 1 row, k 1 row. **Row 4:** P across 5 MC, * 1 CC, 5 MC, repeat from * across. **Rows 5 and 6:** With MC k 1 row, p 1 row. Repeat these 6 rows for Body Pat until 12″ [12½″–13″–13½″] from beg, end Pat Row 6. Continue in stockinette st following chart (see page 33 for Fair Isle knitting), beg and ending on Row 1 as indicated for appropriate size. **At the same time,** when 17¼″ [17½″–17¾″–18″] from beg or desired length to underarm:

Shape Armholes: Keeping to pat at each armhole edge bind off 3 sts once, 2 sts once, 1 st once—95 [101–107–113] sts. Work even until 55 rows of chart have been completed. With MC p next row.

Yoke: Work Body Pat until 8″ (8¼″–8½″–8¾″) above beg of armhole.

Shape Shoulders: Keeping to pat at each armhole edge bind off 8 [9–9–10] sts 3 times, then 8 [7–9–8] sts once—31 [33–35–37] sts. Bind off.

FRONT: Work same as back until 5″ [5¼″–5½″–5¾″] above beg of armhole shaping—95 [101–107–113] sts.

To Shape Neck and Shoulders—Next Row: Keeping to pat work 42 [44–46–48] sts, join another ball of corresponding color and bind off center 11 [13–15–17] sts, finish row. Keeping to pat, working both sides at once, bind off at each neck edge 3 sts once, 2 sts twice, 1 st 3 times—32 [34–36–38] sts each side. When armholes are same depth as on back, shape shoulders as on back.

SLEEVES: With No. 5 needles and MC, cast 50 [52–54–56] sts. Work ribbing as for back for 3″, inc 3 [1–5–3] sts evenly spaced on last row—53 [53–59–59] sts. Change to No. 8 needles. Work in Body Pat as for back, inc 1 st each edge every 8 rows 12 [13–11–12] times, working added sts into Body Pat—77 [79–81–83] sts. Work even until 18½″ from beg or desired length to underarm.

To Shape Cap: Keeping to pat, at each edge bind off 3 sts once, then 2 sts 10 times. Dec 1 st each edge every other row 8 [9–10–11] times—15 sts. Bind off.

FINISHING: Seam right shoulder.

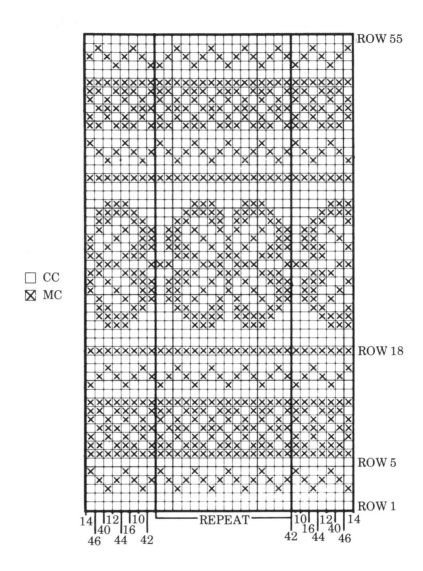

Neckband: With No. 5 needles and MC, pick up 94 [96–98–100] sts around neck edge. Work in k 1, p 1 ribbing for 2¾". Bind off loosely in ribbing. Fold neckband in half to wrong side and sew in place.

Sew left shoulder, side and sleeve seams. Sew in sleeves.

WOMAN'S SWEATER

SIZES: Misses' 10 [12–14–16]. Garment width around underarms, about 33" [35½"–38"–40½"].

MATERIALS: Knitting worsted, 18 [20–22–24] ozs. main color (MC), 4 [4–6–6] ozs. contrasting color (CC). Knitting needles No. 5 and No. 8, **or the size that will give you the correct gauge.**

266

GAUGE: 5 sts = 1"; 7 rows = 1".

BACK: With No. 5 needles and MC, cast on 82 [88–94–100] sts. Work in k 1, p 1 ribbing for 2½", inc 1 st at end of last row—83 [89–95–101] sts. Change to No. 8 needles. Work first 5 rows of chart, beg and ending as indicated by arrows for appropriate size. With MC p next row.

Body Pattern—Row 1 (right side): K across 2 MC, * 1 CC, 5 MC, repeat from * to last 3 sts, 1 CC, 2 MC. **Rows 2 and 3:** With MC p 1 row, k 1 row. **Row 4:** P across 5 MC, * 1 CC, 5 MC, repeat from * across. **Rows 5 and 6:** With MC k 1 row, p 1 row. Repeat these 6 rows for Body Pat until 10" [10½"–11"–11½"] from beg, end Pat Row 6. Continue in stockinette st following chart, beg and ending on Row 1 as indicated for appropriate size. **At the same time,** when 15" [15½"–16"–16½"] from beg or desired length to underarm:

Shape Armholes: Keeping to pat at each armhole edge bind off 3 sts once, 2 sts once, 1 st once—71 [77–83–89] sts. Work even until 55 rows of chart have been completed. With MC p next row.

Yoke: Work Body Pat until 7" [7¼"–7½"–7¾"] above beg of armhole shaping.

Shape Shoulders: Keeping to pat, at each armhole edge bind off 5 [6–6–7] sts 3 times, then 6 [5–7–6] sts once—29 [31–33–35] sts. Bind off.

FRONT: Work same as back until 4" [4¼"–4½"–4¾"] above beg of armhole shaping—71 [77–83–89] sts.

To Shape Neck and Shoulders—Next Row: Keeping to pat work 31 [33–35–37] sts, join another ball of corresponding color and bind off center 9 [11–13–15] sts, finish row. Keeping to pat, working both sides at once, bind off at each neck edge 3 sts once, 2 sts once, 1 st 5 times—21 [23–25–27] sts each side. When armholes are same depth as on back, shape shoulders as on back.

SLEEVES: With No. 5 needles and MC, cast on 44 [46–50–52] sts. Work ribbing as for back for 3", inc 3 [1–3–1] sts evenly spaced on last row—47 [47–53–53] sts. Change to No. 8 needles. Work in Body Pat as for back, inc 1 st each edge every 6 [6–8–8] rows 10 [11–9–10] times, working added sts into Body Pat—67 [69–71–73] sts. Work even until 16½" [16¾"–17"–17¼"] from beg or desired length to underarm.

To Shape Cap: Keeping to pat at each edge bind off 3 sts once, then 2 sts 10 times. Dec 1 st each edge every other row 4 [5–6–7] times—13 sts. Bind off.

FINISHING: Sew right shoulder seam.

Neckband: With No. 5 needles and MC, pick up 86 [88–90–92] sts around neck edge. Work in k 1, p 1 ribbing for 2¾". Bind off loosely in ribbing. Fold neckband in half to wrong side and sew in place.

Sew left shoulder, side and sleeve seams. Sew in sleeves.

Rib and Cable Pullover and Hat

*Classic and yet fashionable—
his and hers rib and zigzag
cable pullover with button-
down turtleneck. There are
hats to match.*

HER PULLOVER

SIZES: Misses, small ([medium–large]). Garment width around underarms, about 33½" [37"–41"].

MATERIALS—For Sweater: Knitting worsted, 22 [24–26] ozs. Knitting needles No. 5 and No. 8, **or the size that will give you the correct gauge.** Cable needle. Crochet hook size F. 3 small buttons. **For hat:** Knitting worsted, 4 ozs. Dp needles No. 5 and No. 8.

GAUGE: 11 sts = 2"; 13 rows = 2" (rib pat on No. 8 needles, slightly stretched).

ZIGZAG CABLE PATTERN: Worked on 11 sts. **Row 1 (right side):** P 8, k 2, p 1. **Row 2:** K 1; sl next 2 sts to cable needle and hold in back, k 1, p sts from dp needle (p 2 left made); k 7. **Row 3:** P 6; sl next st to cable needle and hold at back, k 2, p st from cable needle (k 2 right made); p 2. **Row 4:** K 3, p 2 left, k 5. **Row 5:** P 4, k 2 right, p 4. **Row 6:** K 5, p 2 left, k 3. **Row 7:** P 2, k 2 right, p 6. **Row 8:** K 7, p 2 left, k 1. **Row 9:** P 1, k 2, p 8. **Row 10:** K 7, sl next st to cable needle and hold in front, p 2, k st from cable needle (p 2 right made), k 1. **Row 11:** P 2, sl next 2 sts to cable needle and hold in front, p 1, k sts from cable needle (k 2 left made), p 6. **Row 12:** K 5, p 2 right, k 3. **Row 13:** P 4, k 2 left, p 4. **Row 14:** K 3, p 2 right, k 5. **Row 15:** P 6, k 2 left, p 2. **Row 16:** K 1, p 2 right, k 7. Repeat these 16 rows for cable pat.

BACK: With No. 5 needles, cast on 96 [102–112] sts and work in k 1, p 1 ribbing for 2½". Change to No. 8 needles. **Row 1 (right side):** K 2, * p 3, k 2, repeat from * across. **Row 2:** P 2, * k 3, p 2, repeat from * across. Repeat these 2 rows for Rib Pat. Work even until 19½" [19½"–22½"] from beg, or desired length to underarms.

To Shape Armholes: Keeping pat as established, at each edge bind off 3 [3–4] sts once, 2 sts once, 1 st 0 [2–3] times—82 [88–94] sts. Work even until 6½" [7"–8¼"] above beg of armhole shaping.

To Shape Neck and Shoulders: Mark the 14 [16–20] middle sts. At each shoulder edge, bind off 6 sts 3 [2–3] times, 7 [5–5] sts 1 [3–2] times; **at the same time,** on first shoulder bind-off row, with new strand of yarn, bind off 14 [16–20] middle sts, then at each neck edge bind off 3 sts 3 times.

FRONT: With No. 5 needles, cast on and work in ribbing as for back. Change to No. 8 needles. **Row 1 (right side):** K 1, (p 3, k 2) 2 [3–4] times, work cable pat over next 11 sts, k 2, (p 3, k 2) 9 times, work cable pat over next 11 sts, k 2 (p 3, k 2) 2 [3–4] times. Keeping pats as established, work as for back until 4¼" [4¾"–5¾"] above beg of underarm shaping—82 [88–94] sts.

To Shape Neck and Shoulders: Work 36 [39–42] sts; with another ball of yarn, bind off 10 [10–12] sts, work across. Working both sides at once, at each neck edge bind off 3 [3–4] sts once, 2 sts 3 times, 1 st 2 [3–4] times. When armholes are same as back to shoulder, shape shoulders as on back.

SLEEVES: With No. 5 needles, cast on 42 [46–50] sts. Work in k 1, p 1 ribbing for 2¼"; inc 5 [6–7] sts evenly spaced on last row—47 [52–57] sts. Change to No. 8 needles and rib pat as on back. Inc 1 st each edge every 6 rows 15 times—77 [82–87] sts. Work even until 16¾" [16¾"–18½"] from beg or desired length to underarm.

To Shape Cap: At each edge, bind off 4 sts once, 2 sts 7 times, 1 st 3 [5–6] times, 2 sts 4 [4–5] times, 4 sts once—11 [12–11] sts. Bind off.

FINISHING: Seam right shoulder.

Turtleneck Collar: With No. 5 needles, pick up and k 51 [53–55] sts around front neck edge, 35 [37–43] sts across back—86 [90–98] sts. Work in k 1, p 1 ribbing for 3½". **Dividing Row:** On right side, work 24 [26–27] sts; with another ball of yarn, work next 2 sts tog, work across. Working both sides separately, continue in ribbing until 6½" from beg. Bind off loosely in ribbing. Sew left shoulder and collar seam (collar turns over to outside). Work 2 rows sc around opening, working 3 buttonholes on right front opening. Sew buttons on left front.

HER HAT

With No. 5 dp needles, cast on 112 sts; join, being careful not to twist sts. Work in k 1, p 1 ribbing for 3". Change to No. 8 needles. **Rnd 1:** * P 2, k 2, repeat from * around. Work around in ribbing as established until 9″ from beg. **Dec Rnd 1:** * P 2 tog, k 2, repeat from * around—84 sts. Work 7 rnds even. **Dec Rnd 2:** * P 1, sl 1, k 1, psso, repeat from * around 56 sts. Work 7 rnds even. **Dec Rnd 3:** K 2 tog around—28 sts. K 1 rnd. Cut yarn leaving a 4″ end. Draw end through remaining sts and fasten tightly. Turn up cuff.

HIS PULLOVER

SIZES: Men's small ([medium–large]). Garment width around underarms, about 37″ [41″–44″].

MATERIALS: For Sweater: Knitting worsted, 24 [26–28] ozs. Knitting needles No. 5 and No. 8, **or the size that will give you the correct gauge.** Cable needle. Crochet hook size F. 3 small buttons. **For hat:** Knitting worsted, 4 ozs. Dp needles, No. 5 and No. 8.

GAUGE: 11 sts = 2″; 13 rows = 2″ (rib pat on No. 8 needles, slightly stretched).

ZIGZAG CABLE PATTERN: Worked on 11 sts. **Row 1 (right side):** P 8, k 2, p 1. **Row 2:** K 1, sl next 2 sts to cable needle and hold in back, k 1, p sts from dp needle (p 2 left made), k 7. **Row 3:** P 6, sl next st to cable needle and hold at back, k 2, p st from cable needle (k 2 right made), p 2. **Row 4:** K 3, p 2 left, k 5. **Row 5:** P 4, k 2 right, p 4. **Row 6:** K 5, p 2 left, k 3. **Row 7:** P 2, k 2 right, p 6. **Row 8:** K 7, p 2 left, k 1. **Row 9:** P 1, k 2, p 8. **Row 10:** K 7, sl next st to cable needle and hold in front, p 2, k st from cable needle (p 2 right made), k 1. **Row 11:** P 2, sl next 2 sts to cable needle and hold in front, p 1, k sts from cable needle (k 2 left made), p 6. **Row 12:** K 5, p 2 right, k 3. **Row 13:** P 4, k 2 left, p 4. **Row 14:** K 3, p 2 right, k 5. **Row 15:** P 6, k 2 left, p 2. **Row 16:** K 1, p 2 right, k 7. Repeat these 16 rows for cable pat.

BACK: With No. 5 needles, cast on 102 [112–122] sts and work in k 1, p 1 ribbing for 2½″. Change to No. 8 needles. **Row 1 (right side):** K 2, * p 3, k 2, repeat from * across. **Row 2:** P 2, * k 3, p 2, repeat from * across. Repeat these 2 rows for Rib Pat. Work even until 19½″ [22½″–22½″] from beg, or desired length to underarms.

To Shape Armholes: Keeping pat as established, at each edge bind off 3 [4–4] sts once, 2 sts once, 1 st 2 [3–5] times—88 [94–100] sts. Work even until 7″ [8¼″–9″] above beg of armhole shaping.

To Shape Neck and Shoulders: Mark the 16 [20–24] middle sts. At each shoulder edge, bind off 6 sts 2 [3–4] times, 5 [5–5] sts 3 [2–1] times; **at the same time,** on first shoulder bind-off row, with new strand of yarn, bind off 16 [20–24] middle sts, then at each neck edge bind off 3 sts 3 times.

FRONT: With No. 5 needles, cast on and work in ribbing as for back. Change to No. 8 needles. **Pat Row 1 (right side):** K 1, (p 3, k 2) 3 [4–4] times, work cable pat over next 11 sts, k 2, (p 3, k 2) 9 [9–11] times, work cable pat over next 11 sts, k 2 (p 3, k 2) 3 [4–4] times.

Keeping pats as established, work as for back until 4¾″ [5¾″–6¼″] above beg of underarm shaping—88 [94–100] sts.

To Shape Neck and Shoulders: Work 39 [42–43] sts; with another ball of yarn, bind off 10 [12–14] sts, work across. Working both sides at once, at each neck edge bind off 3 [4–4] sts once, 2 sts 3 times, 1 st 3 [4–4] times. When armholes are same as back to shoulder, shape shoulders as on back.

SLEEVES: With No. 5 needles, cast on 46 [50–54] sts. Work in k 1, p 1 ribbing for 2¼″, inc 6 [7–8] sts evenly spaced on last row—52 [57–62] sts. Change to No. 8 needles and rib pat as on back. Inc 1 st each edge every 6 rows 15 times—82 [87–92] sts. Work even until 16¾″ [18½″–19″] from beg, or desired length to underarm.

To Shape Cap: At each edge, bind off 4 sts once, 2 sts 7 times, 1 st 5 [6–7] times, 2 sts 4 [5–5] times, 4 sts once—12 [11–14] sts. Bind off.

FINISHING: Seam right shoulder.

Turtleneck Collar: With No. 5 needles, pick up and k 53 [55–57] sts around front neck edge, 37 [43–47] sts across back—90 [98–104] sts. Work in k 1, p 1 ribbing for 3½″ [3¾″–3¾″]. **Dividing Row:** On right side, work 26 [27–31] sts; with another ball of yarn, work next 2 sts tog, work across. Working both sides separately, continue in ribbing until 6½″ [7″–7″] from beg. Bind off. Seam left shoulder and collar.

Work 2 rows sc around opening, working 3 buttonholes on left front opening. Sew buttons on right front.

HIS HAT

With No. 5 dp needles, cast on 110 sts; join, being careful not to twist sts. Mark beg of rnds. Work in k 1, p 1 ribbing for 2¼″. Change to No. 8 needles. **Rnd 1:** * K 3, p 2, repeat from * around. Work around in ribbing as established until 9″ from beg.

To Shape Top—Rnd 1: * K 1, k 2 tog, p 2, repeat from * around— 88 sts. Work 10 rnds even. **Rnd 12:** K 2, p 2 tog, repeat from * around —66 sts. Work 10 rnds even. **Rnd 23:** K 2 tog around—33 sts. Place sts on 2 needles and weave tog (see kitchener stitch, p. 32).

Eight Fisherman Sweaters from the Greek Islands

Time-honored, traditional patterns for both men and women, with a basic raglan shoulder/crew-neck design the same for all eight sweaters.

RHODES

A wishbone cable design on a reverse stockinette stitch background.

SIZES: Men's or women's small (34–36) [medium (38–40), large (42–44)].

MATERIALS: Bernat Blarney-Spun, 10 [12–14] (2-oz.) balls; knitting needles, 1 pair No. 6, 1 pair No. 8 (or English needles No. 7 and No. 5) **or the sizes that will give you the correct gauge,** 1 set (4) double-pointed needles No. 6.

GAUGE: When working pattern stitch: 9 sts = 2"; 6 rows = 1".

BACK: With No. 6 needles, cast on 85 [93–102] sts. Work in ribbing of k 1, p 1 for 3″. Change to No. 8 needles and work in pattern as follows: **1st row (right side):** P 7 [11–6] sts, * slip next 2 sts to dp needle and hold in back of work, k next st, k the 2 sts from dp needle, slip next st to dp needle and hold in front of work, k next 2 sts, k the st from dp needle, p 7 [7–6] sts. Repeat from * across, ending last repeat p 7 [11–6] sts. **2nd row:** P across. **3rd row:** P 7 [11–6] sts, * k 6, p 7 [7–6] sts. Repeat from * across, ending k 6, p 7 [11–6] sts. Repeat 2nd and 3rd rows twice more. **8th row:** Repeat 2nd row. Repeat first through 8th rows for pattern. Work even in pattern until piece measures 15½″ [16″–16½″] from beg or desired length to underarm, ending with a wrong side row.

To Shape Raglan Armholes: Keeping in pattern as established, bind off 2 [3–4] sts at beg of next 2 rows. **Next row (dec row):** K 2, sl 1 as if to k, k 1, psso, work in pattern to last 4 sts, k 2 tog, k 2. **Following row:** P across. Repeat last 2 rows 26 [28–30] times more. Place remaining 27 [29–32] sts on a holder for back of neck.

FRONT: Work same as back until 20 [22–24] armhole dec rows have been completed, ending with a right side row (41 [43–46] sts).

To Shape Neck—Next row: P 10 [11–12] sts, place next 21 [21–22] sts on a holder, attach another ball of yarn and p last 10 [11–12] sts. Working on both sides at once, dec 1 st at each neck edge every other row 3 [4–5] times and continue to dec at each armhole edge as before 7 times more.

SLEEVES: With No. 6 needles, cast on 40 [42–44] sts. Work in ribbing of k 1, p 1 for 3″. **Next row:** P across and inc 6 [4–4] sts evenly spaced across row (46 [46–48] sts). Change to No. 8 needles. Work in pattern as follows: **1st row (right side):** P 7 [7–9] sts, * slip next 2 sts to dp needle and hold in back of work, k next st, k the 2 sts from dp needle, slip next st to dp needle and hold in front of work, k next 2 sts, k the st from dp needle, p 7 [7–6] sts. Repeat from * across, ending last repeat p 7 [7–9] sts. **2nd row:** P across. **3rd row:** P 7 [7–9] sts, * k 6, p 7 [7–6] sts. Repeat from * across, ending k 6, p 7 [7–9] sts. Repeat 2nd and 3rd rows twice more. **8th row:** P across. Repeat first through 8th rows for pattern. Work in pattern and inc 1 st at beg and end of row every 1¼″ [1″–¾″] 10 [13–15] times, working added sts in pattern. Work even on 66 [72–78] sts until sleeve measures 18″ [18½″–19″] from beg or desired length to underarm, ending with a wrong side row.

To Shape Raglan Cap: Work same as back armhole shaping. Place remaining 8 sts on a holder.

FINISHING: Sew sleeves to back and front armholes. Sew underarm and sleeve seams.

Neckband: With right side of work facing you, using dp needles, pick up and k 76 [82–88] sts around neck edge, including sts from holders. Work around in ribbing of k 1, p 1 for 14 rnds. Bind off loosely in ribbing. Turn half of neckband to wrong side and slip-stitch in place.

KOS

A sweater worked in vertical bands of arrowheads.

SIZES: Men's or women's small (34–36) [medium (38–40), large (42–44)].

MATERIALS: Bernat Blarney-Spun, 12 [13–15] (2-oz.) balls; knitting needles, 1 pair No. 6, 1 pair No. 8 (or English needles No. 7 and No. 5) **or the sizes that will give you the correct gauge,** 1 set (4) double-pointed needles No. 6.

GAUGE: When working pattern stitch: 9 sts = 2″; 6 rows = 1″.

PATTERN: Multiple of 13 sts, plus 1. **1st row (right side):** * K 1, p 5, k 2, p 5. Repeat from * to last st, k 1. **2nd row and even-numbered rows:** P across. **3rd row:** * K 1, p 4, skip the first st on left-hand needle, k into the front of 2nd st on left-hand needle but do not drop off, k into the front of the first st on left-hand needle, slip both sts off needle (right twist made); k into the back of 2nd st on left-hand needle, k into the front of the first st on left-hand needle, slip both sts off needle (left twist made); p 4. Repeat from * to last st, k 1. **5th row:** * K 1, p 3, make right twist, k 2, make left twist, p 3. Repeat from * to last st, k 1. **7th row:** * K 1, p 2, make right twist, k 4, make left twist, p 2. Repeat from * to last st, k 1. **9th row:** * K 1, p 1, make right twist, k 6, make left twist, p 1. Repeat from * to last st, k 1. **10th row:** P across. Repeat first through 10th rows for pattern.

BACK: With No. 6 needles, cast on 85 [94–102] sts. Work in ribbing of k 1, p 1 for 3″. Change to No. 8 needles and establish pattern as follows: **1st row (right side):** P 3 [1–5] sts, place a marker on needle, work first row of pattern over next 79 [92–92] sts, place a marker on needle, p last 3 [1–5] sts. **2nd row:** P across, slipping markers. Continue in this manner, working pattern on the 79 [92–92] sts between markers and p sts outside markers until piece measures 15½″ [16″–16½″] from beg or desired length to underarm, ending with a wrong side row.

To Shape Raglan Armholes: Keeping in pattern as established, bind off 2 [3–4] sts at beg of next 2 rows. **Next row (dec row):** K 2, sl 1 as if to k, k 1, psso, work in pattern to last 4 sts, k 2 tog, k 2. **Following row:** P across. Repeat last 2 rows 26 [28–30] times more. Place remaining 27 [30–32] sts on a holder for back of neck.

FRONT: Work same as back until 20 [22–24] armhole dec rows have been completed, ending with a right side row (41 [44–46] sts).

To Shape Neck—Next row: P 10 [11–12] sts, place next 21 [22–22] sts on a holder, attach another ball of yarn and p last 10 [11–12] sts. Working on both sides at once, dec 1 st at each neck edge every other row 3 [4–5] times and continue to dec at each armhole edge as before 7 times more.

SLEEVES: With No. 6 needles, cast on 40 [42–44] sts. Work in ribbing of k 1, p 1 for 3″. **Next row:** P across and inc 13 [11–9] sts evenly spaced across row (53 sts). Change to No. 8 needles. Work in pattern and inc 1 st at beg and end of row every 1½″ [1¼″–1″] 7 [10–13] times, working added sts in pattern st. Work even on 67 [73–79] sts until sleeve measures 18″ [18½″–19″] from beg or desired length to underarm, ending with a wrong side row.

To Shape Raglan Cap: Work same as back armhole shaping. Place remaining 9 sts on a holder.

FINISHING: Sew sleeves to back and front armholes. Sew underarm and sleeve seams.

Neckband: With right side of work facing you, using dp needles, pick up and k 76 [82–88] sts around neck edge, including sts from holders. Work around in ribbing of k 1, p 1 for 14 rnds. Bind off loosely in ribbing. Turn half of neckband to wrong side and slip-stitch in place.

CORFU

A chain and check patterned sweater.

SIZES: Men's or women's small (34–36) [medium (38–40), large (42–44)].

MATERIALS: Bernat Blarney-Spun, 12 [14–16] (2-oz.) balls; knitting needles, 1 pair No. 6, 1 pair No. 8 (or English needles No. 7 and No. 5) **or the sizes that will give you the correct gauge,** 1 set (4) double-pointed needles No. 6

GAUGE: When working pattern stitch: 9 sts = 2"; 6 rows = 1".

PATTERN: Multiple of 17 sts, plus 3. **1st row (right side):** K 3, * p 4, slip next 2 sts to dp needle and hold in back of work, k 1, k the 2 sts from dp needle, slip next st to dp needle and hold in front of work, k 2, k the st from dp needle, p 4, k 3. Repeat from * across. **2nd row and all even-numbered rows:** P across. **3rd row:** K 3, * p 4, k 6, p 4, k 3. Repeat from * across. **5th row:** Repeat 3rd row. **7th row:** K 3, * p 4, slip next st to dp needle and hold in front of work, k 2, k the st from dp needle, slip next 2 sts to dp needle and hold in back of work, k 1, k the 2 sts from dp needle, p 4, k 3. Repeat from * across. **9th row:** Repeat 3rd row. **11th row:** P 3, * k 3, p 1, slip next 2 sts to dp needle and hold in back of work, k 1, k the 2 sts from dp needle, slip next st to dp needle and hold in front of work, k 2, k the st from dp needle, p 1, k 3, p 3. Repeat from * across. **13th row:** P 3, * k 3, p 1, k 6, p 1, k 3, p 3. Repeat from * across. **15th row:** Repeat 13th row. **17th row:** P 3, * k 3, p 1, slip next st to dp needle and hold in front of work, k 2, k the st from dp needle, slip next 2 sts to dp needle and hold in back of work, k next st, k the 2 sts from dp needle, p 1, k 3, p 3. Repeat from * across. **19th row:** Repeat 13th row. **20th row:** P across. Repeat first through 20th rows for pattern.

BACK: With No. 6 needles, cast on 90 [96–104] sts. Work in ribbing of k 1, p 1 for 3″. Change to No. 8 needles and establish pattern as follows: **1st row (right side):** P 1 [4–8] sts, place a marker on needle, work first row of pattern over next 88 sts, place a marker on needle, p last 1 [4–8] sts. **2nd row:** P across, slipping markers. Continue in this manner, working pattern on the 88 sts between markers and p sts outside markers until piece measures 15½″ [16″–16½″] from beg or desired length to underarm, ending with a wrong side row.

To Shape Raglan Armholes: Keeping in pattern as established, bind off 4 [4–5] sts at beg of next 2 rows. **Next row (dec row):** K 2, sl 1 as if to k, k 1, psso, work in pattern to last 4 sts, k 2 tog, k 2. **Following row:** P across. Repeat last 2 rows 26 [28–30] times more. Place remaining 28 [30–32] sts on a holder for back of neck.

FRONT: Work same as back until 20 [22–24] armhole dec rows have been completed, ending with a right side row (42 [44–46] sts).

To Shape Neck—Next row: P 10 [11–12] sts, place next 22 sts on a holder, attach another ball of yarn and p last 10 [11–12] sts. Working on both sides at once, dec 1 st at each neck edge every other row 3 [4–5] times and continue to dec at each armhole edge as before 7 times more.

SLEEVES: With No. 6 needles, cast on 40 [42–44] sts. Work in ribbing of k 1, p 1 for 3″, increasing 14 [12–10] sts evenly spaced across last row (54 sts). Change to No. 8 needles. Work in pattern and inc 1 st at beg and end of row every 1½″ [1¼″–1″] 7 [9–12] times, working added sts in pattern. Work even on 68 [72–78] sts until sleeve measures 18″ [18½″–19″] from beg or desired length to underarm, ending with a wrong side row.

To Shape Raglan Cap: Work same as back armhole shaping. Place remaining 6 sts on a holder.

FINISHING: Sew sleeves to back and front armholes. Sew underarm and sleeve seams.

Neckband: With right side of work facing you, using dp needles, pick up and k 76 [82–88] sts around neck edge, including sts from holders. Work around in ribbing of k 1, p 1 for 14 rnds. Bind off loosely in ribbing. Turn half of neckband to wrong side and slip-stitch in place.

MYKONOS

A sweater in lacy fishtail design.

SIZES: Men's or women's small (34–36) [medium (38–40), large (42–44)].

MATERIALS: Bernat Blarney-Spun, 10 [12–14] (2-oz.) balls; knitting needles, 1 pair No. 6, 1 pair No. 8 (or English needles No. 7 and No. 5) **or the sizes that will give you the correct gauge,** 1 set (4) double-pointed needles No. 6.

GAUGE: When working pattern stitch: 9 sts = 2″; 6 rows = 1″.

PATTERN: Multiple of 8 sts, plus 1. **1st row (right side):** * K 1, y o, k 2, sl 1, k 2 tog, psso, k 2, y o. Repeat from * across to last st, k 1. **2nd row and all even-numbered rows:** P across. **3rd row:** K 2, * y o, k 1, sl 1, k 2 tog, psso, k 1, y o, k 3. Repeat from * across, ending k 2 instead of k 3. **5th row:** K 3, * y o, sl 1, k 2 tog, psso, y o, k 5. Repeat from * across, ending k 3 instead of k 5. **6th row:** P across. Repeat these 6 rows for pattern.

BACK: With No. 6 needles, cast on 89 [97–105] sts. Work in ribbing of k 1, p 1 for 3″. Change to No. 8 needles and work in pattern until piece measures approximately 15″ [16″–17″] from beg or desired length to underarm, ending with a fourth row of pattern.

To Shape Raglan Armholes: Keeping pattern as established, work as follows: **1st row:** Bind off 3 sts (the fourth st remains on right-hand needle), k 2 tog, * y o, k 5, y o, sl 1, k 2 tog, psso. Repeat from * across, ending y o, k 3. **2nd row:** Bind off 3 sts, p across (83 [91–99] sts). **3rd row:** K 2, sl 1 as if to k, k 1, psso (first decrease), k 2, * y o, k 2, sl 1, k 2 tog, psso, k 2, y o, k 1. Repeat from * across to last 5 sts, k next st, k 2 tog, k 2 (second decrease). **4th row and all even-numbered rows:** P across. **5th row:** K 2, sl 1 as if to k, k 1, psso, k 2, * y o, k 1, sl 1, k 2 tog, psso, k 1, y o, k 3. Repeat from * across to last 11 sts, y o, k 1, sl 1, k 2 tog, psso, k 1, y o, k 2, k 2 tog, k 2. **7th row:** K 2, sl 1 as if to k, k 1, psso, k 2, * y o, sl 1, k 2 tog, psso, y o, k 5. Repeat from * across to last 9 sts, y o, sl 1, k 2 tog, psso, y o, k 2, k 2 tog, k 2. **9th row:** K 2, sl 1 as if to k, k 1, psso, k 2, sl 1, k 1, psso, * k 2, y o, k 1, y o, k 2, sl 1, k 2 tog, psso. Repeat from * across to last 13 sts, k 2, y o, k 1, y o, k 3, sl 1, k 1, psso, k 1, k 2 tog, k 2. **11th row:** K 2, sl 1 as if to k, k 1, psso, * sl 1, k 2 tog, psso, k 1, y o, k 3, y o, k 1. Repeat from * across to last 7 sts, sl 1, k 2 tog, psso, k 2 tog, k 2 (4 sts decreased on this row). **13th row:** K 2, sl 1 as if to k, k 2 tog, psso, * y o, k 5, y o, sl 1, k 2 tog, psso. Repeat from * across to last 10 sts, y o, k 5, y o, k 3 tog, k 2. **15th row:** K 2, sl 1 as if to k, k 1, psso, k 3, * y o, k 2, sl 1, k 2 tog, psso, k 2, y o, k 1. Repeat from * across to last 6 sts, k next 2 sts, k 2 tog, k 2. **17th row:** K 2, sl 1 as if to k, k 1, psso, * k 3, y o, k 1, sl 1, k 2 tog, psso, k 1, y o. Repeat from * across to last 7 sts, k 3, k 2 tog, k 2. **19th row:** K 2, sl 1 as if to k, k 1, psso, k 3, * y o, sl 1, k 2 tog, psso, y o, k 5. Repeat from * across, ending last repeat k 3 instead of k 5, k 2 tog, k 2. **21st row:** K 2, sl 1 as if to k, k 1, psso, * k 2, sl 1, k 2 tog, psso, k 2, y o, k 1, y o. Repeat from * across to last 11 sts, k 2, sl 1, k 2 tog, psso, k 2, k 2 tog, k 2 (4 sts decreased). **22nd row:** P across. Repeat last 12 rows (from 11th row through 22nd row) until 43rd [47th–53rd] row is completed. Place remaining 31 [31–33] sts on a holder for back of neck.

FRONT: Work same as back until 33rd [37th–43rd] row is completed; last row worked is a right side row (43 [45–47] sts).

To Shape Neck—Next row: P 10 [11–12] sts, place next 23 sts on a holder, attach another ball of yarn and p last 10 [11–12] sts. Working on both sides at once, dec 1 st at each neck edge every other row 3 [4–5] times and continue to dec at each armhole edge as before 7 times more.

SLEEVES: With No. 6 needles, cast on 42 [42–44] sts. Work in ribbing of k 1, p 1 for 3″. Next row: P across and inc 7 [15–21] sts evenly spaced across row (49 [57–65] sts). Change to No. 8 needles. Work in pattern and inc 1 st at beg and end of row every 1½″ 8 times, working added sts in pattern. Work even on 65 [73–81] sts until sleeve measures approximately 18″ [18″–19″] from beg or desired length to underarm, ending with a fourth row of pattern.

To Shape Raglan Cap: Work same as back armhole shaping until 43rd [47th–53rd] row is completed. Place remaining 7 [7–9] sts on a holder.

FINISHING: Sew sleeves to back and front armholes. Sew underarm and sleeve seams.

Neckband: With right side of work facing you, using dp needles, pick up and k 76 [82–88] sts around neck edge, including sts from holders. Work around in ribbing of k 1, p 1 for 14 rnds. Bind off loosely in ribbing. Turn half of neckband to wrong side and slip-stitch in place.

SANTORIN

A bold combination of diamonds and garter-stitch patterns.

SIZES: Men's or women's small (34–36) [medium (38–40), large (42–44)].

MATERIALS: Bernat Blarney-Spun, 11 [13–15] (2-oz.) balls; knitting needles, 1 pair No. 6, 1 pair No. 8 (or English needles No. 7 and No. 5) **or the sizes that will give you the correct gauge,** 1 set (4) double-pointed needles No. 6.

GAUGE: When working pattern stitch: 9 sts = 2″; 6 rows = 1″.

DIAMOND PATTERN: Worked on 16 sts. **1st row (right side):** K 1, p 5, skip the first st on left-hand needle, k into the front of 2nd st on left-hand needle but do not drop off, k into the front of the first st on left-hand needle, slip both sts off needle (right twist made); k into the back of 2nd st on left-hand needle, k into the front of the first st on left-hand needle, slip both sts off needle (left twist made); p 5, k 1. **2nd row and all even-numbered rows:** P across. **3rd row:** K 1, p 4, make right twist, k 2, make left twist, p 4, k 1. **5th row:** K 1, p 3, make right twist, k 4, make left twist, p 3, k 1. **7th row:** K 1, p 2, make right twist, k 6, make left twist, p 2, k 1. **9th row:** K 1, p 1, make right twist, k 8, make left twist, p 1, k 1. **11th row:** K 1, make right twist, k 10, make left twist, k 1. **13th row:** K 1, p into back of 2nd st on left-hand needle, k into the front of the first st on left-hand needle, slip both sts off needle (purl left twist made); k 10, k into the front of the 2nd st on left-hand needle, p first st on left-hand needle, slip both sts off needle (purl right twist made); k 1. **15th row:** K 1, p 1, make a purl left twist, k 8, make a purl right twist, p 1, k 1. **17th row:** K 1, p 2, make a purl left twist, k 6, make a purl right twist, p 2, k 1. **19th row:** K 1, p 3, make a purl left twist, k 4, make a purl right twist, p 3, k 1. **21st row:** K 1, p 4, make a purl left twist, k 2, make a purl right twist, p 4, k 1. **23rd row:** K 1, p 5, make a purl left twist, make a purl right twist, p 5, k 1. **24th row:** P across. Repeat first through 24th rows for pattern.

BACK: With No. 6 needles, cast on 84 [94–104] sts. Work in ribbing of k 1, p 1 for 3". Change to No. 8 needles and establish position of diamond patterns as follows: **1st row (right side):** * P 4 [6–8], place a marker on needle, work first row of diamond pattern over next 16 sts, place a marker on needle. Repeat from * 3 times more; p 4 [6–8]. **2nd row:** P across, slipping markers. Continue in this manner, working diamond pattern on the 16 sts inside markers and p remaining sts until piece measures 15½" [16"–16½"] from beg or desired length to underarm, ending with a wrong side row.

To Shape Raglan Armholes: Keeping in pattern as established, bind off 2 [3–5] sts at beg of next 2 rows. **Next row (dec row):** K 2, sl 1 as if to k, k 1, psso, work in pattern to last 4 sts, k 2 tog, k 2. **Following row:** P across. Repeat last 2 rows 26 [28–30] times more. Place remaining 26 [30–32] sts on a holder for back of neck.

FRONT: Work same as back until 20 [22–24] armhole dec rows have been completed, ending with a right side row (40 [44–46] sts).

To Shape Neck—Next row: P 10 [11–12] sts, place next 20 [22–22] sts on a holder, attach another ball of yarn and p last 10 [11–12] sts. Working on both sides at once, dec 1 st at each neck edge every other row 3 [4–5] times and continue to dec at each armhole edge as before 7 times more.

SLEEVES: With No. 6 needles, cast on 40 [42–44] sts. Work in ribbing of k 1, p 1 for 3". **Next row:** P across and inc 10 sts evenly spaced across row (50 [52–54] sts). Change to No. 8 needles and establish position of diamond pattern as follows: **1st row (right side):** P 17 [18–19] sts, place a marker on needle, work first row of diamond pattern over next 16 sts, place a marker on needle, p last 17 [18–19] sts. **2nd row:** P across, slipping markers. Continue in this manner, working diamond pattern on the 16 sts between markers and p the sts outside markers; **at same time,** inc 1 st at beg and end of row every 1½" [1¼"–1"] 8 [10–13] times, purling the added sts. Work even on 66 [72–80] sts until sleeve measures 18" [18½"–19"] from beg or desired length to underarm, ending with a wrong side row.

To Shape Raglan Cap: Work same as back armhole shaping. Place remaining 8 sts on a holder.

FINISHING: Sew sleeves to back and front armholes. Sew underarm and sleeve seams.

Neckband: With right side of work facing you, using dp needles, pick up and k 76 [82–88] sts around neck edge, including sts from holders. Work around in ribbing of k 1, p 1 for 14 rnds. Bind off loosely in ribbing. Turn half of neckband to wrong side and slip-stitch in place.

HYDRA

An over-all design of ribs and ridges in p 2, k 1 pattern.

SIZES: Men's or women's small (34–36) [medium (38–40), large (42–44)].

MATERIALS: Bernat Blarney-Spun, 10 [12–14] (2-oz.) balls; knitting needles, 1 pair No. 6, 1 pair No. 8 (or English needles No. 7 and No. 5) **or the sizes that will give you the correct gauge,** 1 set (4) double-pointed needles No. 6.

GAUGE: When working pattern stitch: 4 sts = 1″; 6 rows = 1″.

PATTERN: Multiple of 3 sts, plus 1. **1st row (right side):** K 1, * p 2, k 1. Repeat from * across. **2nd row:** P across. Repeat first and 2nd rows for pattern.

BACK: With No. 6 needles, cast on 76 [85–91] sts. Work in ribbing of k 1, p 1 for 3″. Change to No. 8 needles and work in pattern until piece measures 15½″ [16″–16½″] from beg or desired length to underarm, ending with a wrong side row.

To Shape Raglan Armholes: Keeping in pattern as established, bind off 2 [3–3] sts at beg of next 2 rows. **Next row (dec row):** K 2, sl 1 as if to k, k 1, psso, work in pattern to last 4 sts, k 2 tog, k 2. **Following row:** P across. Repeat last 2 rows 23 [25–27] times more. Place remaining 24 [27–29] sts on holder for back neck.

FRONT: Work same as back until 17 [19–21] armhole dec rows have been completed, ending with a right side row (38 [41–43] sts).

To Shape Neck—Next row: P 10 [11–12] sts, place next 18 [19–19] sts on a holder, attach another ball of yarn and p last 10

282

[11–12] sts. Working on both sides at once, dec 1 st at each neck edge every other row 3 [4–5] times and continue to dec at each armhole edge as before 7 times more.

SLEEVES: With No. 6 needles, cast on 36 [38–40] sts. Work in ribbing of k 1, p 1 for 3". **Next row:** P across and inc 7 [8–9] sts evenly spaced across row (43 [46–49] sts). Change to No. 8 needles. Work in pattern and inc 1 st at beg and end of row every 1¼" [1"–1"] 9 [11–12] times, working added sts in pattern. Work even on 61 [68–73] sts until sleeve measures 18" [18½"–19"] from beg or desired length to underarm, ending with a wrong side row.

To Shape Raglan Cap: Work same as back armhole shaping. Place remaining 9 [10–11] sts on a holder.

FINISHING: Sew sleeves to back and front armholes. Sew underarm and sleeve seams.

Neckband: With right side of work facing you, using dp needles, pick up and k 72 [78–84] sts around neck edge, including sts from holders. Work around in ribbing of k 1, p 1 for 14 rnds. Bind off loosely in ribbing. Turn half of neckband to wrong side and slip-stitch in place.

PATMOS

Garter-stitch stripes appear on the diagonal to distinguish this Greek motif.

SIZES: Men's or women's small (34–36) [medium (38–40), large (42–44)].

MATERIALS: Bernat Blarney-Spun, 11 [12–14] (2-oz.) balls; knitting needles, 1 pair No. 6, 1 pair No. 8 (or English needles No. 7 and No. 5) **or the sizes that will give you the correct gauge,** 1 set (4) double-pointed needles No. 6.

GAUGE: When working pattern stitch: 9 sts = 2″; 6 rows = 1″.

PATTERN: Multiple of 8 sts plus 4. **1st row (right side):** K 4, * p 4, k 4. Repeat from * across. **2nd row and all even-numbered rows:** P across. **3rd row:** P 1, * k 4, p 4. Repeat from * across to last 3 sts, k 3. **5th row:** P 2, * k 4, p 4. Repeat from * across to last 2 sts, k 2. **7th row:** P 3, * k 4, p 4. Repeat from * across to last st, k 1. **9th row:** P 4, * k 4, p 4. Repeat from * across. **11th row:** K 1, * p 4, k 4. Repeat from * across to last 3 sts, p 3. **13th row:** K 2, * p 4, k 4. Repeat from * across to last 2 sts, p 2. **15th row:** K 3, * p 4, k 4. Repeat from * across to last st, p 1. **16th row:** P across. Repeat first through 16th rows for pattern.

BACK: With No. 6 needles, cast on 84 [92–100] sts. Work in ribbing of k 1, p 1 for 3″. Change to No. 8 needles and work in pattern until piece measures 15½″ [16″–16½″] from beg or desired length to underarm, ending with a wrong side row.

To Shape Raglan Armholes: Keeping in pattern as established, bind off 2 [3–4] sts at beg of next 2 rows. **Next row (dec row):** K 2, sl 1 as if to k, k 1, psso, work in pattern to last 4 sts, k 2 tog, k 2. **Following row:** P across. Repeat last 2 rows 26 [28–30] times more. Place remaining 26 [28–30] sts on holder for back neck.

FRONT: Work same as back until 20 [22–24] armhole dec rows have been completed, ending with a right side row (40 [42–44] sts).

To Shape Neck—Next row: P 10 [11–12] sts, place next 20 sts on a holder, attach another ball of yarn and p last 10 [11–12] sts. Working on both sides at once, dec 1 st at each neck edge every other row 3 [4–5] times and continue to dec at each armhole edge as before 7 times more.

SLEEVES: With No. 6 needles, cast on 40 [42–44] sts. Work in ribbing of k 1, p 1 for 3″. **Next row:** P across and inc 9 [7–5] sts evenly spaced across row (49 sts). Change to No. 8 needles and work sleeve pattern as follows: **1st row (right side):** (K 4, p 4) 3 times; k 1, (p 4, k 4) 3 times. **2nd and all even-numbered rows:** P across. **3rd row:** P 1, (k 4, p 4) twice; k 4, p 3, k 1, p 3, k 4, (p 4, k 4) twice; p 1. **5th row:** P 2, (k 4, p 4) twice; k 4, p 2, k 1, p 2, k 4, (p 4, k 4) twice; p 2. **7th row:** P 3, (k 4, p 4) twice; k 4, p 1, k 1, p 1, k 4, (p 4, k 4) twice; p 3. **9th row:** (P 4, k 4) 3 times; k 1, (k 4, p 4) 3 times. **11th row:** K 1, (p 4, k 4) twice; p 4, k 7, p 4, (k 4, p 4) twice; k 1. **13th row:** K 2, (p 4, k 4) twice; p 4, k 5, p 4, (k 4, p 4) twice; k 2. **15th row:** K 3, (p 4, k 4) twice; p 4, k 3, p 4, (k 4, p 4) twice; k 3. **16th row:** P across. Repeat first through 16th rows for pattern and inc 1 st at beg and end of row every 1″ [¾″–¾″] 9 [12–15] times, working added sts in pattern. Work even on 67 [73–79] sts until sleeve measures 18″ [18½″–19″] from beg or desired length to underarm, ending with a wrong side row.

284

To Shape Raglan Cap: Work same as back armhole shaping. Place remaining 9 sts on a holder.

FINISHING: Sew sleeves to back and front armholes. Sew underarm and sleeve seams.

Neckband: With right side of work facing you, using dp needles, pick up and k 76 [82–88] sts around neck edge, including sts from holders. Work around in ribbing of k 1, p 1 for 14 rnds. Bind off loosely in ribbing. Turn half of neckband to wrong side and slip-stitch in place.

TENOS

A sweater in an easy-to-work checkerboard pattern.

SIZES: Men's or women's small (34–36) [medium (38–40), large (42–44)].

MATERIALS: Bernat Blarney-Spun, 10 [12–14] (2-oz.) balls; knitting needles, 1 pair No. 6, 1 pair No. 8 (or English needles No. 7 and No. 5) **or the sizes that will give you the correct gauge,** 1 set (4) double-pointed needles No. 6.

GAUGE: When working pattern stitch: 9 sts = 2″; 6 rows = 1″.

PATTERN: Multiple of 8 sts, plus 4. **1st row (right side):** K 4, * p 4, k 4. Repeat from * across. **2nd row:** P across. **3rd through 8th rows:** Repeat first and 2nd rows. **9th row:** P 4, * k 4, p 4. Repeat from * across. **10th row:** P across. **11th through 16th rows:** Repeat 9th and 10th rows. Repeat first through 16th rows for pattern.

BACK: With No. 6 needles, cast on 84 [92–100] sts. Work in ribbing of k 1, p 1 for 3". Change to No. 8 needles and work in pattern until piece measures 15½" [16"–16½"] from beg or desired length to underarm, ending with a wrong side row.

To Shape Raglan Armholes: Keeping in pattern as established, bind off 2 [3–4] sts at beg of next 2 rows. **Next row (dec row):** K 2, sl 1 as if to k, k 1, psso, work in pattern to last 4 sts, k 2 tog, k 2. **Following row:** P across. Repeat last 2 rows 26 [28–30] times more. Place remaining 26 [28–30] sts on a holder for back of neck.

FRONT: Work same as back until 20 [22–24] armhole dec rows have been completed, ending with a right side row (40 [42–44] sts).

To Shape Neck—Next row: P 10 [11–12] sts, place next 20 sts on a holder, attach another ball of yarn and p last 10 [11–12] sts. Working on both sides at once, dec 1 st at each neck edge every other row 3 [4–5] times and continue to dec at each armhole edge as before 7 times more.

SLEEVES: With No. 6 needles, cast on 40 [42–44] sts. Work in ribbing of k 1, p 1 for 3". **Next row:** P across and inc 4 [2–8] sts evenly spaced across row (44 [44–52] sts). Change to No. 8 needles. Work in pattern and inc 1 st at beg and end of row every 1" [¾"–1"] 11 [14–13] times, working added sts in pattern. Work even on 66 [72–78] sts until sleeve measures 18" [18½"–19"] from beg or desired length to underarm, ending with a wrong side row.

To Shape Raglan Cap: Work same as back armhole shaping. Place remaining 8 sts on a holder.

FINISHING: Sew sleeves to back and front armholes. Sew underarm and sleeve seams.

Neckband: With right side of work facing you, using dp needles, pick up and k 76 [82–88] sts around neck edge, including sts from holders. Work around in ribbing of k 1, p 1 for 14 rnds. Bind off loosely in ribbing. Turn half of neckband to wrong side and slip-stitch in place.

yarn sources

If you have difficulty in obtaining any of the yarns specified for these garments, you can write to the following addresses for mail orders:

AMERICAN THREAD
> Richfield Yarn Products
> 469 Central Avenue
> Jersey City, N. J. 07307

BEAR BRAND, BUCILLA
AND FLEISHER
> Merchandise Mailing Service
> Box 144
> East Meadow, N. Y. 11554

BERNAT
> Art Needlecraft Inc.
> Box 394
> Uxbridge, Mass. 01569

BRUNSWICK
> Windyways
> Brandwood Station
> Greenville, S. C. 29610

REYNOLDS
> International Creations
> Box 55
> Great Neck, N. Y. 11023

UNGER
> Scandinavian Import Corp.
> P.O.B. 347
> Madison Square Station
> New York, N. Y. 10010

KENTUCKY YARNS
> Edgemont Yarn Service
> RR 2, Box 14
> Maysville, Ky. 41056

Write directly to the following manufacturers for the location of your nearest dealer:

COATS AND CLARK'S
> 75 Rockefeller Center
> New York, N. Y. 10019

COLUMBIA-MINERVA CORP.
> 295 Fifth Avenue
> New York, N. Y. 10016

FREDERICK J. FAWCETT
> 129 South Street
> Boston, Mass. 02111

LILLY MILLS CO.
> Shelby, N. C. 28150

PHENTEX U. S. A. INC.
> P.O.B. 99
> Plattsburgh, N. Y. 12901

SPINNERIN
> 230 Fifth Avenue
> New York, N. Y. 10001

Design Credits

Ake, M.—pages 139, 148.
Bahrt, A.—pages 209, 212.
Biasiny, N.—pages 111, 184, 250.
Bodenstein, B.—pages 48, 66, 69, 82, 90, 94, 98, 101, 109, 114, 117, 154, 155, 157, 204, 218, 245, 247, 254.
Bullett, H.—pages 189, 192, 194, 226.
Claiborne, L.—page 57.
Columbo, M.—page 176.
Credrins, I.—page 215.
Daniels, M.—pages 86, 179.
Dutkus, M.—page 159.
de Gaetano, S.—page 146.
Emott, M.—page 229.
Hobbs, L.—pages 72, 163.

Jacksier, R.—page 201.
Kohn, N.—page 78.
Lawrence, P.—pages 119, 129, 221.
Loeb, E.—pages 54, 75, 143.
Maeda, L.—pages 60, 106.
Maitles, J.—page 207.
Olson, J.—page 238.
Rosenstark, E.—page 136.
Taylor, J.—page 152.
Woman's Day Staff—pages 50, 53, 56, 160, 161, 168, 170, 182, 198, 240.

Crochet diagrams on pages 40 and 41 have been reprinted courtesy of Columbia-Minerva Corporation.

Photo Credits

Dorot, D.—page 60.
Eberstadt, F.—page 57.
Levy, P.—pages 139, 143, 148.
Maucher, A.—pages 50, 52, 72, 119, 163, 165, 198, 240.
McLaughlin-Gill, F.—pages 209, 212, 215, 221.
Pinney, D.—pages 176, 182, 192, 194, 226.

Schiavone, C.—pages 47, 48, 66, 69, 75, 78, 82, 86, 90, 94, 98, 106, 108, 109, 111, 113, 117, 136, 146, 152, 154, 159, 179, 201, 204, 207, 218, 229, 238, 243, 245, 247, 250, 254.
Svensson, S.—pages 109, 129, 155, 157.